Dame Edith Evans as the Countess Rousillon in the
1959 Stratford on Avon production

JOSEPH G. PRICE

The Unfortunate Comedy

A STUDY OF
ALL'S WELL THAT ENDS WELL
AND ITS CRITICS

UNIVERSITY OF TORONTO PRESS
1968

Published in Canada by
UNIVERSITY OF TORONTO PRESS

Copyright 1968 by Joseph G. Price

*No part of this book may be reproduced
in any form without permission from
the publishers, except for the quotation
of brief passages in criticism*

8020 1526 3

First published 1968

*Printed and bound in Great Britain by
Hazell Watson & Viney Ltd
Aylesbury, Bucks*

TO

ARTHUR COLBY SPRAGUE

He brought her down full forty pound
  Tyed up within a glove,
'Fair maid, I'll give the same to thee
  Go seek another love.'

'O I'll have none of your gold,' she said,
  'Nor I'll have none of your fee;
But your fair bodye I must have,
  The king hath granted me.'

Sir William ran and fetched her then,
  Five hundred pounds in gold,
Saying, 'Fair maid, take this to thee,
  My fault will ne'er be told.'

' 'Tis not the gold that shall me tempt'
  These words then answered she;
'But your own bodye I must have,
  The king hath granted me.'

'Would I had drank the water clear,
  When I did drink the wine,
Rather than any shepherd's brat
  Should be a ladye of mine.'

Selection from
The Knight and Shepherd's Daughter,
a ballad described by Bishop Percy as popular
'in the time of Queen Eliz., being usually
printed with her picture before it'.

PREFACE

SHAKESPEARE'S *All's Well that Ends Well* has been a neglected play. In the past, critics have generally dismissed the play in a few pages of sketchy analysis. More detailed criticisms have appeared in recent years, but they have examined the play from single viewpoints. Among these, Mr. G. Wilson Knight's essay, 'The Third Eye', is perhaps the most extensive, yet it is restricted to an analysis of theme. So too, *All's Well* has been neglected by the literary historians. We have no 'New Variorum Edition'. In the 'New Arden Edition' published in 1959, Mr. G. K. Hunter includes a selection of critical comments; the selection, however, is determined by Mr. Hunter's discussion of problems. In the theatre, the play has been produced infrequently, and the productions have received scant critical attention. The most accurate account of the stage history is a brief summary of one and a half pages written by Harold Child for the 'New Cambridge Edition' in 1929. As a result of this neglect, *All's Well*, unlike other Shakespearian plays, has been given no historical framework in which director, critic, and student may examine the play. My purpose is to provide that framework through an exhaustive theatrical and critical history to 1964 and to suggest an interpretation which is attentive to that framework.

Throughout the history, I have used the terms romance and realism as they are employed by literary historians to mark the trends of critical and popular taste. Despite the objections of critics who insist that the ambiguity in the terms makes them useless in defining the nature of a specific work, the very scope of the terms makes them useful descriptions of recognizable literary attitudes which characterize an age. The term romance characterizes that literature which inflates the human spirit, which stresses the capacity and the capability of man for life. The term realism assumes a deflation of the human spirit. It argues against the capability of man and imposes tight restraints upon the literary character with grand aspirations. Romance insists that the price which society must pay for individualism is worth while; realism denies that individualism is worth the cost to society. For this reason, romantic interpretations of *All's Well* admire both the capacity of Helena for love and the capacity of Parolles for life. Realistic interpretations see both as individual excesses which violate some code of society and are to be condemned. From such assumptions spring the controversy of the 'bright' or 'dark' comedy.

In presenting the critical history of the play, I have adopted two techniques, one in arrangement of the material and one in documentation, which require explanation. To avoid imposing the burden of summary and analysis upon the reader, I have followed a loose rather than a strict chronological order. Instead of a year by year or decade by decade survey, I have grouped by topic in each age those critics whose judgements are similar. For example, the eighteenth-century delight in Parolles remained constant from 1700 to 1775; consequently, I have discussed expressions of that delight throughout those years and then returned to earlier conflicting judgements upon other elements in the play. In documenting material in the history, since criticism of the play is limited to a few pages in any one source, I usually have identified only my first reference. Whenever following references are not clearly identified by that reference, I have added specific notes. Thus, I have supplied a note for only the first reference to *The Times* review of the 1852 Phelps production although I refer to the source several times. On the other hand, I have indicated the precise page for each reference to Mr. Knight's long essay. In a few instances, as in quotations from the 'Bell Acting Edition', I have included page numbers in my text for the convenience of readers who wish to collate the material. I have used the 'New Arden Edition', London, 1959, for all references to *All's Well* and its source.

I gratefully acknowledge the kindness of Miss Helen Willard of the Harvard Theatre Collection and the gracious assistance of the staffs of the Folger Shakespeare Library, and the Bryn Mawr College Library. I acknowledge the editors of the *Shakespeare Jahrbuch* and *Theatre Survey* for permission to reproduce a portion of the stage history which I have published in two articles: 'From Farce to Romance', *Shakespeare Jahrbuch*, xcix (1963) and '*All's Well that Ends Well* in the American Theatre', *Theatre Survey* (May 1966). I appreciate the permission of the Folger Shakespeare Library and the Library for the Performing Arts, Lincoln Center, to reproduce the illustrations of playbills and actors.

JOSEPH G. PRICE

Bowling Green State University
Bowling Green, Ohio

CONTENTS

ILLUSTRATIONS

PART I

The Stage History of
All's Well that Ends Well

I

PAROLLES AND FARCE
(1741–1785)

SHAKESPEARE'S *All's Well that Ends Well* probably was written and first acted between 1601 and 1604.[1] There is no record of a subsequent production until 1741. A gap of approximately a century and a half in the production of a Shakespearian play may seem startling to the modern reader who, in the past fifteen years, has had opportunity to see the entire canon on the stages of Shakespearian repertory companies. But the gap is not so surprising when we consider the tastes of the seventeenth-century audience, especially in comedy. Within the first forty years of the century, the imaginative freedom of the Elizabethan Age had been checked by the critical, often cynical, probings of the Jacobean. The realistic and satirical comedies of Jonson, Fletcher, and later Jacobean dramatists were evidence in the theatre of those same forces which were fashioning a 'metaphysical' poetry. Interest in the early romantic comedies of Shakespeare waned. Whatever the satirical connotations of the term 'dark comedy' which modern critics have applied to *All's Well*, the play, with its miraculous cure of a king, with its fabulous fulfilment of a wifely task, with its optimistic title and happy ending, certainly differed in tone from the popular comedy of Jonson and his disciples. The tone of *All's Well* was no more appealing in the moral and social rebellion of the Restoration after the theatres were reopened in 1660. Audiences 'demanded a reflex of their own gay immoral lives as well as a series of plays full of personal satire. The comedy of manners was the answer to this demand, faithfully reproducing the upper-class wit, licentiousness and social ideas of the time'.[2] When theatre managers sought old plays to supplement the new comedy, they turned back less frequently to Shakespeare than to Jonson and Beaumont and Fletcher whose plots and satirical characters of humours satisfied the taste of the age.[3] Few Shakespearian comedies were produced and these were for the most part altered. Off stage as well,

---

1. For a summary of the controversy concerning the date of the play, see G. K. Hunter (ed.), *All's Well that Ends Well*, London, 1959, pp. xviii–xxv.
2. Allardyce Nicoll, *A History of Restoration Drama: 1660–1700*, Cambridge, England, 1923, p. 20.
3. See n. 1, p. 174.

the plays were regarded indifferently; there are relatively few extant allusions to them in the seventeenth century.[1]

Restoration preference for the comedy of manners and the plays of Ben Jonson continued into the early eighteenth century. Theatrical records for the first forty years confirm as representative the judgement of Charles Gildon, who concluded that there was very little comedy in English drama before Jonson, 'for no Man can allow any of Shakespear's Comedies, except the Merry Wifes of Windsor'.[2] An examination of the repertory at Drury Lane during this period gives a rather accurate guide to the tastes of the times. None of Shakespeare's comedies was played at that theatre in its original form until a production of *The Merry Wives of Windsor* in December 1734. Two of his more realistic comedies, *The Merry Wives* and *The Taming of the Shrew*, had been produced in alterations throughout the first few decades, along with an adaptation of *The Merchant of Venice*. Productions of *The Tempest*, as altered by Dryden and Davenant, and then by Shadwell, and *Troilus and Cressida*, as altered by Dryden, demonstrated the compromise between Shakespeare and Restoration interests. Only *Love in a Forest*, a blending of parts of *As You Like It* and *A Midsummer Night's Dream*, which was produced in 1723, sought the spirit of fantasy intended by Shakespeare in his romantic comedy.

Although the offerings at Drury Lane reflect the popular taste, there is some evidence of interest in Shakespearian comedy during this period. In 1720, *The Merry Wives* and *Measure for Measure* were revived in their original forms at Lincoln's Inn Fields. Odell suggests that the productions were due to a less popular theatre seeking to attract an audience by revivals of rarely performed plays.[3] But the comedies enjoyed sufficient success to remain in the theatre's repertory. In 1733, both plays were acted for the first time at Covent Garden, and the productions initiated a policy of Shakespearian revivals at that theatre. Between 1736 and 1738, the original text of *Much Ado* was performed as well as the full texts of the histories, *Henry V*, *King John*, and *Richard II*. In 1737, Drury Lane added *Measure for Measure* to its repertory. It was not until the 1740–1 season at Drury Lane, however, that a deliberate effort was made to revive the romantic comedies. *As You Like It*, *Twelfth Night*, and *The Merchant of Venice* were produced perhaps at the prodding of Charles

1. Gerald Bentley, *Shakespeare & Jonson: Their Reputations in the Seventeenth Century Compared*, Chicago, 1945, i. 137.

2. *The Life of Betterton*, London, 1710, p. 173. For the statistics concerning the stage history of *All's Well* and other plays of Shakespeare in the eighteenth century, I am indebted to Charles Beecher Hogan's *Shakespeare in the Theatre: 1701–1800*, Oxford, 1952 ·7, vols i–ii.

3. George C. D. Odell, *Shakespeare from Betterton to Irving*, New York, 1920, i. 227.

Macklin, who played Malvolio, Shylock, and in the following year Touchstone.[1] It was in this first revival of the original *Merchant* that Macklin surprised the dramatic world with his interpretation of a villainous Shylock and won such acclaim for himself and the play. The Drury Lane productions were an immediate success, and interest in the romantic comedies of Shakespeare blossomed. In the same season, a minor theatre in London attempted to capitalize on this interest by offering two Shakespearian comedies which had not been acted in over a century.

Henry Giffard had reopened his theatre at Goodman's Fields after a lapse of five years.[2] In his bid for the London audience, he presented in the first three months of the 1740–1 season the five most popular Shakespearian plays of the age: *Hamlet, Macbeth, Othello, 1 Henry IV*, and *The Merry Wives*. Whether he was unable to compete with the rival productions of these plays at Drury Lane and Covent Garden or whether he saw greater advantage in the appeal of romantic comedy, Giffard challenged the first-night performance of *Twelfth Night* at Drury Lane by introducing on the same night, 15 January 1741, *The Winter's Tale*. Then, on 7 March 1741, he presented *All's Well that Ends Well*, 'written by Shakespeare and not acted since his time'.[3] Both plays proved attractive; each had a run of eight performances throughout the season; each was added to the repertory of a major theatre in the following season. Giffard, in fact, selected *All's Well* as his first Shakespearian production of the 1741–2 season on 28 September. But any plans for a season of comedy were hastily discarded by the happy manager when, a few weeks later, he introduced to the London stage a young man, David Garrick, as Richard III. The acclaim which greeted the performance dictated a repertory of tragedy for Goodman's Fields.

We know very little about this first revival of *All's Well* beyond the cast of characters. From the cast and from Odell's analysis of similar revivals, however, two points of historical interest to the play emerge.[4] First, it is most probable that the text was kept intact. This is significant in that, apart from the few following productions, *All's Well* was not performed again as Shakespeare wrote it for 170 years, not until Benson restored the text at Stratford on Avon in 1916.

1. Ibid., p. 228. See also Arthur H. Scouten, 'The Shakespearean Revival', *The London Stage: Part 3, 1729–1747*, Southern Illinois University Press, 1961, i, pp. cxlix–clii.

2. Mr. Scouten has an interesting discussion of Giffard's success as a producer both in the management of the theatre and in the training of young actors. See his introduction to *The London Stage: Part 3, 1729–1747*, i, pp. lxxx–lxxxv.

3. John Genest, *Some Account of the English Stage from the Restoration in 1660 to 1830*, London, 1832, iii. 641.

4. See n. 2, p. 174.

Second, the response of the audience may have surprised Giffard; it certainly indicated the appeal which the play would maintain throughout the eighteenth century. In casting the play, Giffard and his wife quite naturally took for themselves the roles of hero and heroine. Parolles was assigned to Joseph Peterson, an actor who had been entrusted with only minor parts. But, we may conjecture, Parolles delighted the audience and dominated the play. For Peterson enjoyed such success that he took the part to the provinces in later years; Theophilus Cibber and Charles Macklin fought for the role in the Drury Lane production in the following year; and no other leading actor in a London company chose to play Bertram again until John Philip Kemble attempted the part in 1794. Until that date, the interest of the audience was in the comedy of the play, and the eighteenth-century theatre-goer shared the earlier view of King Charles I, who had penned in 'Monsieur Parolles' next to the Shakespearian title in his copy of the second folio.

The success of this first production was such that the play was added to the Drury Lane repertory in the following season. A stroke of ill luck had already fallen upon *All's Well* when it had been supplanted at Goodman's Fields by the tragedies produced for David Garrick. The difficulties which the Drury Lane revival now encountered foreshadowed the turbulent history of the play on the stages and critical pages of later generations. It was performed on 22 January, but Davies records: '*All's well that ends well* was termed, by the players, the unfortunate comedy, from the disagreeable accidents which fell out several times during the acting of it.'[1] After the first night, scheduled performances were cancelled because of the illness of the vastly popular Peg Woffington, who had played Helena. The management then listed the play for 27 January, but the sickness of William Milward who was cast as the King forced another postponement. *All's Well* belied its title and earned its epithet, 'unfortunate comedy', when a second attack proved fatal to Milward. He had played his role, we might well imagine, with gracious nobility:

Milward, who acted the King, is said to have caught a distemper which proved fatal to him, by wearing, in this part, a too light and airy suit of clothes, which he put on after his supposed recovery. He felt himself seized with a shivering; and was asked, by one of the players, how he found himself? 'How is it possible for me,' he said, with some pleasantry, 'to be sick, when I have such a physician as Mrs. Woffington?'[2]

1. Thomas Davies lists the date incorrectly as Oct. 1741, in *Dramatic Miscellanies*, London, 1783, ii. 7. He also assigns the roles of the Clown and Interpreter to Chapman, but Charles Macklin played the Clown. See Hogan, i. 88; Genest, iii. 645–6; and Scouten, ii. 961.   2. *Dramatic Miscellanies*, ii. 7.

Not Acted these *EIGHTEEN YEARS.*

TheatreRoyal in *Drury-Lane,*

This present *Tuesday,* being the 24th of *February,* 1756
Will be *Reviv'd* a COMEDY, call'd

All's Well that Ends Well,

(Written by SHAKESPEAR.)
Capt. *PAROLLES*

By Mr. WOODWARD,

Bertram by Mr. PALMER,
Lafeu by Mr. BERRY,
King of *France* by Mr. DAVIES
Clown by Mr. YATES,
Duke of *Florence* by Mr. BURTON,
Steward by Mr. SIMSON,
Lords by Mr. *Bransby,* Mr. *Walker,* &c.
Interpreter by Mr. BLAKES,
COUNTESS of *ROUSILLON*

By Mrs. PRITCHARD,

Diana by Mrs. DAVIES,
Widow of *Florence* by Mrs. CROSS,
Helena by Miss MACKLIN.

End of Act II. a *Comic* DANCE.

To which will be added (in Two PARTS)
An ARABIAN NIGHT's ENTERTAINMENT, call'd

The GENII.

Harlequin by Mr. WOODWARD,

The Other CHARACTERS by
Miss HAUGHTON, &c.

The DANCES by
Mr. *Dennison,* Mr. *Mathews,* Mr. *Granier,*
Mrs. *Vernon,* Mrs. *Preston,* &c.

✝ On *Account of the Machinery, no Persons whatever can be admitted
behind the Scenes.* *Vivat Rex.*

To-morrow *(By Desire)* K. RICHARD III, & on *Thursday* the TEMPEST.

Eighteenth-century interest in *All's Well that Ends Well* is illustrated by this
playbill which features Harry Woodward as Parolles

J. Roberts ad Vivam del.   *Publish'd for Bell's Edition of Shakespeare Dec 1, 1776.*   *Grignion sc.*

MISS MACKLIN in the Character of HELENA
— *'tis but the shadow of a Wife you see.*

Maria Macklin was associated with the role of Helena
from 1746 to 1774

A new attempt was made at production on 16 February, but in the first act, Mrs. Woffington 'fainted away, as she stood at the scenes, ready to come on; after a proper Apology being made, the Audience with great Humanity and Patience, waited till another person dress'd to read the part'.[1] By 1783, Davies had added two more illnesses, but the evidence suggests that theatrical legend and superstition had magnified the misfortunes of this production.[2]

The difficulties of the play were not limited to sickness and death. The revival was also threatened by a dispute over the casting of Parolles. Theophilus Cibber had enjoyed the leading comic roles at Drury Lane for a number of seasons. In 1738, however, he had joined Covent Garden after attempting to stir a rebellion among the players against the manager, Charles Fleetwood. In Cibber's absence, Charles Macklin had not only assumed the comic roles but also ingratiated himself with Fleetwood through his theatrical knowledge. Cibber returned to Drury Lane in the autumn of 1741 after Macklin's great success in Shylock. Despite Macklin's strong position in the company, despite the fact that Fleetwood had promised the role of Parolles to Macklin, Cibber insisted on the part and 'by some sort of artifice, as common in theatres as in courts, snatched it from him, to his great displeasure'.[3] Macklin settled for the role of Lavache, the Clown.

Even with the illness of the cast, the death of Milward, the quarrel over casting, and 'the superstition of some of the players, who wished and entreated that it might be discontinued',[4] *All's Well* enjoyed its second successful season. It was given ten performances at Drury Lane that year. The objections of the players were overruled, according to Davies, because the play 'had such a degree of merit, and gave so much general satisfaction to the public'. The satisfaction appears to have been derived primarily from the comic elements of the play. Concerned with neither the romantic melodrama of the plot nor the moral tone of the bed-trick, audiences responded with delight to Parolles and farce. In his comments on the production, written in 1783, Davies devotes more space to the braggart-soldier than to any other part: 'Cibber's Parolles, notwithstanding his grimace and false spirit, met with encouragement. This actor, though his vivacity was mixed with too much pertness, never offended by flatness and insipidity.' Much more enthusiasm is registered by Cibber's contemporary, William Shenstone. In a letter to Richard

1. Scouten, ii. 968. There is some confusion over the date of this incident. Both Genest (iii. 645) and Augustin Daly (*Woffington*, Troy, New York, 1890, pp. 31–32) list the illness for the first performance, 22 Jan. 1742, but Hogan (i. 88) and Scouten correct the error.
2. See n. 3, p. 174.
3. *Dramatic Miscellanies*, ii. 9. 4. Ibid., p. 10.

Graves concerning the 1742 production, Shenstone wrote what is probably the first recorded criticism of *All's Well* on stage:

If you enquire after the stage,—I have not seen Garrick; but, more fortunately for *you*, your brother *has*. Me nothing has so much transported as young Cibber's exhibition of Parolles, in Shakespear's '*All's well that ends well.*' The character is admirably written by the author; and, I fancy, I can discover a great number of hints which it has afforded to Congreve in his Bluff. I am apt to think a person, after he is twelve years old, laughs annually less and less: less heartily, however; which is much the same. I think Cibber elicited from me as sincere a laugh as I can ever recollect. Nothing, sure, can be comparable to this representation of Parolles in his bully-character; except the figure he makes as a shabby gentleman. In his first dress he is tawdry, as you may imagine; in the last, he wears a rusty black coat, a black stock, a black wig with a Ramillie, a pair of black gloves; and a face!—which causes five minutes laughter.[1]

Comic possibility was exploited in other roles as well. Davies comments that 'Berry's Lafeu was the true portrait of a choleric old man and a humourist'. Lafeu has been played very differently in many later productions. Lavache may have been played by Macklin with 'humour, vulgarity, rusticity, and cunning'.[2]

There are a few pieces of negative evidence as well which suggest that the appeal of the play was in its comedy. The demand for the continuation of this production was most insistent after the second performance, but it was in this performance that Mrs. Woffington fainted in the first act and the part of Helena was merely read. The audience was attracted to other elements in *All's Well* than its heroine. Even after Peg Woffington, 'the most captivating comedienne of her time',[3] returned to the role, her representation of Helena inspired no critical comment. There is abundant material on her career in biographies and in memoirs of fellow actors, yet none records any success for her in a play whose plot stresses the heroine. The testimony of the following forty years confirms the evidence that it was Parolles, not Helena, who delighted eighteenth-century audiences.

Once again, the addition of David Garrick to a theatrical company forced *All's Well* from the repertory. When Garrick joined Drury Lane in 1742, emphasis shifted to tragedy and history plays. The Giffards, whose theatre was threatened under the Licensing Act, closed Goodman's Fields and moved to Lincoln's Inn Fields for the 1742–3 season. As their only offering in Shakespearian comedy, they

---

1. Marjorie Williams (ed.), *The Letters of Wm. Shenstone*, 1939, p. 42.
2. William Cooke, *Memoirs of Charles Macklin*, London, 1804, p. 409.
3. *Shakespeare From Betterton to Irving*, i. 336.

produced *All's Well* on 2 and 4 February 1743. Success was insured with the appearance of Cibber as Parolles. Peterson, who had played the role in the original revival, yielded to the reputation of Cibber.

Because of frequent disputes with managers and actors, Theophilus Cibber moved from theatrical company to company. In March of 1746, he was appearing at Covent Garden. It was probably at his suggestion that the management decided on the first revival of *All's Well* at that theatre. The first performance was scheduled for the night of 20 March 1746, for the benefit of Cibber.[1] John Rich, the manager of Covent Garden, had gathered an excellent cast for the production. Theophilus Cibber, of course, was given the part of Parolles. Oliver Cashell, a man who had played a great number of Shakespearian roles, was cast as the King; Lafeu was assigned to Bridgwater, an actor of like experience. Sacheverel Hale was designated Bertram. Thomas Chapman, whom Davies describes as 'admirable in the clowns of Shakespeare', drew Lavache. The role of the Countess was given to an experienced actress, Mrs. Horton; and, most fortunate, Helena was to be played by a leading actress of the age, Mrs. Pritchard. But once again, the 'unfortunate comedy' suffered serious problems. Cibber advertised that the play would be temporarily postponed because of 'an Assembly'. Within the next few days, however, Cibber left Covent Garden and returned to Drury Lane. *All's Well* had lost its major attraction.

Despite the desertion of Cibber, the rehearsal of the cast and perhaps the production expenses forced a presentation of the play. An actor in the company was trained hastily for the part of Parolles, and the revival took place on 1 April. Whether the actor had too little time to master the role or whether the cast, disgruntled by the betrayal of Cibber, objected to additional performances, or whether the play simply failed to please, *All's Well* was given only a single performance and it was not added to the repertory of the theatre. Yet the actor who substituted for Cibber was Harry Woodward, the comedian who soon would dominate *All's Well* and its braggart-soldier Parolles for thirty years. We may wonder if the tag 'unfortunate comedy' was not tied more firmly to the play by the actors of this production. Cibber's betrayal was an ominous sign. Probably within the month of the single performance, Sacheveral Hale died.[2] Within a year, Thomas Chapman died. These deaths surely recalled the death of Milward within the month of the first performance at

1. Genest, iv. 192–3.
2. Genest last lists Hale in a production for 18 April 1746 (iv. 194); a benefit for Hale and Rosco is listed for 23 April, but Hale does not appear in the cast. The benefit may have been the customary tribute to him either at the time of a fatal illness or after his death.

Drury Lane in 1742. It is not unlikely that superstitions enveloped the play. Whatever the cause, *All's Well* was not repeated in a London theatre until 1756, a span of ten years.

During the first five years of its revival, 1741–6, *All's Well* compared favourably with other Shakespearian comedies in stage productions. It was performed 22 times in 4 theatres in 4 separate seasons. A very popular comedy, *As You Like It*, received 65 performances during the same period in 3 theatres in 6 seasons. But *Twelfth Night* had only 10 performances in one theatre in 2 seasons. The *Winter's Tale* had been revived originally at the same time and by the same theatre as *All's Well*; it was dropped, however, after 14 performances in 2 theatres after its second season. The statistics for *All's Well* assume additional significance when coupled to Odell's discussion of the revival of these neglected Shakespearian plays:

> But note that, just as the day seemed won, appeared, in 1741–2, David Garrick, the greatest of tragic stars, and brought back to Hamlet, Lear, Richard and Macbeth something of the glory they seemed to have lost in the passing of Booth and Wilks. . . . None of the newly revived works of Shakespeare quite disappeared from view, again, but none experienced entirely the success it deserved unless the all-eclipsing David took part in the performance.[1]

David Garrick did not act in the play; yet *All's Well's* success was at least moderate.

Although the play was not produced again on the London stage until 1756, its initial popularity spread through the provincial theatre. Between 1750 and 1758, the Norwich Company performed the play nine times.[2] Among Shakespearian plays in the company's repertory, *All's Well* shared second place in number of productions with *Hamlet* and *King John*; *Romeo and Juliet* led the list with 18 performances in this period. *Measure for Measure*, a play frequently regarded as a companion piece to *All's Well*, had only 4 performances. Of the 4 leading plays, then, *All's Well* was the sole comedy; its rank may have been caused by the success of Joseph Peterson as Parolles. Peterson, as I have noted, acted the part in the original London revival in 1741. Elsewhere in the provinces, the appeal of the play was likewise in its braggart-soldier. In York, Bridge Frodsham, whom Miss Rosenfeld notes was known as the 'York Garrick', played Parolles in 1763.[3] Despite his reputation as a tragedian, Frodsham also played young sparks in comedy. In Parolles, he may have represented both comedy and tragedy.

---

1. *Shakespeare from Betterton to Irving*, i. 228–9.
2. Sybil Rosenfeld, *Strolling Players & Drama in the Provinces: 1660–1765*, Cambridge, England, 1939, pp. 93–94.   3. Ibid., p. 143.

In 1756, *All's Well* was produced in a second major revival on the London stage in an altered form which catered to the eighteenth-century delight in Parolles and farce. The alteration, in all probability, was prepared by David Garrick who was then manager at Drury Lane. As early as 1752, Garrick had been at work on a text of the play.[1] On 24 February 1756, he produced an acting version which became the standard adaptation of *All's Well* in the theatre for the next twenty years. The adaptation is of interest not only to the stage historian but also to the literary historian as well, for it gives insight into the changing standards and tastes of an age which even then felt the birth pangs of Romantic concepts and Victorian ethics.

As an adapter, Garrick's chief concern seems to have been the pacing of his plays. To quicken the pace of *All's Well* and to focus upon Parolles simultaneously, Garrick cut sharply into the poetry, the motivation, and the dramatic force of the original play. The result is a series of scenes which highlight Parolles as he struts to his downfall, but all else is lost in shadows. The deep incisions make more difficult those controversial points of plot and character in Shakespeare's play; with *neither* romantic justification *nor* psychological realism, the characters are one-dimensional and the plot is hopelessly inane. Nowhere is the loss of motivation and credibility more apparent than in the heroine. Garrick has drawn the character in miniature. Interestingly, what he has discarded are just those marks of determination and aggressiveness so highly regarded by Shaw but so blindly neglected by the Romantics. If Garrick's Helena was not yet the sentimental heroine, the Shakespearian ideal of womanhood which the Romantics imagined, it was only because he had so reduced her role and importance in the play. But the seed was planted; Helena in this alteration is a colourless heroine, but she suggests the passive, long-suffering wife who will dominate the play for over a century.

Garrick's technique in adjusting the play to Parolles and farce may be traced in the altered characterization of Helena. The omissions shift the balance of a scene repeatedly. In the first scene where Shakespeare constructs the character of his heroine by emphasizing her virtue, Garrick deletes the substance and is content with mere outline. In relating this virtue to a dominant theme of the play, natural goodness and inherited nobility, Shakespeare stresses in the speech of the Countess:

1. See G. W. Stone's unpublished dissertation (Harvard, 1938), 'Garrick's Handling of Shakespeare's Plays and His Influence Upon the Changed Attitude of Shakespearean Criticism During the Eighteenth Century', i. 230.

I have those hopes of her good that her education promises her dis-
positions she inherits—which makes fair gift fairer; for where an unclean
mind carries virtuous qualities, there commendations go with pity; they
are virtues and traitors too. In her they are the better for their simpleness:
she derives her honesty and achieves her goodness.   (I. i. 36–42)

Garrick reduces this to the bald statement, 'I have those hopes of her
good that her education promises her'. Again, the adaptation sacrifices not only substance in characterization but dramatic force and
poetry as well in the compression of Helena's first soliloquy to nine
lines; it eliminates the intensity of her love and the obstacles to that
love:

> I am undone; there is no living, none,
> If Bertram be away; 'twere all one
> That I should love a bright particular star
> And think to wed it, he is so above me.
> In his bright radiance and collateral light
> Must I be comforted, not in his sphere.
> Th' ambition in my love thus plagues itself:
> The hind that would be mated by the lion
> Must die for love.   (I. i. 82–90)

The virginity duologue between Helena and Parolles is brought to a
close not by the reverie of Helena, 'Not my virginity; yet . . .' (I. i.
161–82), but by the entrance of the page seeking Parolles. The first
scene ends with 'little Helen' merely walking off stage behind the
swaggering Parolles, with the audience still laughing at his jests on
virginity. Thus Garrick accomplishes his two goals: he hands the
scene to Parolles and he reduces his heroine to passive sentimentality
by omitting entirely her closing soliloquy:

> Our remedies oft in ourselves do lie . . .
>   (I. i. 212–25)

Such is Helena's fate throughout the alteration. In the scenes
which follow, Garrick continually undermines the force of his
heroine's character and the depth of her love. Her dramatic and
spirited wordplay with the Countess on the term 'mother' is con-
densed; in the same scene, her touching confession of love at the
knees of the sympathetic Countess is reduced by eighteen lines (I. iii).
In the next act, instead of dominating the attention of the assembled
court as she deliberates over the choice of husband, Helena merely
announces her selection of Bertram (II. iii. 65–101 omitted).
Because the audience is already aware of her decision, the adaptation
sacrifices characterization and theatrical suspense to move along the
plot. So uninterested is Garrick in the heroine that he ignores lines
which aid his interpretation of her; he omits her maidenly hesitation:

Please it your majesty, I have done already.
The blushes in my cheeks thus whisper me:
'We blush that thou should'st choose; but be refused,
Let the white death sit on thy cheek for ever,
We'll ne'er come there again.'   (II. iii. 67–72)

He likewise omits her less maidenly but affecting plea for a kiss from her departing husband at the end of the act (II. v. 78–87). Illustrative of his intention and technique is his rearrangement of Helena's final soliloquy. In the Shakespearian scene, Helena, the Countess, and the two lords discuss the news of Bertram's desertion. While Helena, distracted, ponders Bertram's letter, the Countess questions the lords and condemns Parolles's part in her son's conduct. Then the Countess and the lords leave the stage to the grieving Helena, who expresses her love, her fears, and finally her plan to flee France for her beloved's sake. The soliloquy ends the scene. In the Garrick adaptation, after a few words with Helena, the Countess turns away and talks quietly with the lords while Helena, in an aside only half as long as the soliloquy, announces to the audience her plan. The heroine leaves the stage and the scene ends with the Countess speaking aloud her condemnation of Parolles to the lords. Again, the emphasis has been shifted from the heroine to Parolles.

Deletions in characterization may have speeded up the play and focused attention upon Parolles, but they weakened the structure of the plot at the same time. Garrick has severely compressed the dialogue in which Helena persuades the King of her power to cure him. The resultant minimal reference to the medical skill of her father and the intercession of heaven strip away Shakespeare's attempt at credibility (II. i). Here and elsewhere, the structural parallel between the seemingly impossible cure of the King and the seemingly impossible fulfilment of Helena's love is obscured. So too, the omission of the Duke of Florence scenes (III. i and iii) and several references to the Florentine war makes less credible Bertram's appearance as the general of the troop. The character of the King is weakened by the deletion of his remonstrance against modern youth (I. ii. 31–45) and his jests about 'those girls of Italy' (II. i. 19), but there is a structural weakening as well in the loss of Shakespeare's forewarning of Bertram's actions. The elimination of the Clown's ironic 'That man should be at woman's command . . .' (I. iii. 89–93) strikes at a theme of the plot, as the elimination of Diana's ironic 'You have won / A wife of me' (IV. ii. 64–65) strikes at a technique of the dramatist. Perhaps, the very tone of the play, even in its comic elements, suffers in the omission of the final lines of Parolles's soliloquy. For the comedy of Shakespeare's Parolles is sustained through his easy acceptance of the conditions of life. But the farce of Garrick's adaptation crushes the braggart harshly. Garrick ends the exposure scene with the lines:

> for it will come to pass
> That every braggart shall be found an ass.
> (IV. iii. 324–5)

But Shakespeare adds:

> Rust, sword; cool, blushes; and Parolles live
> Safest in shame; being fool'd by fool'ry thrive.
> There's place and means for every man alive.
> I'll after them.   (IV. iii. 326–9)

Apart from this effect, the character of Parolles undergoes little change. He does lose some of his bawdiest lines in the virginity scene. But Garrick appears to have satisfied any new moral standard not by deleting Parolles's puns but by reducing Helena's participation. The Shakespearian duologue becomes almost a monologue, and we can imagine the actress standing aloof, perhaps musing on her departed Bertram, while Parolles jests with the audience. In addition to this preservation of Helena's decorum, decency dictated some changes in the language of the play: some of the Clown's *double entendres* are gone; overt references to sexual acts, such as 'take possession of the bride' (II. v. 25) are omitted; 'courted her' is substituted for 'boarded her' (v. iii. 210). And discreetly, the King's disease is no longer identified as a fistula. But both Parolles with his virginity jests and the bed-trick remain; these are targets for a later age. Garrick emphasizes the intention of his adaptation by assigning the epilogue to Parolles rather than to the King as Shakespeare had written it.

For the first performance of the Garrick adaptation on 24 February 1756, the Drury Lane playbill gave top billing to 'Capt. Parolles by Mr. Woodward'; this was printed just below the title of the play.[1] The playbill indicates the appeal not only of the character but of the actor as well. Very probably, Garrick had prepared his adaptation as a vehicle for Harry Woodward, who had substituted for Cibber in the part of Parolles in the ill-fated 1746 production at Covent Garden. Since that time, Woodward had become the leading comedian at Drury Lane. Parolles became one of his great successes. From 1756 to his retirement in 1777, Woodward led the rascally braggart from theatre to theatre. He dominated the part on the London stage and was responsible for the enthusiastic response which

1. Uncatalogued playbill in the Library of the Performing Arts, New York Public Library.

All's Well received during this period. Characteristic of critical reaction is Davies's description of Woodward in the drum scene:

The unbinding Parolles, who looked about him with anxious surprize and terror, redoubled the bursts of laughter which echoed round the theatre. Woodward was excellent in the whole scene, but particularly in characterizing Bertram and the Dumaines, whose feelings, upon the unexpected heap of slander which he threw upon them, served to heighten the scene. Bertram was most angry, because Parolles deviated very little from the truth in what he said of him; his lasciviousness, and his intrigue with Diana, he could not deny.

In all our comic writers, I know not where to meet with such an odd compound of cowardice, folly, ignorance, pertness, and effrontery, with certain semblance of courage, sense, knowledge, adroitness, and wit, as Parolles. He is, I think, inferior only to the great master of stage gaiety and mirth, Sir John Falstaff.[1]

Despite the comic talent of Woodward, the first performance of Garrick's *All's Well* appears to have been unsuccessful. Richard Cross, Sr., the theatre's prompter, merely noted in his diary, 'Play went off dull'.[2] Difficulties in the plot may have been responsible, for Garrick made changes in his adaptation before the second performance. The omission of the Duke of Florence, with perhaps other modifications, lessened the importance of the major plot. Garrick then offered to the public in sharper focus what had probably attracted them in the first performance, 'Capt. Parolles'. *All's Well* was added to the repertory and was given seven performances from 1756 to 1758.

Garrick had assembled an excellent company at Drury Lane, and the cast for this production was superior. Berry, who had played Lafeu in the 1742 revival, repeated the role. Richard Yates, famous for his portrayals of Shakespearian clowns, acted Lavache. The celebrated Mrs. Pritchard, who had played Helena in 1746, now assumed the part of the Countess. As a young actress, Maria Macklin, daughter of Charles Macklin, impersonated Helena. Of the cast, Miss Macklin was the weakest. Although the altered role offered only limited potential, 'unfortunate' may again be applied to the play in its heroine. Miss Macklin represented Helena for the next twenty years in London, yet her talent as an actress was such that at no time did she bring the role into prominence. A Helena of ability equal to that of Woodward might have restored the text of the play and perhaps have established a reputation for *All's Well* which would have altered its rather dark stage history. But both the warmth and resoluteness of Helena were beyond Miss Macklin:

1. *Dramatic Miscellanies*, ii. 40.
2. The Diary is in the Folger Shakespeare Library collection.

Though Maria had achieved a modest success on the stage, her contemporaries, without exception, found her chilly and remote. She was somewhat small, like her mother, with a good figure, an agreeable, light voice, and her father's expressive eyes. Yet she was evidently colorless, almost cataleptic in manner, both on and off stage. . . . Until 1759 she remained an exemplary member of Drury Lane but from the time of her transfer to Covent Garden until her retirement in 1776 she became increasingly languid and diffident.[1]

It is as well that Miss Macklin was not exposed to the irony of Helena's analysis of Parolles, for Garrick had dropped the lines:

> Yet these fix'd evils sit so fit in him
> That they take place when virtue's steely bones
> Look bleak i' th' cold wind.   (I. i. 100–2)

That 'these fix'd evils' did 'take place' over 'virtue's steely bones' is evident from a rather long and interesting review of *All's Well* which appeared in the London *Chronicle* on 1 December 1757. The review has particular value as the first theatrical criticism of the play in a London newspaper. It has more general interest as an exception to Mr. Gray's summary of theatrical criticism in London that as late as 1770 newspaper criticism was usually limited to short notes added to plot summaries of new plays.[2] The reviewer for the *Chronicle* not only discussed Woodward's success but commented upon the character Parolles and a scene which troubled him:

There is not one of Shakespear's Comedies where he has exerted a greater share of the *Vis comica* than in this, and I do not imagine there is to be found in all that great Master's Works, if you except his Falstaff, a truer, pleasanter, and more striking Character than that of Paroles. Yet one thing I have observed in it which I never could answer to myself; it is when, after one of his Scenes with Losen [Lafeu], the Bragart in a Soliloquy talks of wiping out the disgraces put upon him by that old Lord by fighting his Son, and a good deal more to that Purpose; everywhere else Paroles is thoroughly sensible of his Cowardice; why then should be just at that Instant lack that Consciousness, and strive, as it were, to cheer himself into a Notion of his being brave? Besides that it answers no Purpose, and breaks off the Continuity of the Character, is not this perverting the End of Soliloquies, which are in themselves but too absurd, and have only been allowed for Conveniency, that by their Means the Audience may get an Insight into Characters and Designs of a Nature that requires a Theatrical Secrecy; that is to say, a Secrecy relative only to the Business of the Play and the Parties concerned in the Plot? This only I offer as my Doubt, and rather incline to think it my Mistake, than imagine that

---

1. William Appleton, *Charles Macklin: An Actor's Life*, Cambridge, Massachusetts, 1960, p. 201.

2. *Gray*, p. 190.

incomparable Writer defective in that very point which was always esteemed his particular Excellence. However, that Character, even admitting that Reproach to be well grounded, is one of the greatest on the English Stage; and Mr. Woodward's exhibition of it fell in nothing short of its Beauties and Humour; as to the rest of the Parts, they are rather just than striking, and, I think, as much may be said of the performance.

We may wonder at the failure of the critic to see the dramatic effectiveness of Parolles's soliloquy when it is followed by the re-entrance of Lafeu and the dissolution of Parolles's brave front. But we can believe that his observations on the excellence of Woodward's Parolles and the mere 'just' presentations of the other performances reflect the nature of this production.[1]

It is not surprising that Woodward dominated the play and was responsible for its appeal. The audience of this age associated parts with actors. A play's success depended upon the appeal of a particular actor in a particular role. The audiences of the mid century went to see Garrick as Hamlet, Barry as Othello, Macklin as Shylock, Quin as Falstaff, and Woodward as Parolles. Woodward's hold upon the entire play remained unchallenged because the role of Helena was not identified with an actress of artistic stature. Whether the altered text discouraged the actresses, whether Miss Macklin's association with the part deterred them, or whether the comic force of Woodward resisted the competition, Helena did not become a vehicle of success.

As You Like It was saved to the stage by a succession of great Rosalinds— Mrs. Pritchard, Mrs. Woffington, Mrs. Barry, Mrs. Yates. *Measure for Measure* was revived at times to give these same fair ladies an opportunity to appear as Isabella.[2]

The comedy in *All's Well*, unlike that of *As You Like It*, was masculine; and the tragic potential of Isabella was not matched in the emaciated Helena of Garrick's text. Consequently, the *All's Well* of the eighteenth century was shaped by the comic force of Parolles.

At the end of the 1757–8 season, Woodward left Drury Lane and joined Spranger Barry in opening the new Crow-Street Theatre in Dublin. A rather turbulent rivalry broke out between the new theatre and the Smock Alley Theatre. A truce was reached just prior to the opening of the 1760–1 season. To show that all was well between the theatres, Woodward seems to have selected Shakespeare's

---

1. See n. 4, p. 174.

2. *Shakespeare from Betterton to Irving*, i. 338–9. Odell confirms the association of actors with parts, 'In every case the repertoire was regulated by the presence or the absence in the company of actors capable of drawing the public in certain characters.'

comedy as the first production for the sake of its title. The play was performed at Crow Street on 24 October 1760, but 'the house was far from being crowded'.[1] The partnership with Barry failed, and in 1762 Woodward returned to London and signed with Covent Garden.

Perhaps incensed that Woodward had joined the rival theatre, Garrick decided upon a daring revival of *All's Well* at Drury Lane. Since Miss Macklin, too, was now with Covent Garden, Garrick relied upon a new cast. Thomas King was given the role of Parolles, Mrs. Palmer that of Helena. The production was performed on 23 October 1762, and repeated on 25 November. Woodward and Covent Garden took up the challenge. On 29 November, *All's Well* was produced for the first time at Covent Garden in eighteen years. Woodward was featured as 'Capt. Parolles'; Miss Macklin appeared as Helena; the famous clown, Edwin Shuter, was cast as Lavache; and a rising sixteen-year-old actress, Miss Hallam (later Mrs. George Mattocks), was assigned the role of Diana. The competition between the two rival productions was short-lived. Garrick withdrew the play from his repertory, and it was not seen again at Drury Lane until the Kemble production of 1794.[2] The Woodward production enjoyed a highly successful season; performances were repeated in December, January, February, March, and April. It remained in the repertory at Covent Garden until 1774, three years before the death of Woodward. During that time, it was performed seventeen times in seven seasons.[3] The attraction of *All's Well* was Woodward, and it is significant that only the names of Mrs. Ward as the Countess and Miss Hallam as Diana are added occasionally to Woodward's name in newspaper advertisements for the play.[4]

Woodward had continued to use the Garrick adaptation of *All's Well* even after joining the rival company at Covent Garden.[5] Evidence of this is included in the two editions of the adaptation which have come down to us. In 1774, the 'Bell Acting Edition' of *All's Well* was published; it printed the text of the play 'As Performed

1. Robert Hitchcock, *An Historical View of the Irish Stage*, Dublin, 1788, ii. 45.

2. Mr. Stone concludes that *All's Well* was not a success at Drury Lane since it was dropped from the repertory in 1762, but he fails to consider Woodward's performances at Covent Garden (i. 333).

3. Mr. Pedicord is in error in the appendix entitled 'Repertoire at Covent Garden Theatre, 1747–1776'. He lists thirteen performances in six seasons. There is an additional error in his tabulation of *All's Well* at Drury Lane; the play was produced there in four seasons, but he records only three. See Appendix C, pp. 210–11 and 224–5.

4. See n. 5, p. 174.

5. Such piracies were most common; some minor changes may have been made by Woodward to prevent accusations. The 1764 production, for example, reinstated the Duke of Florence either as an experiment or to forestall a Garrick claim that the version was stolen from him.

at the Theatre-Royal, Drury Lane'. The edition listed the cast for the last production at that theatre, that by Garrick in 1762. In addition, it gave the cast for the most recent production of *All's Well* at Covent Garden, that in which Woodward played Parolles in 1772. The implication is that both casts used the adaptation printed therein. More conclusive, however, is the title-page of a second edition published in the *Theatrical Magazine* in 1778. This edition presents the play, 'As it is Acted at the Theatres Royal in Drury Lane and Covent Garden'. In substance, the texts of the adaptation are the same in both editions, but there are differences in the stage directions. The 1778 edition records the stage business of the productions at Covent Garden. For example, Parolles is led on stage by the Clown in the last scene rather than by guards as the 1774 direction reads. In general, the presence of the Clown serves to lighten the oppressive mood of the trial; in particular, the direction brings back on-stage at Covent Garden the extremely popular comedian, Edwin Shuter. We can conclude then, that although there were separate traditions of stage business at each theatre, Woodward did use the Garrick text, and that text was the sole acting version of *All's Well* on the London stage from 1756 to 1774.

The first recorded criticism of the adaptation is contained in the 'Bell Acting Edition' in an introduction and notes written by Francis Gentleman. His comments provide a contemporary verdict upon the acting version in the very year in which it was last produced; they reveal as well attitudes which would soon alter the treatment of *All's Well* in the theatre. First reflecting the popular taste of the previous twenty years, Gentleman defends the emphasis which the adaptation has given to Parolles, Shakespeare's 'chief object, and inducement to undertake this piece'.[1] He gives high praise to the comedy of the play:

It is a stroke of humour to represent *Parolles* making so much ado about the loss of a drum, though victory has been on their side.   (p. 334)

The sonorous jargon uttered in this scene, to rouse the timidity of *Parolles*, is well introduced, and extremely farcical.   (p. 342)

The terrible, but just dilemna, *Parolles* appears in, through this scene, the progress of his interrogation, his treacherous, slanderous, pusillanimous answers, all combined, give great scope for comic merit, and are excellent food for mirth.   (p. 345)

---

1. These general comments are a part of Gentleman's 'Introduction' to the 'Bell Acting Edition' of *All's Well that Ends Well*, London, 1774, p. 297. Other references in this section are to his notes throughout the edition and are indicated by a page number in parentheses in my text.

But his approval of the comedy is not without qualification, for Gentleman has already been affected by the trend toward sentimentality and prudery. Of the virginity scene, he writes, 'This scene, as it stands originally, is not only indelicate, but trifling: above half of it is omitted, and indeed the whole might very well be spared' (p. 302). He would eliminate such offensive lines as Diana's 'his wife grew big with child' (p. 358) and the 'impertinent quibbling matter, between the Countess and Clown' (p. 315).

Especially in his remarks about Helena do we foresee the dilemma which *All's Well* presented to the nineteenth-century stage. On the one hand, Gentleman imagines the sentimental heroine fashioned by the Romantic critics. Helena confesses her love of Bertram to the Countess 'in terms of the most modest, pleasing sensibility' (p. 310); of her proposed pilgrimage, he writes: 'The idea of *Helena's* mitigating, by chaste prayers, the errors of her husband, is exceedingly beautiful' (p. 329). On the other hand, he cannot reconcile her agressiveness with this concept. She wins her husband, 'it must be confessed on terms very ungracious to delicate or generous feelings' (p. 319); after Bertram's desertion, 'Helena, resolving to have the man, whether he will or not, somewhat abates our pity for her situation' (p. 327). Gentleman is forced to conclude that the play, in its original form, 'can hardly live on the stage; yet we are of the opinion, that by judicious alterations and additions, it might be made much more tolerable' (p. 297). For a century, the stage history of *All's Well* records the attempts at 'judicious alterations and additions'.

The farcical approach to *All's Well* was attempted once more in the eighteenth century; the result was an even greater distortion of Shakespeare's play than Garrick's version. On 26 July 1785, the *Gazetteer and New Daily Advertiser* announced that there 'will be revived a Comedy, in Three Acts (altered from Shakespeare) called *All's Well that Ends Well*' that same evening at the Haymarket. The alteration was prepared for John Bannister, who was 'the chief support of farce, and of course of the Haymarket—the House of Farce'.[1] The first performance was a benefit for Bannister who played Parolles. The adapter, Frederick Pilon, had compressed the material to highlight the role. Reviews of the production generally credit Pilon with giving Bannister a *tour de force*. Unfortunately, the text of the alteration has not been preserved, and we are dependent upon the reviews for our knowledge of the version. Seemingly, the plot was reduced to two incidents, the exposure of Parolles and the exposure of Bertram. Helena, as a passive instrument in these

1. John Roach, *Authentic Memoirs of the Green Room*, London, 1796, p. 9.

incidents, hovered in the background; 'the most interesting picture can hardly be imagined of grace, dignity, and beauty'.[1] It was not Shakespeare's picture, however, for Pilon omitted almost all of the first three acts:

The whole of the story of the King's cure, and all the circumstances preliminary to the marriage of Bertram and Helena are past over, and the piece commences with the entrance of Helena in her pilgrim's dress. He [Pilon] has properly reserved, however, many of the poetical beauties of the first three acts, which he has connected by some sentences of his own writing.[2]

Genest does not give a full cast, but a playbill lists a sufficient number of actors to suggest that Pilon retained the major characters of the original play.[3] One clue to the fashioning of minor roles is the introduction of Lafeu with Bertram in Florence; Lafeu absorbs the role of one lord and participates in the exposure of Parolles.

The character was admirably adapted to his talents, and beneficial to his reputation. In the first part he had to display a vain coxcomb, an empty traveler, a bragging coward, and an obsequious sycophant, patient of affronts, and enduring to be termed an imposter and a knave. In all these scenes Bannister exhibited the pertness, presumption, and uneasy bustle of such a mind, with the pretended fever of simulated indignation, when reproach touched him too nearly to be misapprehended or devade. His dress was that of a point-de-vice soldier; and his bearing alert, petulant, and confident. In a subsequent scene, where his presumptious folly leads him into an ambuscade, he is captured and blindfolded by a party of his friends, bent on disclosing him in his true colours, who speaking a pretended language (a good specimen of the unknown tongues) through the organ of a mock interpreter, draw from him all the secrets of his meanness, and leave him overloaded with disgrace and scorn. Degraded and baffled, he still attempts to be considered as an adherent of those with whom he had before claimed equality; and in a mean habiliment, and with corresponding humbleness of speech and gesture, he so far works on the good feelings of an honourable old lord, the great contemner of his former pretensions, as to be retained in a very humble situation. In this portion of the play, the actor's style was no less masterly than in those which preceded: there was a base humility in his address, a prompt alacrity in his complaisance, a total extinction of everything like pretension which made the spectator well pleased that the wretch should find a

---

1. *The Morning Post and Daily Advertiser*, 27 July 1785.
2. *Gazetteer and New Daily Advertiser*, 27 July 1785. This rather detailed and enthusiastic review appears to have been overlooked by stage historians. Hogan does not list it (ii. 110). Frederick W. Kilbourne, in *Alterations and Adaptations of Shakespeare* (Boston, 1910), wrote that he could learn nothing about the Pilon version.
3. Uncatalogued playbill in the Library for the Performing Arts, New York Public Library.

comfortable though servile refuge in the charity of the old Lord Lafeu. Bannister received, throughout the piece, warm and well-deserved applause.[1]

The majority of reviewers praised the alteration. *The Morning Post & Daily Advertiser* considered it an improvement, 'a compression of matter, too diffusely disposed of, for the strength of its humour, its character, and interest'. Yet we may suspect that the extravagant praise was caused more by the attraction of Bannister at his own benefit than by the text. At least one critic objected to the 'mangling' of Shakespeare, to the negligible parts assigned to Helena and Bertram, and to the 'injudicious omissions' even in Parolles.[2] He concludes that only 'the liberty allowed in such benefits' justified the alteration. His judgement was validated by the fate of the play; the Pilon *All's Well* was repeated two nights later, but was never acted again.

1. *Memoirs of John Bannister, Comedian*, London, 1839, i. 124–5.
2. *European Magazine and London Review*, viii (Aug. 1785), 150–1.

For the Benefit of Mr. Bannister, Jun.

At the Theatre-Royal, Hay-Market,

This present TUESDAY, JULY 26th, 1785,

Will be reviv'd a COMEDY, in Three Acts, (altered from SHAKESPEARE) call'd

All's well that ends well.

The Principal CHARACTERS by

Mr. E D W I N,
Mr. B A D D E L E Y,
Mr. W I L I A M S O N,
Mr. B U R T O N,
Mr. G A R D N E R, Mr. R. P A L M E R,
And Mr. B A N N I S T E R, Jun.
Mrs. I N C H B A L D,
Mrs. C U Y L E R, Mrs. P O U S S I N,
And Miss F A R R E N.

A new Prologue to be spoken by Mr. BANNISTER, Jun.

After the Play, will be perform'd (acted but once) a Comic Sketch, in 1 Act, with Alterations, call'd

The Green Room;

Or, CUT AND COME AGAIN.

In which Mr. BANNISTER, Jun. will introduce various
IMITATIONS, Vocal and Rhetorical.

The CHARACTERS by

Mr. PALMER, Mr. BADDELEY, Mr. AICKIN, Mr. WEWITZER,
Mr. R. PALMER, Mr. BURTON, and Mr. BANNISTER.

After which will be perform'd a Musical Farce, in Two Acts, call'd

GRETNA GREEN.

The Principal CHARACTERS by

Mr. B A N N I S T E R,
Mr. R. P A L M E R, And Mr. B O O T H.
Signora S E S T I N I,
Miss G E O R G E,
Mrs. W E B B,
And Mrs. B A N N I S T E R.

To-morrow (Ninth Night) TURK, AND NO TURK;
With HARLEQUIN TEAGUE; or, The Giant's Causeway.

Playbill for the 1785 Pilon adaptation at the Haymarket

2

THE KEMBLE TEXT:
SENTIMENT AND DECENCY
(1794–1895)

In 1793, a third adaptation of the play was published under the title, *Shakespeare's All's Well That Ends Well; With Alterations by J. P. Kemble, As it is performed by His Majesty's Servants, of the Theatre-Royal, Drury Lane*. The title is deceiving, for the adaptation had not yet been produced in the theatre. The old Drury Lane had been demolished in 1791. From 1791 to 1793, the company performed at the King's Theatre and at the Theatre Royal, Haymarket. It is probable that Kemble prepared his version of *All's Well* during this period. But the company was disbanded for the 1793–4 season while it awaited the opening of the new Drury Lane, and Kemble was unable to produce his alteration. With a production date uncertain, Kemble, we may conjecture, published his text. The play was performed for the first time on 12 December 1794. Undoubtedly, the production followed the published version, for a second edition of the text was printed in 1795 with only two, perhaps careless, changes in stage directions.

The Kemble alteration has had a long history in the theatre. A revised version which was used as the acting text for a Charles Kemble production at Covent Garden in 1811 was published in the same year. This text was reprinted in 1815 and, with only a few additional stage directions, was published in 1838 as the 'Cumberland Acting Edition'. The Cumberland, in turn, was reprinted exactly in 'Lacey's Acting Edition'. The Kemble tradition has been brought down to modern times in the 'French Acting Edition' of *All's Well*, which reproduces Lacey's with only one change, the shifting of a single stage direction. Conceivably, the text is still used by amateur producers of the play. In the professional theatre, it was used in a performance at Bath in 1821, and most probably, in the Samuel Phelps production in London in 1852.

There are differences between the Kemble versions published in 1793 and 1811. The 1793 text is closer to the original play; its cuts are determined primarily by Kemble's interest in compression; it is more concerned with plot than character, unlike the later version; it is less governed by the demands of 'decency'.[1] Nevertheless, the

1. See n.1, pp. 174–5.

approach and technique are the same in both editions. These are sharply delineated if the 1811 edition is considered the basic Kemble text. Not only does it represent his final concept of the play, but also it incorporates the stage experience gained in the 1794 production.

Kemble's approach to *All's Well* reflects the trend which the theatre and the age were following. Where Garrick had moulded a farce, Kemble now fashioned a sentimental comedy. He was much more interested in the plot of the play, in the heroine, in the potentiality for theatrical pomp than Garrick had been. Kemble focused his adaptation upon Helena and the plight of her selfless love. He cut severely into the comic elements of the play by diminishing the parts of Parolles and the Clown. To avoid any distortion of his focus, he reduced the roles of the Countess, the King, and Lafeu to mere instruments in the attainment of the heroine's love. But that attainment is not the result of an aggressive Helena; on the contrary, Kemble deleted all dialogue and action which might be offensive in the long-suffering, virtuous heroine of romance. In effect, the adapter presented to his audience a Helena as she was conceived by the Romantics and epitomized by Coleridge twenty-four years later as Shakespeare's 'loveliest character'.[1]

Helena dominates the first act of the alteration, yet without a semblance of that aggressiveness which many critics of Shakespeare's play have attributed to her. Kemble makes her love less forward in the first scene by narrowing the gap between the young lord of the household and the poor dependent. In his departure for the Court, Bertram takes leave of Helena warmly. In lines usually addressed to his mother, Bertram bids farewell to Helena: 'The best wishes, that can be forg'd in your thoughts, be servants to you, Helen!' (i. i. 71–72). Kemble deliberately obscures the heroine's position as an inferior at Rousillon by the deletion of Bertram's charge: 'Be comfortable to my mother, your mistress, and make much of her' (i. i. 73–74). His exit is marked by only five lines of Helena's original soliloquy in which she first expresses her love for him; the remaining lines which convey the hopelessness of her love are postponed to the end of the scene. This brief expression of love is followed by the entrance of Parolles, who interrupts her reverie, as he does in Shakespeare's play fourteen lines later. But the interruption is momentary, for the entire virginity duologue is omitted (i. i. 102–86). Instead of dominating the scene as he did in Garrick's version, Parolles merely exchanges a few lines with the virtuous heroine before he follows Bertram to Court. Helena returns to her reverie and concludes the

1. Thomas Middleton Raysor (ed.), *Coleridge's Shakespearean Criticism*, London, 1930, i. 113. See my Chapter 5, p. 84.

scene as the unloved heroine of melodrama musing on the obstacles to her love. In Shakespeare's play, Helena had pondered these obstacles before the entrance of Parolles. Perhaps prompted by her wordplay with Parolles on the loss of virginity, Helena concludes the scene with a second soliloquy which reveals her determination to attain her love. Kemble transposes any hint of such action until after the Countess has encouraged his heroine.

To maintain his focus upon Helena, Kemble transposes Bertram's arrival at Court (I. ii) to his second act. Thus, the heroine's revelation of her love is followed by the confession of that love to Bertram's mother (I. iii). The compression of dialogue in this scene has three effects. The expurgation of the Clown's reasons for marrying rejects an anticipatory parody and preserves the decorum of the confession (I. iii. 25–61). The elimination of forceful lines in the interrogation of Helena by the Countess weakens, but makes more modest, the characterizations of both women: Helena offers so little resistance that the Countess's charge of 'hellish obstinacy' is understandably cut (I. iii. 175). Finally, the strength of Helena's resolution is modified in keeping with her docility. She commands attention at the end of Act I not by her determination but through a change in stage business. Unlike Shakespeare's *All's Well* where the Countess and the heroine go off stage together, the adaptation leaves Helena alone to form her plan in a sharply curtailed and enigmatic soliloquy:

> Our remedies oft in ourselves do lie,
> Which we ascribe to chance. Who ever strove
> To show her merit, that did miss her love?
> The king's disease—my project may deceive me:
> But my intents are fix'd, and will not leave me.
>
> (I. i. 212–25)

Kemble balances the roles of hero and heroine by the transposition of one scene and the compression of two others in the beginning of his second act. As Helena dominates the two scenes of Act I, Bertram dominates the first two scenes of Act II. To forewarn the audience of a flaw in his romantic hero, Kemble opens the act with Bertram's refusal to accept Lafeu's caution against Parolles (II. v. 1–11). But the brief scene is only a forewarning, for it is followed by a favourable impression of the hero in a blending of the two Shakespearian Court scenes (I. ii and II. i). For Kemble's purpose, the blending is an effective compression. In a single scene, Bertram is introduced to the King; mention is made of the Florentine war; the King inquires about the physician at Rousillon, Helena's deceased father; the lords leave for the war; and the young hero bravely vows to slip away after them. Kemble has balanced the roles and the opposing forces of his romance: as Helena has determined to seek out love, Bertram has determined to seek out war.

After the crowded action of the first four scenes, Act II, scene iii provides the first interlude. Probably for comic relief, Kemble advances the 'O Lord, Sir' jest between the Countess and the Clown (II. ii); he places the scene before the King's acceptance of Helena's cure instead of after it. The acceptance is substantially the same as in the original play. The deletions are intended to make less bold Helena's persuasion of the King; she remains in character as the submissive heroine of melodrama.

That character is amplified in Act III. In the first scene, Kemble's only significant omission is Helena's deliberation before each of the young lords prior to her choice of Bertram (II. iii. 76–102). Garrick appears to have cut the scene because of his focus upon comedy; Kemble's motive is the preservation of maidenly modesty. In the second scene, lines are deleted to maintain the sobriety of the heroine. As Helena had been denied her repartee on virginity with Parolles, so here she is denied her quibbling with the Clown (II. iv. 2–7). Only minor cuts are made in the third scene, but, in the fourth scene, the conception of a child is expurgated from Bertram's letter of conditions (III. ii. 57–58). The moral taste of the age demanded a heroine consistent with its notion of purity, and the sexual pursuit of a male was outside that notion. Kemble satisfied the moral taste and the dramatic taste as well by closing the third act with a soliloquy in which Helena vows to sacrifice herself for her beloved (III. ii. 99–129).

Perhaps indicative of the age's satisfaction with the mere appearance of morality, the expurgation of the condition of a child does not alter the plot. For the removal of this explicit charge does not spare the heroine the 'shameful deceit' of the bed-trick. Kemble has eliminated any overt mention of the bed-trick and the conception of a child, but only a naïve or wilfully blind audience would miss the implication in the alteration that Bertram sleeps with his wife in an attempted seduction of Diana. Besides more discreet Shakespearian allusions, Kemble retains Helena's proposal to the Widow, Bertram's wooing of Diana, and Diana's subsequent charge that Bertram has misused her (v. iii. 139–45). Nineteenth-century morality read into the plot what Shakespeare had made specific.

After eliminating the second Duke of Florence scene (III. iii), in which Bertram is commissioned general of the troop, Kemble composed a fourth act of seven scenes which follow rather closely the parallel scenes in Shakespeare (III. iv–IV. iii). There are omissions and compression, but they are dictated by Kemble's general intentions: a focus upon romantic melodrama and an inoffensive text.

Thus, Helena's letter to the Countess in which she explains her flight is dismissed as unnecessary repetition (III. iv. 4–18); the moralizing of the lords is reduced for pacing, and consequently, the thematic speech, 'The web of our life is of a mingled yarn, good and ill together', is lost (IV. iii. 59–81); indelicate lines such as Bertram's plea, 'But give thyself unto my sick desires' (IV. ii. 35), are dropped; Parolles loses his irrepressible acceptance of life after his exposure (IV. iii. 326–9). Farce had crushed the ambushed soldier in the Garrick adaptation; morality demanded the chastisement of the evil companion in the Kemble text.

Unlike the original play, the 1811 *All's Well* places all the events which lead immediately to the reconciliation in the last act. Act v begins with Lafeu's defence of Bertram before the Countess (IV. v). To build swiftly to his climax, Kemble eliminates most of the quibbling between Lafeu and the Clown. The omissions forfeit the touching explanation by the Countess of the Clown's presence in her household (IV. v. 61–64) and the Clown's characterizing lines: 'I am a woodland fellow . . .' (IV. v. 44–52). Instead of two scenes depicting the journey of Helena, Diana, and the Widow (IV. iv and v. i), Kemble combines them as his second scene and sacrifices both realism and characterization. The final two scenes of both plays correspond except for the usual compression of dialogue and expurgations. But despite these expurgations, as I have noted above, the seduction of Diana is implicit in the trial of Bertram. The entrance of Helena is not preceded by Diana's lines:

> He knows himself my bed he hath defil'd;
> And at that time he got his wife with child,
>> (v. iii. 294–5)

but the effect of the entrance upon Bertram is the same in both plays. It is a desperate and repentant husband who falls before the heroine. There is a difference, however, in the character of the heroine. In the Kemble version, it is not the clever wife, but the long-suffering, scorned wife who raises her husband to his redemption. The bright world of Shakespeare's romance has been shaded by the moral tone of sentimentalism. As Virtue Rewarded, the Kemble Helena turns to the audience and delivers the epilogue.

Again, we see the assignment of the epilogue as a touchstone of the alteration. For Garrick, the epilogue and the play belonged to Parolles; by the end of the century *All's Well that Ends Well* was Helena's. In the view of most critics, the change in focus and the adaptation itself were improvements. The London *Star*, on 29 December 1794, reported, 'The alterations chiefly consist in judicious compressions and transpositions.' The verdict echoes through the centuries. In the nineteenth century, Genest wrote:

His alteration is very judicious—he has omitted the weak parts, and transposed some speeches with good effect—by not attempting to do too much he has fitted this C[omedy] for representation without injuring it.[1]

In the twentieth century, Harold Child agreed: 'In or about 1794 John Philip Kemble took the play in hand and made a judicious version of it which brought it back pretty nearly to the original.'[2] Among the commentators, only Halliwell-Phillips in 1857 attacked the adaptation: 'It is scarcely a matter of surprise that the performance of the drama, in this vitiated form, should not have met, at any recent period, with the success that it probably commanded on the Shakespearean stage.'[3] Kemble had discarded motivation, characterization, comedy, and poetry; only a melodrama remained. But the nineteenth century gave a grudging preference for the sentimentality of Kemble to the indelicacy of Shakespeare.

Although production of the Kemble adaptation was delayed until the completion of a new Drury Lane in 1794, the text published in 1793 included a cast of characters as 'performed by His Majesty's Servants, of the Theatre-Royal, Drury Lane'. The emphasis which *All's Well* now reflected may be noted in Kemble's assignment of Helena to Mrs. Siddons and Bertram to himself. For the first time since the play's revival in 1741, the 'stars' of a company were cast as hero and heroine. The casting of Mrs. Siddons as Helena suggests, as it would have suggested to the London audience, a serious, perhaps a tragic heroine. From about 1790, the leading female roles in Shakespearian plays at Drury Lane had been divided between Mrs. Siddons, who acted the tragic heroines, and Mrs. Jordan, who acted the comic. Earlier, in 1786 and 1787, Mrs. Siddons had challenged the reputation of Mrs. Jordan in comedy by appearing as Rosalind in *As You Like It*, Mrs. Jordan's most famous part. But the challenge had failed. In the first few months of the 1794–5 season before *All's Well* was finally produced, Mrs. Siddons played in *Macbeth*, *Henry VIII*, and *Othello*; Mrs. Jordan acted in *As You Like It* and *Twelfth Night*. The audience was prepared for a melodramatic Helena. Surprisingly, at the first performance of the play on 12 December 1794, Mrs. Jordan appeared as Helena!

Why Kemble substituted Mrs. Jordan for Mrs. Siddons is open to unlimited conjecture. Did Kemble or Mrs. Siddons decide the comic

1. vii. 183–4.
2. 'The Stage History', *All's Well that Ends Well*, ed. Sir Arthur Quiller Couch and Dover Wilson, Cambridge, England, 1929, p. 188.
3. J. Q. Halliwell-Phillips, *Memoranda on All's Well that Ends Well*, etc., Brighton, 1879, p. 20.

characters of Parolles, Lafeu, and Lavache still restricted the tragic potential of the heroine despite the tone of the adaptation? Did Mrs. Jordan insist on the part as a comic role? Did Kemble prefer Mrs. Jordan for the part once the play moved from his imagination to the stage? Or was the change made simply out of some theatrical necessity? One other fact qualifies a conclusion. *All's Well* was followed by another Shakespearian revival on 30 December 1794. Kemble produced *Measure for Measure*, which, like *All's Well*, had not been seen in London since 1785. Mrs. Siddons, who had played Isabella very much like a tragic heroine in 1785, repeated the role. Since the two 'companion' plays were revived in the same month by the same theatre after the same lapse of years, we may conclude tentatively that *Measure for Measure* was considered more suited to the dramatic talent of Mrs. Siddons, despite the earlier publication of her name as Helena. It is of some significance that Helena and *All's Well*, in spite of the comic deletions, were considered to be brighter than Isabella and the 'dark comedy', *Measure for Measure*.

We should imagine that *All's Well that Ends Well* was at last fortunate in the casting of its heroine. The play had been altered to spotlight Helena, and, here at last an actress of great beauty and merit might 'create' a character which would live in theatrical memory. In tragedy, Mrs. Siddons had done this with her portrayal of Lady Macbeth; why not Mrs. Jordan with Helena? Her charm as an actress blossomed into legend among Romantic critics. Hazlitt thought of her as 'the child of nature, whose voice was a cordial to the heart';[1] Leigh Hunt rhapsodized, 'In the girl, what hey-day vivacity, what bounding eagerness, what tip-toe spirits and expectation, what exquisite ignorance of received habits!'[2] Perhaps most pertinent to the qualities in Helena is the comment of Lamb: 'Her childlike spirit shook off the load of years from her spectators; she seemed one whom care could not come near,—a privileged being sent to teach mankind what he most wants, joyousness.'[3] Here was a Helena, then, who might well teach Bertram love and the audience acceptance of that love.

Yet, a set of circumstances similar to the misfortunes of the first Drury Lane revival some fifty years before haunted the play. As the first performance of that revival was marred by the illness of Peg

1. William Hazlitt, 'Dramatic Essays from the London Magazine', *The Collected Works of William Hazlitt*, ed. Arnold Glover and A. R. Waller, London, 1903, viii. 389. The essay first appeared in the *London Magazine*, Jan. 1820.

2. Lawrence H. and Carolyn W. Houtchens (eds.), *Leigh Hunt's Dramatic Criticism: 1801–1831*, New York, 1949, p. 88. The comment first appeared in an essay by Hunt, 'The Comic Actresses', 8 Jan. 1815.

3. Brander Matthews (ed.), *The Dramatic Essays of Charles Lamb*, New York, 1891, p. 246.

Woffington, so this production was hampered by the illness of Kemble—which must have made more emphatic Bannister's description of Kemble in comedy, 'He was as *merry* as a funeral, and as *lively* as an elephant.'[1] So too, this production was troubled by a dispute in casting Parolles. King had played the role in the 1762 performances at Drury Lane after Woodward's departure; Bannister had played the role in the two performances of 1785. Each wanted the part. Years later, Bannister's biographer records the comedian's magnanimity in yielding the role to King, but this is not true.[2] Contemporary reviews show that Bannister won the part. Finally, Mrs. Jordan, at the time, was undergoing a wearying pregnancy; of a performance two weeks before, she wrote to the Duke of Clarence, 'I was very unwell and c^d not speak the epilogue.'[3] She appeared infrequently on the stage until the birth of her baby on 16 April 1795. If these circumstances did not recall the superstition surrounding *All's Well* in the theatre, both cast and audience were reminded by a review in the London *Star* which gave a brief history of the play and its epithet, 'unfortunate comedy'.[4]

Perhaps because of the political and military events of the time, there are few dramatic reviews of the production, but all are favourable. The *European Magazine and London Review* reported that the play was revived 'in a style very creditable to the Manager'.[5] On the day following the performance, the *Star* noted that the revival 'received much applause'. In a more detailed review on 19 December, the *Star* praised the alteration and the cast:

> Bannister is deficient in nothing but personal importance—Woodward certainly surpassed him in figure, but not in conception of the character. Mrs. Jordan's appearance, 'tis true, bespeaks not the virgin bride of Bertram; but her tones and manner are irresistibly interesting . . . King makes the Fool a 'kind of wit' and insinuates his jokes successfully through the house.

The *Sun* reported that the house was very respectably filled, applauded the revival of old comedies, singled out Miss Miller, who had recently been raised from the chorus and now appeared as Diana, and promised, 'Of the propriety of the alterations we shall speak hereafter'.[6] The promise implies that the reviewer fully expected the play to be added to the repertory of the theatre. But *All's Well* was given only one performance; Kemble dropped the play.

Kemble's illness explains why *All's Well* was not repeated immediately; he does not appear in Genest's list of casts until 30 December. But it does not explain why the play was dropped entirely from the

1. *Oxberry's Dramatic Biography*, London, 1825, N.S. i. 120.
2. John Adolphus, *Memoirs of John Bannister, Comedian*, London, 1839, i. 347.
3. See n. 2, p. 175.   4. 29 Dec. 1794.   5. xxvii (Jan. 1795), 48.   6. 13 Dec. 1794.

repertory. The pregnancy of Mrs. Jordan certainly operated against the plot of the play; the longer a second performance was delayed, the more ludicrous her appearance as Helena would be. Yet, this only increases our wonder at Kemble's replacing Mrs. Siddons with Mrs. Jordan in the part. Furthermore, Kemble had much at stake in the production. The adaptation was his work; the acting edition had been published a year in advance of performance. He produced the play 'with his usual care'.[1] At a new theatre with new stage machinery, the phrase 'usual care' implies considerable expense. For a production of *Macbeth* in the same season, 'Among the novelty of scenery that efficiently rose and smoothly descended upon the stage of the new Drury Lane, Kemble had introduced a lake of real water, to the admiration of all spectators'.[2] Production costs would necessitate repeat performances even for a play which had been poorly received. Yet, receipts for the single performance show that the play drew a larger audience than had the premieres of eight of the ten previous Shakespearian productions. Its box-office receipts were larger than the first night of the succeeding revival, *Measure for Measure* with Mrs. Siddons. Despite this, *Measure for Measure* was repeated; *All's Well* was dropped. All this would be quite comprehensible if the play had proved a wretched failure, but the evidence of contemporary critics refutes this. The evidence is scant; nevertheless, it receives some support in later years in the delight with which Lamb recalled the performance of Mrs. Jordan as Helena—if we can trust his memory.[3] We can only conclude that circumstances other than the reception of the play closed this carefully prepared production. It may well be that the illness of Kemble, the apparently forced withdrawal of Mrs. Jordan, and the dispute over casting revived the superstitions of the theatre.[4]

Seventeen years later, on 24 May 1811, a second attempt at a successful production of Kemble's alteration was made. Charles Kemble, the younger brother of John and manager of Covent Garden, produced the play and published the acting text shortly after. Charles Kemble had acquired a reputation for lavish productions:

At no theatre, and during no season, have so many of the best Plays of Shakespeare, and of our great English Dramatists, been revived, and brought forward with so much elegance and magnificence, as at Covent Garden, during the last Winter and Spring.[5]

1. James Boaden, *Memoirs of the Life of John Philip Kemble, Esq.*, London, 1825, ii. 137.
2. Yvonne French, *Mrs. Siddons, Tragic Actress*, London, 1936, p. 178.
3. *The Dramatic Essays of Charles Lamb*, p. 44.
4. We may also wonder what effect the recent military disaster in France might have had upon an English audience as they watched a play with a French setting, French characters, and victorious French soldiers.   5. *Bell's Weekly Messenger*, 7 July 1811.

In the revival of *All's Well*, he surpassed his own standards and the meticulous care displayed by his brother in 1794:

> We observed, that, upon no similar occasion, had greater attention been paid to the due preparation of a Play than was evinced upon this occasion. The performers were all perfect in the dialogue. The Florentine *costume* of the age was well attended to in the dresses of the character; and the scenery was illustrative of the subject.[1]

Comparable care was given to the selection of the cast. As his brother had done, Charles Kemble played Bertram. Helena was acted by Mrs. H. Johnston. The charming Mrs. Weston represented the Countess. Two of the greatest character actors of the age, Joseph Munden and John Fawcett, Jr., played Lafeu and Parolles respectively. Charles Lamb's famous tribute to Munden suggests a wonderful portrayal of Lafeu:

> He, and he alone, literally makes faces; applied to any other person, the phrase is a mere figure, denoting certain modifications of the human countenance. . . . But in the grand grotesque of farce, Munden stands out as single and unaccompanied as Hogarth. . . . Can any man *wonder* like he does?[2]

That sense of wonderment must have been particularly effective in *All's Well* where Lafeu must express amazement at the cure of the King, the arrogance of Parolles, and the revelations of Diana and Helena in the last scene.

The imaginative impression which we can paint of Munden in the role of Lafeu is of more interest to the 'ideal' production of *All's Well*, however, than the actual performance was to the refined sensibilities of the 1811 audience. Even the relatively tolerant attitude of the reviewer in the *European Magazine and London Review* suggests a spirit of sentimentality fatal to the play:

> Though we are far from considering this Comedy as one of those upon which the renown of our immortal Bard is eminently dependent, yet there are such instances of superior merit, in various parts of it, as leaves but little doubt that he was the Editor of it. The character of *Parolles* is wrought up with the hand of a master, and the situations of *Helena* are so delicately supposed and finished, that the auditor follows her, in the vicissitudes of her fortunes, with sympathy. In the *enclaircissement*, which occurs in the fifth act, there is so much mystery and enigma, that the judgment is not entirely satisfied, though the reconciliation which so happily ensues between *Bertram* and his maltreated wife, is so perfectly satisfactory and

1. J. M. Williams (ed.), *The Dramatic Censor: or, Critical and Biographical Illustration of the British Stage. For the Year 1811*, London, 1812, pp. 276–7. The same review appeared in the *European Magazine and London Review*, lix (June 1811), 380. A description of the costumes appears in the 'Cumberland Acting Edition', p. 8.

2. See n.3, p. 175.

pleasing, that we are inclined to turn aside from analysing the mode in which that event is brought about; and content ourselves with the knowledge that the virtue of Helena is eventually rewarded in the necessary repentance of her unfeeling husband. The Performers deserve much credit for the ability and ardour which they exhibited; and this praise is strongly due to Mr. Munden, Mr. Fawcett, and Mrs. H. Johnston, whose characters required greater exertion than the rest of the Dramatic Personae.[1]

There is not yet the objection to Helena and her boldness; Kemble has presented the long-suffering heroine whose methods are lost in 'mystery and enigma', whose methods need no analysis since virtue is rewarded—the maltreated wife has redeemed her erring husband. But we find no delight in the comedy, no vivid descriptions of Parolles, no interest in the comic scenes. In fact, Genest disputes the reviewer's praise for the performance of Parolles:

Yet Fawcett is said to have been hissed—when he came off the stage he put the part in Kemble's hands, and declared that he would not play it again—'then,' said Kemble, 'you will knock up the play'—Fawcett was however prevailed on to act Parolles a second time on June 22.

(viii. 237)

If the story is true, it points up most dramatically the swing of taste from the broad comedy of the Woodward era. The play was repeated on 22 June, but it was then dropped by Covent Garden. Almost a century of darkness was beginning for *All's Well*. Both its comedy and theme offended an audience whose judgement was based upon a rigid code of decency and a sentimental criterion of drama. Not only *All's Well* suffered from that judgement. A clear warning was sounded for the theatrical world in the *Examiner*'s summary of Charles Kemble's season at Covent Garden: 'The New Theatre closed on Tuesday last after a season more degrading to the views of the Managers and the indulgence of the public, than has been known for many years.'[2]

The play was next presented on 23 May 1821 at Bath. It may have been suggested by Mrs. Weston, who had played the Countess in the 1811 performance and now repeated the role. Genest praised the management for reviving *All's Well* but commented that the play 'has rarely proved attractive—it was acted on this evening in a respectable manner—Mrs. Weston was everything that could be wished' (ix. 131–2). What is intriguing about the production is that Genest himself apparently prepared the prompt-book which he based upon the 1793 Kemble rather than the 1811 edition.[3] In the

1. lix (June 1811), 380.
2. 28 July 1811.
3. The prompt-book is a 1793 Kemble edition with manuscript notes prepared by Genest. It is now located in the Furness Room of the University of Pennsylvania.

prompt-book manuscript notes include stage directions, call signals, lighting effects, change of costumes, changes in act divisions, time of production, and the initials of the Bath cast pencilled next to the appropriate character in Kemble's *dramatis personae*. The prompt-book appears to be unique among Genest's theatrical interests.

If Kemble's adaptation had not sufficiently purified *All's Well* for nineteenth-century audiences, still the play was written by Shakespeare, and the Romantic veneration of his genius would not permit the play to die. If the play was defective, then revitalize it with healthy tissue grafted from the Shakespearian corpus! Cover the blemishes with 'beauties' from other plays; inject song and dance into its veins! Thus, on 11 October 1832, *The Times* and the *Theatrical Observer* posted advertisements for a performance of *All's Well that Ends Well* as an opera. The notice in the *Theatrical Observer* boasted inaccurately, 'It has, since the death of Garrick, been almost entirely laid on the shelf, it having been acted at Drury Lane only twice in 1793, and once at Covent Garden in 1807.' The critic for the *Court Journal*, who had not yet seen the performance, wrote enthusiastically:

> The comedy of *All's Well that Ends Well* has been arranged for representation at Covent Garden by the most successful of modern dramatists, Frederick Reynolds. The music introduced . . . does not interfere with the plot or leading characters of the play; among which Parolles is to be personated by Jones, and is likely to form a pendant to his unique delineation of Mercutio.[1]

The play was performed on 12 October 1832. Despite the absurdity of the attempt, the production does have importance for the stage history of *All's Well*. The attempt, of course, shows the attitude of the age to the play, but the purpose of the adaptation has wider significance. Frederick Reynolds, the arranger, strove to blend the comic with sentimental elements against a background of romantic fairy-tale. He is the first of several producers who adopted this approach in their productions of the play. He purged the play of all 'bitter' plot machinations, realistic character motivations, offensive dialogue, and farce. To reinforce the sentimental and comic, Laporte, the manager, engaged the celebrated Miss Inverarity to act (and to sing) the role of Helena and induced the famous actor Jones to return to the stage after six years' absence to play Parolles. To create a background of fairy-tale, Oberon, Robin Goodfellow, and a chorus of fairies were whisked from *A Midsummer Night's Dream* and dropped into the opera. To lighten the 'dark' motives of the original and to replace offensive lines, songs were composed from verses in the sonnets, *Romeo and Juliet*, *Othello*, *A Midsummer Night's Dream*,

1. 13 Oct. 1832.

Love's Labour's Lost, Two Gentlemen of Verona, and *Twelfth Night*.[1] We can create a rather vivid image of the production if we imagine Bertram singing 'Love is a smoke . . .' (*R & J*, I. i. 196–200); Helena intoning mournfully, 'I am St. Jacques' Pilgrim . . .' (*All's Well*, III. iv. 1–10); and the entire chorus accompanied by Helena, Diana, the Astringer, and Falconers (!) bursting into 'If music be the food of love . . .' (*TN*, I. i. 1–5).

The critic for the *Theatrical Observer* was momentarily deceived. On 13 October, the day following the performance, he gave a brief summary of the plot (since the play 'as an acting Drama' is unknown to the 'present race of play-goers'), praised the loveliness and singing ability of Miss Iverarity, and concluded:

The Play has been got up with great care, and was on the whole well acted; its announcement for Tuesday [October 16th] was hailed with considerable applause, mixed with hisses.

In justice to the critic, he did condemn a masque in the first act as unbearable. Upon reflection, however, his entire view hardened. On 17 October he wrote:

We know not to whom the merit of having selected this play for revival belongs, but this we do know, that it shews extreme ignorance of the taste of the town, on the part of the person choosing it, for though the original Comedy contains some beautiful poetry and several cleverly drawn characters, the plot is in itself so objectionable to modern refinement, that it has long been acknowledged not to be fit for representation. . . . It has been said the play was got up almost expressly for Jones, if so, that was an error, for that lively comedian does not appear to advantage as *Parolles*; he lacks humour for the part, and in vain tries to make up for the deficiency, by blustering and swagger.

We might suspect that a moral wave of wrath against *All's Well* even in this purified form prompted the reversal of the critic's evaluation. For the other major reviews follow the same pattern. *The Times* of 13 October, with some objectivity, ascribed part of the blame to the age: 'It has, however, long been felt, that with reference to the taste of the times in which we live, it is not an acting play.' The reviewer also notes the dilemma of any producer of the play, 'To leave out all that makes it unfit for representation would be to leave a little behind', and he regrets 'that the scissors of the adapter have been so liberally applied' to Parolles. But such regrets were not the sentiments of the majority of the reviewers. More typical is an attack in the *Court Journal* which laid *All's Well* to rest for twenty

1. *Airs, Duets, Choruses, &C. Introduced in Shakespeare's Revived Comedy of All's Well that Ends Well or Love's Labour Won! As Performed at the Theatre Royal, Covent Garden, Friday, October 12, 1832*. Music composed, selected, and arranged by Rophino Lacy, London, 1832.

years. Because it is representative of critical opinion and indicative of the fate of the play in any alteration, I quote extensively from it:

Miserable blunders in taste and feeling are not always miserable failures in effect; but the revival, or adaptation, or alteration, or what you will, of *All's Well that Ends Well*, is signally as it ought to be in this particular. The revival at all, at this time of day, of the *only* play of Shakespeare that is really exceptionable in its moral tone and tendency, is a sufficient blunder; to unite that play in a forced marriage with the most touchingly pure, innocent, and pastoral, and at the same time most exquisitely and exclusively poetical, and most divinely human and beautiful, of all the same writer's plays, *A Midsummer Night's Dream*, was a still further stretch of that art of doing wrong, in which some people so remarkably excel;—and to reach the climax of ill-doing, nothing was needed but to set the divine verses of Shakespeare to that peculiar class of musical composition which may be taught as readily as 'reading, writing, and the use of the globes.'

That all this has been the work of so experienced and once popular a dramatist as Mr. Reynolds, we cannot persuade ourselves; . . . Conceive of an enquiring foreigner hastening to witness and judge of the *All's Well that Ends Well* of Shakespeare and listening to the farrago of mingled dullness and indecency presented to him by Mr. Laporte! What must be his impressions of us, and of our idol bard?[1]

There are few instances, I think, when the history of the stage criticism of a play acts as such a valid documentary of the ethical and sociological attitudes of English culture. To the interest in sentimental melodrama, to the objections to broad comedy, to the refinement of moral taste, we may add a growing nationalistic pride as characteristic of this period of the nineteenth century. The impression which this production gives the 'enquiring foreigner' is insulting to England. With *All's Well* considered as an affront to each of these attitudes, only a daring manager would risk a new production. Until the last decade of the century, only one manager dared that risk—Samuel Phelps.

Samuel Phelps revived the play at his theatre, Sadler's Wells, on 1 September 1852, twenty years after the operatic version. It was daring, and the press emphasized the risk. The issue of 4 September of the *Illustrated London News* reported, 'The mere announcement was calculated to excite great curiosity. It is one of those perilous adventures which, on this stage, have furnished the most remarkable successes'. The *Critic* called it 'a bold experiment: . . . Four times has this comedy been reproduced, and four times has it fallen'.[2] But

1. 20 Oct. 1832.

2. 15 Sept. 1852. For quotations taken from the numerous reviews of this production, I shall footnote only the first entry for each review. All further references are to the single date of the review.

such risks were common to Phelps, whom *John Bull* described as 'a diligent laborer in the vineyard of old plays'.[1] His reputation in the theatrical world of London is delineated in a review of *The Times*:

At any other theatre besides Sadler's Well, we should be surprised to see a revival of *All's Well that Ends Well*, but the Islington establishment is a sort of museum for the exhibition of dramatic curiosities, and we have no more right to be astounded at finding some Elizabethan crudity within its precincts than at finding a Buddhist idol in a missionary collection.[2]

And the *Spectator* shifts the image somewhat to describe the particular audience which attended Sadler's Wells:

There we have a public soundly educated in the faith that the Elizabethan fountain is all of pure if not medicinal water, and that the manager's judgment is infallible. A piece that is odd or dull beyond the ordinary level no more startles the genuine Islingtonian, than an extraordinary miracle in the Romish Church disturbs the devotion of the faithful.[3]

Despite the reputation of Phelps and the 'cultivated tolerance' of his audience, the risk remained in presenting a play whose plot was universally condemned. In the view of the *Athenaeum*, 'The rude nature of the plot has banished this play . . . from the modern stage. The manners represented are exceedingly gross'.[4] The *Critic* thought the plot so indecent that it should not be introduced to any modern audience and concluded that, if *All's Well* were the work of a contemporary dramatist, 'it would have been hissed off the stage on the first night of its production'. *The Times* attacked the plot as 'indelicate, even beyond the limits usually conceded to Elizabethan dramatists'. Furthermore,

If a young lady were to ask a gentleman to give her some notion of it, the latter would be given at once to a *nonplus*, unless he took refuge in the evasive reply that it resembled the episode of Angelo and Mariana, in *Measure for Measure*.

Phelps attempted to forestall such objections to his production of *All's Well* by three methods: the expurgation of the text, the refinement of his heroine, and an extremely dignified style. In all probability, he used the Kemble text. If he did not, he at least made the same concessions to the taste of the audience. He eliminated the bedtrick and the preliminary demand for the conception of Bertram's child; he omitted offensive lines. *The Times* commented, 'The offensive peculiarities are kept so far in the background that nothing is left to shock the ordinary spectator.' In spite of the considerable weeding in the text, Phelps did not succeed in smoothing the moral irritations of the press. The *Critic* felt the plot to be so offensive that

1. 4 Sept. 1852.   2. 2 Sept. 1852.   3. 4 Sept. 1852.   4. 4 Sept. 1852.

the play could never meet with success. *Bell's Weekly Messenger* expressed a similar belief, 'But no amount of cutting or transposition can eradicate the main idea, which crops up at every turn, and in every scene.'[1] *John Bull* termed it 'the most utterly hopeless' of all Phelps's revivals because the plot was not a fit subject in female society, nor could the play, 'alter it as you will, be made presentable to an audience of which decent females form a portion'.

But if Phelps did not forestall criticism with his expurgated text, he was more successful with his other methods. In these instances, he was aided by the taste of his audience. Miss Cooper, his choice for Helena, played the role with the modesty of a heroine so pleasing to the age. *Bell's Weekly Messenger* reported that 'genuine outbursts of applause' interrupted her characterization which was marked by 'great delicacy, feeling and effect'. The *Athenaeum* had high praise for the sentiment of Helena and the Countess, and the grace with which it was expressed:

> There is much natural refinement in the persons of Helena and the Countess. The purity of these two characters sheds an influence over the entire drama, and breathes about it a poetic atmosphere. The success of the present representation must in a great measure be referred to the delicate and efficient manner in which these parts were impersonated by Miss Cooper and Mrs. Ternan.

The sentiment was accentuated by a style unusual in its formality and dignity. It was achieved both by the staging, 'picturesque' in its decorum, and by the ceremonial delivery of dialogue:

> The whole drama had evidently been carefully rehearsed,—and a calm, quiet, and dignified tone prescribed to the different elocutionists. The parts were rather spoken than acted, and an air of polite reserve appeared to have been imposed on all the actors, save one [Parolles].[2]

If such polite reserve and decorum glossed over the unseemly details of the plot, if it created an aura around the 'loveliest character' of Shakespeare, by deliberate contrast it brought out the indecorous conduct of Parolles. Despite the predominant interest in romance, the contrast partially restored Parolles to the glory of the Woodward era. Phelps was so successful in the part that critics unanimously predicted that it would be regarded as one of his best impersonations. Typical of the praise and illustrative of Phelps's method is the review in the *Illustrated London News*:

> The feature of the evening was the *Parolles* of Mr. Phelps, whose nervous temperament well expressed the comic uneasiness of the braggart, whose tongue outruns his thoughts and deeds, even sometimes its words, which

1. 4 Sept. 1852.   2. *Athenaeum*, 4 Sept. 1852. See also *The Times*, 2 Sept. 1852.

THEATRE ROYAL,

Sadler's Wells.

Lessees, Messrs. GREENWOOD and PHELPS.

UNDER THE MANAGEMENT OF
MR. PHELPS.

On WEDNESDAY, Sept. 6th. & THURSDAY 7th, 1852.

Will be presented FIRST TIME SHAKESPEARE's Comedy of

ALL'S WELL
THAT
ENDS WELL.

With New Scenery, Dresses and Decorations.

King of France, -	Mr GEORGE BENNETT
Bertram, - (Count of Rousillon)	- Mr FREDERIC ROBINSON
Lefeu, (an Old Lord)	Mr BARRETT
Dumain, Mr T. C. HARRIS	Lewis, Mr C. MORTIMER
Berin, Mr MEAGRESON	Jaquez. Mr COURTNEY
Parolles, - (a Follower of Bertram)	Mr PHELPS
Tourville, Mr KNIGHT	
Rinaldo,—(Steward) Servants to the Countess	Mr H. MELLON
Clown, - of Rousillon	Mr LEWIS BALL
First Soldier, Mr WILKINS Second Soldier,	Mr FRANKS
Countess of Rousillon, (Mother to Bertram)	Mrs TERNAN
Helena, (a Gentlewoman protected by the Countess)	Miss COOPER
An old Widow of France, - -	Mrs H. MARSTON
Diana, - Neighbours and Friends	Miss T. BASSANO
Mariana, - to the Widow	Mrs DIXON
Polka, — "HEATHER BELL." —	Montgomery.

Published by CHARLES OLLIVIER, 41, New Bond Street.

To be followed by the Successful Comic Drama, in Two Acts, by Mr JOHN DALY, entitled

YOUNG
HUSBANDS.

Mrs Carey, - (of Littledot Villas, Brixton)	-	Mrs H. MARSTON
Matthew Fagg, (married to her eldest Daughter)	Mr LEWIS BALL	
Mr Digby Spooner, (married to her Second Daughter)	Mr F. ROBINSON	
Alfred Vacil, (the Bridegroom of the third Daughter)	Mr WALLIS	
Mr Gadbury, (Mrs Carey's Brother) Mr BARRETT	Wat,	Mr WILLIAMS
Mrs Fagg,	Miss ELIZA TRAVERS	
Mrs Spooner,	Miss STEPHENS	
Anna, Mrs Carey's Daughters	Miss T. BASSANO	
Sophia,	Miss LAMBE	
Jane,	Miss F. YOUNG	
Mary, (Servant of All-Work) Miss PEVENSEY	Mrs Dauder, (Charwoman)	Mrs DIXON

The New Successful Comic Drama, entitled
YOUNG HUSBANDS
WILL BE REPEATED EVERY EVENING.

On FRIDAY and SATURDAY will be revived the Play of The

MERCHANT's WEDDING
Or, LONDON FROLICS IN 1637.

KING LEAR
With New Scenery, Dresses, &c. will be performed
ON MONDAY NEXT.

PRICES:—First Circle, 3s.   Second ditto, 2s.   PIT, 1s.   GALLERY, 6d.
Half-price to Boxes only, at Nine o'Clock.
Private Boxes, £1 1s. and £1 11s. 6d.

To be obtained on application of Mr AUSTIN, Jun., at the Box Office of the Theatre.
And at Mr SAMS Library, St James St.; Mr MITCHELL, Royal Library, Old Bond St.; Mr ANDREWS, New Bond Street
Mr EBERS's dond St., Mr ALCROFT, Bond St.; at the Carlton Library, 12, Regent St.; & of CAMPBELL RANSFORD, &c
New Bond Street. The BOX-OFFICE open from 11 till 3, under the direction of Mr AUSTIN, Junr. Bill Inspector, Mr PHILLIP
Children under Three Years of Age cannot be admitted, and all Children entering the PIT must pay the Full Price of Admission.
Doors open at half-past 6, the Performances to commence at 7.
All Applications relative to the Hab' of the Theatre to be made to Mr GREENWOOD at the Box-Office.

Playbill for the 1852 Phelps production at Sadler's Wells

Mrs Ternan and Lewis Ball appeared as the Countess and the
Clown in the 1852 Phelps production

it has to borrow from others' mouths. The continual propelling of the arms was as curious as it was artistic and provocative of mirth. In the affair of the drum he was admirable; and, in the scene of the exposure, acted with an aptitude which realised the situation most thoroughly.

But the Parolles of Phelps was not the Parolles of Woodward. Against the background of romantic melodrama and before an audience of inflexible ethical standards, farcical jauntiness was transformed into 'empty vaunting' and the will to live into 'abject servility'. The difference in portrayals is indicated in a remark by F. G. Tomlins, who said of Phelps's performance, 'that he would rather it had had a little more of the Falstaff in it and less of the Pistol'.[1] The arm-swinging poltroon does suggest the ranting of Pistol in the tavern, and Pistol's exit before the sword of Falstaff has the same smack of degradation that we find in Phelps's exposure scene. 'The picture of the coward turned traitor was complete. The mental prostration of the culprit was fearfully true. There are touches in this dramatic portrait which are eminently Shakespearean.'[2] This 'dramatic portrait' is not the comic interpretation of Woodward.

The enthusiastic reception of the first-night audience for this tempered version of *All's Well* insured a moderately successful run. The play was performed eleven times during the 1852-3 season. Critics had equal praise for the performers and the careful detail of the production. *The Times* concluded: 'The applause of the audience, which was bestowed on the revival of the piece last night, showed that the manager's exertions had not been in vain.' The entire cast was praised by *Bell's Weekly Messenger*. After commending the delicacy and feeling of Helena and the cleverness of Parolles, the reviewer wrote:

Mr. Bennett, as the *King*, was emphatic and forcible. Mr. Barrett, as *Lafeu*, was characteristic and pointed. Mr. Mellon was judicious in the little he had to do as the *Steward*. Mr. Lewis Ball was quaint and pointed as the *Clown*. Mr. F. Robinson, as *Bertram*, rather under-acted the violent young *Count*. Mrs. Ternan, as the *Countess*, was sensible and lady-like; and Mrs. Marston, as ever, clever and characteristic in the old *Widow* of *Florence*. Miss Bassano gave a spirited emphasis to the speeches of Diana.

We might assume that, with concessions to the taste of his audience, with the meticulous attention given to the details of production, with the general capability of the cast, with the 'incessant roars of laughter'[3] for the modified buffoonery of Parolles, Phelps had at last lifted the tag, 'unfortunate comedy', from the play. Indeed, the

---

1. W. May Phelps and John Forbes-Robertson, *The Life and Life-Work of Samuel Phelps*, London, 1886, p. 124.　　2. *Athenaeum*. 4 Sept. 1852.　　3. *The Times*, 2 Sept. 1852.

drama critic of the *Illustrated London News* assumed just that, for he called this version 'one of the most pleasing of plays'. He thought that 'the success of this experiment will, no doubt, give rise to amended criticism on this play, the elements of which have been much mistaken'.

But the plot of *All's Well*, so universally condemned in all the reviews and so offensive to the audience in spite of the Phelps purgations, could hardly win approval in the Victorian Age as the basis for 'one of the most pleasing of plays'. And although an 'amended criticism' had already begun a defence of 'elements' of the play among Shakespearian scholars, only Gervinus, a German critic whose pronouncements had little effect upon the contemporary English stage, defended *All's Well* in the theatre. Scholars of the mid century were expressing guarded praise for the particular aspects— the loveliness of Helena, the realism of Bertram, the lofty theme of the supernatural, the social theme, the humour of the Clown, the soft regality of the Countess—but these disparate elements lacked a catalyst which might persuade a manager to undertake another risky production.[1] After the qualified success of the 1852–3 season, Phelps dropped the play from his repertory, and it was not produced again until 1895. Rather than the hopeful promise offered by the *Illustrated London News*, *All's Well* finally fell before the verdict of the aptly titled *John Bull*, which dismissed this 'most utterly hopeless' revival:

> The play is bad. *Bertram*, the hero of the piece, exhibited as a *preux Chevalier*, and made the chief object of interest, is a sneaking, paltry, odious scoundrel whose whole character can inspire nothing but disgust; and *Helena*, the heroine, is a love-sick fool, whose affection is wholly irrational, and therefore can inspire no sympathy. The plot, too, [already described in the review as grossly indelicate] is in the highest degree confused and incoherent.

Not only does the review reflect the opinion of the early Victorian audience, but it foreshadows a new objection to the heroine—Helena —the love-sick fool. As the century turned slowly from romanticism to realism, the 'wholly irrational' love of Helena offered a new target to the critics of the 'unfortunate comedy'.

On 22 and 24 January 1895, *All's Well* was presented for only the fourth time in the nineteenth century on the London stage. The Irving Dramatic Club produced a poor version which revealed a continuing concern for moral taste and an increasingly realistic approach among the critics. The expurgation failed to please, for 'the text had been so carefully bowdlerised for the Irving Club that the

---

1. See below, Chapter 6, for my discussion of the critical studies of the age.

story would scarcely have been comprehensible to any one who did not know it beforehand'.[1] The play itself failed to please, for the new mood of the critics condemned Helena as an adventuress whose actions, if done by a man, would brand him a 'villain of the deepest dye'. By the 1890s, the hero and heroine of the early nineteenth-century sentimental romance had been stripped of their fantasy to expose the base snobbery of Bertram and the cunning boldness of Helena. The production, however, had one happy effect; it prompted Shaw's famous review of *All's Well*.

If the critics now chose to evaluate characters and plot realistically, then a powerful voice boomed out a defence of *All's Well* even from that point of view. Shaw first attacked the text and the tampering with the simplicity of the original setting:

The passage of the Florentine army beneath the walls of the city was managed in the manner of the end of the first act of Robertson's *Ours*, the widow and the girls looking out of their sitting-room window, whilst a few of the band gave a precarious selection from the orchestral parts of Berlioz's version of the Rackoczy March. The dresses were the usual fancy ball odds and ends, Helena especially distinguishing herself by playing the first scene partly in the costume of Hamlet and partly in that of a waitress in an Aerated Bread shop, set off by a monstrous auburn wig which could by no stretch of imagination be taken for her own hair. Briefly, the whole play was vivisected, and the fragments mutilated, for the sake of accessories which were in every particular silly and ridiculous.[2]

From his analysis of the performances emerge his interpretations of the original characters and his opinion of the play:

The cool young woman, with a superior understanding, excellent manners, and a habit of reciting Shakespeare, presented before us by Miss Olive Kennett, could not conceivably have been even Helena's thirty-second cousin. Miss Lena Heineky, with the most beautiful old woman's part ever written in her hands, discovered none of its wonderfully pleasant good sense, humanity, and originality: she grieved stagily all through in the manner of the Duchess of York in Cibber's *Richard III*. Mr. Lewin-Mannering did not for any instant make it possible to believe that Parolles was a real person to him . . . Lafeu is hardly a part that can be acted: it comes right if the right man is available: if not, no acting can conceal the makeshift. Mr. Herbert Everitt was not the right man; but he made the best of it. The clown was evidently willing to relish his own humor if only he could have seen it; but there are few actors who would not have gone that far. Bertram (Mr. Patrick Munro), if not the most intelligent of

1. *The Theatrical 'World' of 1895*, London, 1896, pp. 39–41. The review appeared originally in *Pall Mall Budget*, 31 Jan. 1895.

2. John F. Matthews (ed.), *Shaw's Dramatic Criticism (1895–98)*, New York, 1959, pp. 12–18. The review appeared originally in the *Saturday Review*, 2 Feb. 1895.

Bertrams, played the love scene with Diana with some passion . . . But I should not like to see another such performance of *All's Well* or any other play that is equally rooted in my deeper affections.

For Shaw, the merit of Shakespeare's play lay in its realism, in its Ibsen-like elements:

> *All's Well that Ends Well* stands out artistically by the sovereign charm of the young Helena and the old Countess of Rousillon, and intellectually by the experiment, repeated nearly three hundred years later in *A Doll's House*, of making the hero a perfectly ordinary young man, whose unimaginative prejudices and selfish conventionality make him out a very mean figure in the atmosphere created by the nobler nature of his wife.

Helena is neither the sentimental heroine of melodrama, nor the aggressive adventuress of realistic satire, nor the implausible Griselda of fairy-tale. She is the enlightened modern woman, and Shaw concluded, 'Few living actresses could throw themselves into the sustained transport of exquisite tenderness and impulsive courage which makes poetry the natural speech of Helena.' The challenge was there for the twentieth-century actress.

3

THE DIRECTOR AND
THE SEARCH FOR UNITY
(1916–1964)

A STATISTICAL summary of the theatrical history of *All's Well that Ends Well* prior to the twentieth century offers little encouragement to the modern producer. We have no record of a production in Shakespeare's time nor in the entire seventeenth century. In the eighteenth century, the theatres of London presented only 51 performances in contrast to 274 performances of *As You Like It*, or 133 performances of *Measure for Measure*. Of these 51 performances of *All's Well*, 19 were given in the first two seasons of its revival, possibly as a result of the play's novelty. Of the remaining 32 performances, 25 appear to have been prompted by the extraordinary success of Harry Woodward as Parolles. In the ninteenth century, the play had 5 revivals and only 17 performances, 11 of which were presented in the 1852–3 Phelps production. All five revivals used altered texts. Despite the extensive cuts and transpositions, despite the expurgations, the play was so distasteful to audiences that none of the revivals escaped harsh criticism. The shift of emphasis from farce and the dominance of Parolles to sentimental comedy and the dominance of Helena failed to placate critics and audiences. The judgement of the age is apparent in the forty years of silence which the play endured from 1852 to 1895. Even the enthusiasm of Shaw was tempered by his belief that *All's Well* could not be popular on the stage until an audience had been prepared for it and like experiments in realism. As late as 1928, he wrote: 'In Shakespeare there are parts—like that of Helena in *All's Well* for instance—which are still too genuine and beautiful and modern for the public.'[1]

Yet since its revival in 1741, elements of *All's Well* have proved popular with audiences, and critics have expressed surprise, sometimes delight, at the dramatic interest of a scene, a character, a speech which quickened on stage. In separate instances, Helena has pleased audiences with the humility and sincerity of her love, with the courage and determination of her will, with the eloquence and passion of her poetry. In separate instances, audiences have responded to the amusing braggadocio of Parolles, to the farcical

1. E. J. West (ed.), 'How to Lecture on Ibsen', *Shaw on Theatre*, New York, 1959, p. 56.

comedy of the drum scenes, to the moral satisfaction of his exposure. At various times, critical approval has been claimed by almost all the minor characters: Lafeu and the Clown particularly in the eighteenth century; the Countess and the King in the nineteenth; Diana throughout the stage history of the play. Even Bertram has had his defenders when he is acted in the theatre. And repeatedly, critics have been struck by the dramatic excitement of the last scene —a scene which the reader often finds tedious in its complications.

The stage history prior to 1900, then, has demonstrated dramatic potential in particular elements of *All's Well*; it has not shown a sustained theatrical success for the play as Shakespeare wrote it. It is not surprising that, in the twentieth century, the new voice in the theatre, the director, should turn to the play as a challenge. If the play, as Mr. Trewin noted in his review of a 1935 production, was 'more brilliant in its parts than in its whole',[1] then was it not the precise function of the director to blend the parts into a theatrically successful whole? The stage history of *All's Well* in the twentieth century is, with a few exceptions, a record of the attempts of directors to thread the brilliant parts with a unifying, appealing theme. But theatrical tradition offered only remnants as guides, and scholarly analysis had failed to fashion a coherent pattern. The threading was difficult, and early experiments did little to change the general distaste for the play. Only in the last two decades have the parts been unified in successful productions.

Sickness and death had attended several productions of *All's Well* in the eighteenth century and shrouded the play with superstitions. Royal honours attended two revivals in the early twentieth century and proved equally distracting. The play was not produced until the spring of 1916. The Shakespeare Theatre at Stratford on Avon had been founded thirty-five years before to establish a permanent site for the dramatist's plays. By 1916, only *Titus Andronicus* and *All's Well* remained unplayed at the theatre. Frank Benson, who had enjoyed great success as manager of the company, decided to produce the long-neglected comedy and elected to play Parolles. His wife was cast as Helena. Both enjoyed such reputations that *All's Well* seemed assured of a fortunate trial before an audience devoted to Shakespeare. Once again, however, circumstances surrounding the production obscured the potentiality of the play. Just prior to the first performance, Frank Benson was summoned to London to be knighted by the King for his services to the theatre. The award and the accompanying ceremonies so dazzled the Bensons and others in

1. T. C. Kemp and J. C. Trewin, *The Stratford Festival*, Birmingham, England, 1953, pp. 176–7.

the company that Lady Benson wrote: 'The next day we were to appear at Stratford in "All's Well that ends Well". . . . A business like rehearsal of the new production . . . seemed very tame after all this delightful adulation.'[1] The delight in Benson's honour spread to the audience as well, and little attention was paid to the addition of *All's Well* to the Stratford repertory. The play was held up for some minutes by the unrestrained applause which greeted the appearance of the Bensons on stage.[2] And Lady Benson noted that the audience joined with the cast in singing 'Auld Lang Syne' at the end of the play. Understandably, *All's Well* could not compete with its celebrated cast.

Benson is not representative of the producers of *All's Well* in the twentieth century, for he was still part of the tradition of actor-manager rather than a member of the theatre's new profession, the director. His dual function as actor-manager and the distraction of his recent honour negated any forceful direction of the play. More typical of experiments in finding a theme to thread the 'brilliant parts' is the production of William Poel on 20 May 1920, at the Ethical Church, Bayswater. Poel had already established a reputation by his revivals of Elizabethan plays. But Poel's interest in *All's Well* went beyond that of the antiquarian. He saw in the play a social theme with modern significance. Through this theme, he hoped to produce a social morality play. He imposed upon the characterizations and plot an interpretation more extreme than Shaw's:

He saw a plea for the removal of class barriers where the affections between men and women were in question. He believed that the play might have been inspired by the imprisonment of Shakespeare's patron, Southampton, in 1598, for having secretly married Elizabeth Vernon, one of the Queen's Maids of Honour. Helena's wooing of Bertram was free from any restraint of code; it was the expression of a love, religious in impulse, which no convention could repress. For Poel the play had an ethical significance which gave it a place in the history of woman's emancipation; in 1919 this freedom had at last been won and the exploits of Miss Sylvia Pankhurst were a recent memory.[3]

If this interpretation had an ominous ring, the preparations for the production sounded more dismal tones. For the role of Captain Dumain, Poel selected Miss Evans, an actress who was making a career of male impersonations. Winifred Oughton accompanied her as a second French lord. On the night of the performance, 'she and

1. Lady Constance Benson, *Mainly Players*, London, 1926, pp. 287–8.
2. *The Stratford Festival*, p. 113.
3. Robert Speaight, *William Poel and the Elizabethan Revival*, London, 1954, p. 233. The following descriptions are from Mr. Speaight's study, pp. 233–4.

Miss Evans played one of their scenes in the dark to give the impression that they were sleepily talking after "lights out".' But an even more amazing example of Poel's casting is reported by Mr. Speaight:

For the part of Parolles Poel tried to secure the services of Clare Greet. Miss Greet was a delightful character actress who had endeared herself to a large public by her performance of Cockney landladies, charwomen, and mothers-in-law. What possessed Poel to imagine that she could play Parolles is beyond the boundaries of surmise. However, she duly turned up to rehearse, but was not unnaturally dismayed by the character she was expected to interpret and the language she was called upon to speak. She had not read the play and for once Poel's blue pencil had remained in his pocket. She quickly burbled her excuses and left him to his fantasy. Frustrated and chagrined, he eventually played Parolles himself.

Poel also added a modern but eccentric touch to the stage business. At one rehearsal, he called for a bath chair; when asked why, he replied: 'I want the King to be wheeled on to the stage by a nurse in V.A.D. uniform in order that the audience may be in no doubt about the condition of his health.'

With such an interpretation, cast, and stage business, we are not surprised that 'the unrelieved humility' of Helena made the play 'curiously devoid of humour', nor are we surprised by the director's devices of a sombre setting and dull lighting to strengthen the thread of his theme.[1] Unfortunately, Poel had dimmed even the brilliant elements of *All's Well* in his attempt to portray the emancipation of woman and her love. The tone of the production may have prompted the dramatic critic of the *Athenaeum* to his remark, 'Helena has her counterpart in Hamlet',[2] for certainly there was much more of problem drama than comedy in the Poel revival.

A more traditional presentation was offered by the Old Vic on 28 November 1921. This was the first of three productions of *All's Well* directed by Robert Atkins, who had a great fondness for the play. His approach to the comedy was threefold; he revived the comic emphasis of the eighteenth century; he restored the 'indelicate' passages which had been deleted in the various alterations; but he retained the sweetness and delicacy of the nineteenth-century Helena. Interestingly, his success varied with each. The comic scenes won high praise; the restored text had a qualified success; the heroine failed to please. Such uneven merit made the play 'well worth while', but the director had not imposed a unity on the parts; *All's Well* was still not a 'convincing play'.[3]

Much more convincing than the production itself was a review

1. T. Moult, 'All's Well that Ends Well at Bayswater', *Athenaeum*, 4 June 1920, p. 745.
2. Ibid.   3. See n.1, p. 175.

written by John Francis Hope for *The New Age*.[1] In the stage history of *All's Well*, it is one of the few excellent critiques which analyse the nature of the play. Its value lies in its clear analysis of the revival, its commonsense rejection of earlier subjective critical standards, its provocative interpretation of characters, and its anticipation of later critical judgements. Hope called the production 'both interesting and disappointing'. He agreed with the stress placed upon the comic and the restoration of the text, but he was disappointed that Atkins did not give scope to his convictions. Parolles was played 'far too lightly'. He was too much the courtier; the Shakespearian Parolles 'is a sort of younger brother of Pistol, and should exhibit much more of his Mars, even if it were retrograde'. Atkins restored the indelicate passages to the text but seemed embarrassed by them. He failed to give them the sweep of broad humour demanded by the play:

Much of these comic scenes are definitely and distinctly 'smutty' a characteristic quality of English humour; Parolles discussing virginity with Helena, for example, although expressing sound common sense in his reaction against ascetic ideals, is definitely playing for the guffaws. We ought to be as shocked and amused as we are by, say George Robey, who embodies our national type of humour, which is Elizabethan not only in parody but in very nature. But Mr. Ernest Milton got through this scene without once provoking a laugh; he played it like someone skating on very thin ice, as though he were trying to spare Helena's blushes instead of provoking them. The scene is not merely illustrative of the frankness with which men and women discussed sexual matters in those days; it is comic, and is intended to be comic, in the grouty, fleshly English fashion. Shakespeare was a popular playwright tickling the ears of the groundlings in such passages; and it is absurd to bowdlerise him in spirit while giving the text.

If Atkins failed to develop the humour, he was even more guilty in not developing the characterization. Objecting to 'what a sculptor calls "one-view studies"', Hope condemned the lack of internal conflict and passion in the Atkins revival and in the interpretations of Victorian critics. He maintained that the characters in *All's Well* 'are quick and extreme in feeling'. He cites the physical change in the King from the extremity of his sick-bed to his dancing a coranto with Helena; he cites the emotional change from his pleasing affection for Bertram to his blazing wrath at the refusal to marry Helena. The same extremities are apparent in the Countess and Helena. The Countess has not only a maternal dignity but a quick, autocratic temper displayed in her forcing Helena to a confession of love and in the banishment of Bertram from her parental benevolence. She has a merry nature as well, as indicated in her repartee with the

1. 15 Dec. 1921.

Clown. In fact, the Clown 'set up a conflict in the Countess between her will to maintain morality and her unregenerate interest in natural human desires; he makes her laugh herself out of her judgement'. Helena, too, displays a great deal of variety; 'she is not simply a one-view study of sweetness and delicacy'. Her emotional range includes her sorrow in the opening scene, her merry banter with Parolles, her shyness and affection with the Countess passing to confidence and purpose, and her grand manner reserved for the King. If Helena is at times shy, she is also 'a woman who knows what she wants, and how to get it, and uses every faculty of a very capable nature to achieve her purpose. One is sorry that she wasted herself on Bertram—but that is her affair.'

Hope's objection to the bowdlerizing spirit of the revival is just; his interpretation of the characters is interesting; his judgement that the Atkins production lacked passion appears valid. But his cry for delight in the comic and for passionate vitality in the dramatic was too advanced for an age that had just restored the text and now saw in it the dark problems of Shakespeare's bitter mood. It was a cry, however, that would be heard some thirty years hence.

There was little vitality in the second production of *All's Well* at Stratford on Avon. The play was selected as the Shakespeare 'birthday play' for April 1922, and was directed by Bridges-Adams. As in 1916, the production was dwarfed by ceremony; for the first time since the Garrick Jubilee of 1769, the King sent a special representative to Stratford. The first-night audience included a number of celebrities who were presented a refined production of the 'seldom revived *All's Well That Ends Well*'. Mr. Trewin described Maureen Shaw as a 'decorative, red-haired Helena' and reported: 'Someone said that Maurice Colbourne's Bertram looked like an armoured knight in a Burne-Jones window: a figure too beautiful to be taken seriously.'[1] Still, he termed the play 'a pleasant performance'. The revival had a moderate success. Including repeat performances in the Summer Festival, it was played ten times during the season at Stratford.[2] And part of its success again was due to Parolles; St. John Ervine called Baliol Holloway's representation 'a piece of comic acting as fine as I have seen for some time'.[3]

Despite the refinement of the Bridges-Adams production, the praise for Parolles is another indication that the comic elements were regaining some of their past fame and were creating new interest in the play. *All's Well* was revived at a new theatre, the

1. *The Stratford Festival*, p. 128.
2. William Jaggard, *Shakespeare Memorial: Stratford-on-Avon*, Stratford on Avon, 1925?, p. 35.   3. *The Stratford Festival*, p. 128.

Maddermarket, September 1924, and the review in the *London Times*, 27 September, gave special mention to the Clown, a part which had not drawn favourable notice for over a century. Interest was also stirred by a production in modern dress at the Birmingham Repertory Theatre in 1927. The play opened 'in a delightful French atmosphere with the Countess swathed in the crepe so beloved of Gallic widows'.[1] What appealed to Shaw, however, was the 'buoyant humour' of Parolles, who was played as 'an amiable, too smart young man, a sommelier's scourge'.[2] The youthful actor was Laurence Olivier. Robert Atkins demonstrated his continued concern by a second production of *All's Well* at the Arts Theatre Club in November 1932. Although Atkins repeated the interpretation of Helena as all 'sweetness and delicacy', E. H. Williams expressed the contemporary view that the play was 'a bitter, cruel piece of work'.[3] Yet he thought the play was rather excellent medicine and should be acted more frequently because 'it makes an acid test for much modern thought'. The interest in all these productions, however, was due to experiment rather than accomplishment. None of them succeeded in changing the essential view of scholars and theatre-goers. James Agate left the Arts Theatre Club 'with no idea in [his] head except that it was Shakespeare botching and bungling at his worst'.[4]

All's Well, now produced by Mr. B. Iden Payne, was repeated as the 'birthday play' at Stratford on Avon in 1935. Despite the fact that the production failed in the totality of its effect, it was this revival which suggested to Mr. Trewin that the play was 'more brilliant in its parts than in its whole'.[5] Special attention was given to the individualization of each character. Bertram's moral defects were mollified by the physical attractiveness of the actor. Miss Catherine Lacey, as the Countess, strove for that loveliness which Shaw attributed to the role. Lafeu, as he had been played in the eighteenth century, was depicted as a humorous old man, though not a buffoon. Contrast was set up between the charm of Helena and the boisterous vulgarity of Parolles. Perhaps influenced by the 'bitter comedy' charge of the critics, the Clown lost much of his broad humour:

> The Clown in this play is really rather a bore, and Kenneth Wicksteed rubbed this in by giving, in a dry, sententious manner, a life-like portrait of a professional funny man who is not very successful in his profession.[6]

1. Sir Barry Jackson, 'Producing the Comedies', *SS*, viii (1955), 79.
2. J. C. Trewin, *The Birmingham Repertory Theatre: 1913–63*, London, 1963, p. 90.
3. *Four Years at the Old Vic*, London, 1935, p. 175.
4. *Brief Chronicles: A Survey of the Plays of Shakespeare and the Elizabethans in Actual Performances*, London, 1943.
5. *The Stratford Festival*, pp. 176–7.
6. Gordon Crosse, *Shakespearean Playgoing: 1890–1952*, London, 1953, p. 82.

Diana was most sharply delineated; Rosamund Merivale played the role with a 'gay and joyous' spirit; she 'had an acceptable air of modernity which brought a welcome breath of life'.[1] Through this spirit, she dominated the last scene. But this fact may only illustrate that the characters of this production were travelling their separate ways; the audience saw no coherent relationship among the players. To Gordon Crosse, the play in its total effect, was comparatively dull.[2]

So many of the revivals of *All's Well* were marked by circumstances which marred the performance or obscured the production that it seems an ironic necessity that the play should have its most favourable setting produced by a war. As if he seized the opportunity to thrust an old favourite upon a theatrically starved public, Robert Atkins presented his third revival as the only production in London's West End in October 1940. Ivor Brown, in a review in *Punch*, recorded the 'fortunate' opportunity of the comedy:

> Professional productions of *All's Well* happen once in a lifetime, and it is an odd chance which has just given to this unregarded piece the sole tenancy of the West End stage. Now, it might be thought, is the ugly duckling's chance to prove itself a true cygnet of Avon. It has no rivals in its region and anyone intending 'to see a show' becomes the conscript of *Helena* and *Bertram*.[3]

But neither ugly duckling nor true cygnet emerged from the production. Atkins at last achieved the sense of loveliness in Helena which he had sought in previous productions. Miss Catherine Lacey, who had won applause for her portrayal of the Countess in 1935, now as Helena, prompted Mr. Brown to conclude that Shakespeare had 'lost his heart to his heroine. Such losses are infectious. When genius adores, all must capitulate. . . . You need not believe in her, but love her you must—and love her you will.' But again, the total effect of the production was disappointing. Atkins attempted to use Lafeu as his thread to hold the 'brilliant parts'. He played the role himself 'and made him the central character of the play, a kind of grave Sir Toby'.[4] The comic scenes were toned down, and *All's Well* became melodrama. The mood of World War II and two air-raids during the performance (Parolles added an 'all-clear' to one of his lines) perhaps cancelled any advantage which the production enjoyed as London's only play. For Mr. Brown, only Helena and the poetry of the play made the production worthwhile. Mr. Alan Dent denied even this: the play was 'too grim, unwitty, and disconcerting to be called comedy at all; . . . anybody heard defending its poetry should be asked point-blank to quote two consecutive lines'; *All's Well* 'may be

---

1. *The Stratford Festival*, p. 176.   2. *Shakespearean Playgoing*, p. 81.
3. cxcix (16 Oct. 1940), 388.   4. *Shakespearean Playgoing*, p. 149.

put by for another twenty years without great loss'.[1] Mr. Dent's prescription was very nearly carried out. It was not until 1953, thirteen years later, that *All's Well* was granted another major production in London.

Although the experiments conducted by Poel with his social drama, Bridges-Adams with his stylized refinement, Barry Jackson with modern dress, Payne with highly individualized characterization, and Atkins with emotional intensity failed to produce a successful play, they did eliminate stultifying stage traditions and attitudes. Most important, the full text was restored. This, aided by the increasing tolerance of the audience, brought back the comic force of Parolles, the intricacies of the plot, and the long-neglected Clown. No single production satisfied the demands set up in Hope's review for complex, rounded portrayals, but the variety of approaches to *All's Well* suggested the potentiality for more dramatically exciting depictions of Helena and Bertram, the Countess and the King, Lafeu and Diana. The leading figures of the London stage had not yet been attracted to these parts, but others had won approval for competent performances. At last, *All's Well* was being tested in the theatre. In the first forty years of the century, there were eight major productions of the play; only in Woodward's day with a stereotyped interpretation had that number been surpassed.

But the experiments of directors had not resolved what critics considered the jarring elements of the full text. Could the romantic and realistic portions ever blend in the theatre to satisfy any one of the numerous critical interpretations of the play? Could the full text produce a coherent comedy, a sentimental romance, a modern problem play, a dark and bitter satire, a philosophical commentary? Regardless of approach, could Bertram ever be played as an attractive mate for Helena? Could Helena herself ever yield to a consistent interpretation when the 'ribaldries' of her repartee with Parolles on virginity are enclosed by two soliloquies of touching beauty? Should the surprising deceits of Helena be applauded, ignored as mere convention, or decried? Should the unpleasant deceits of Bertram be treated comically or tragically? Should the humorous deceits of Parolles suffer a tragic denouement or a flippant reconciliation with life? How should the minor characters be played —Lafeu as the meddling buffoon or the King's confidant, Lavache as the playful clown or the bitter fool, the King as the impulsive tyrant or the fatherly ruler, Diana as an impudent schemer or virtuous maiden, the Widow as the greedy opportunist or the maternal sympathizer? To such problems the directors of the 1950s turned.

1. *Preludes and Studies*, London, 1942, pp. 121–2.

They continued the search for unity; more intensely, they sought focus which would at least cast into deeper shadows the disparate elements of the play. And in a Canadian town removed by distance but not by influence from the London stage, the focus produced a theatrical success.

On 13 July 1953, in the first year of the Shakespeare Festival at Stratford, Ontario, Tyrone Guthrie followed the initial production, *Richard III*, with *All's Well that Ends Well*. Technically, the production is American, and I have reserved consideration of its critical reception until my treatment of *All's Well* in the American theatre. So too, I have postponed analysis of Mr. Guthrie's specific purposes and techniques until they were given a second test at Stratford on Avon in 1959.[1] Nevertheless, the production deserves mention here as a provocative success managed to a great extent by a staff recruited from the London stage. Mr. Guthrie's general intention was to produce a high comedy free of the 'bitter' unpleasantries without altering the text. Rather than purging the play of either its romantic or realistic elements, he wanted to build the romantic machinations of the plot upon the realistic motives of the characters. Stage business was to provide the focus for his audience. To cite one example, he staged the play in Edwardian costume. The fantastic turns of the plot, of Helena's traps, became much more acceptable in modern dress to a contemporary audience which had been saturated with aggressive heroines, often 'career women' who had won reluctant males in innumerable romantic comedy films during the 1930s and 1940s. In addition, the modern audience accustomed to feminine allurements publicized as necessities by the advertising world, has accepted entrapment as a condition of romance. Critics debated the success of such innovations, but clearly the production was a substantial contribution to the stage history of *All's Well*. For the first time, an approach was attempted which extracted as much as possible from the play rather than pruned it to a particular shape. The eighteenth century had cut deeply into the comic. In this Canadian production, Mr. Guthrie attempted a balance.

Two months later in Great Britain, another attempt was made to impose unity upon the seemingly jarring elements of the play. In the words of one reviewer, 'the producer was able to offer a coherent, convincing, and as far as I know, a new view of Shakespeare's play, at least to those who are prepared to allow that in theatrical affairs the end may justify the means'.[2] Michael Benthall gained coherence

1. See p. 65 for the Canadian production and p. 57 for the Stratford on Avon production.
2. Richard David, 'Plays Pleasant and Plays Unpleasant', *SS*, viii (1955), 134.

in his Old Vic production at Edinburgh on 15 September 1953, by staging the play as a comic fairy-tale. As with the Guthrie production, the focus was provided by stage business, but this time the serious moments of the play suffered badly. Shakespeare's characters became caricatures out of Grimm. Cinderella and her wayward Prince Charming were played off against pasteboard figures cut with physical quirks and comic deformities. The Countess lost that aristocratic decorum so long associated with the role; 'she was bent and crabbed, her gestures had an arthritic awkwardness, her utterance was creaky, abrupt, arbitrary'.[1] In his illness, the King became 'a figure of fun, a fretful invalid, bundled up in nightshirt and cap, with crown askew, and attended by doctors who hovered round with potions and basins'.[2] Lafeu appeared as an aged Polonius who was made ridiculous in the last scene by the appearance on stage of his daughter Maudlin, 'a simpering and quite pathetically ugly damsel'.[3] Lavache shuffled about as a white-haired little hunchback who spoke timidly. In the bright contrast which fantasy allows, Helena was played by Claire Bloom as the fairyland princess, straight long blonde hair, wide-eyes, an ethereal tone of voice—'even that trick of making her exit lines trail off on a rising intonation, like a great bird taking wing, gave an other-wordly quality to her story'.[4] If Bertram is not the ideal hero of fairy-tale, still John Neville managed the role 'with the nobility and dash of a ducal seducer in Technicolor'.[5] An unpleasantness in his character was blamed upon Parolles, who assumed a greater influence upon the youth than the text assigns. A significant example of this occured when Helena requested a kiss from Bertram at her departure for Rousillon. Bertram was about to yield when a whisper from Parolles hurried him away. Indeed, the fairy-tale approach to the plot was reinforced by a morality pattern of the goodness of Helena vying with the demonic influence of Parolles. Both themes were acted out against Disney-like sets, and strangely artificial lighting.

The undermining of the serious elements of the play by comical stage business may be illustrated by Mr. Benthall's management of the King. No longer the dignified and authoritative figure of stage tradition, he was treated as a butt of contempt and coarse humour. In his first scene at court, the young lords tolerated the whims of the sick old man with ill-concealed boredom and disrespect. Just before Helena's arrival to cure him, the King was attended by a monk 'who

1. Ibid., pp. 134–6.
2. Mary Clarke and Roger Wood, *Shakespeare at the Old Vic*, London, 1954, p. 58.
3. Ibid.   4. David, p. 136.
5. Eric Keown, 'All's Well that Ends Well', *Punch*, ccxxv (30 Sept. 1953), 416.

burst into terrified chanting at his royal master's every spasm'.[1] The contortions of the King and the farcical bungling of his doctors created a scene in which 'both pain and the Last Sacrament were treated as subjects for buffoonery interspersed with attacks of vomiting in the worst of comic taste'.[2] Helena's mission could not escape the vulgarity.

I have treated Mr. Benthall's direction of the play with more severity than is warranted by the reaction of both critics and audience. On the one hand, an understanding of his approach may be gained more simply by recording the extravagances of the production, those details that were often condemned even in favourable reviews. Such extravagances show clearly the extent of the director's attempt to create a tone, a unity, in a play which so challenges the imposition of a single theme. On the other hand, I do not think the Old Vic production was the artistic success ascribed to it by a majority of the drama critics. It is true that the play had its most successful run in the theatrical history of the play in England, a total of thirty-five performances in a single season. It is true that the audiences laughed at the farcical gimmicks. The justification for those gimmicks, however, is much like the critical attitude of the nineteenth century towards the Kemble text. If *All's Well* must be played, then play it as removed as possible from the original. If the public is to be lured to *All's Well*, then this defective play of Shakespeare's must be garnished with entertaining business to divert them. The defence of Mr. Benthall's interpretation was phrased for the majority of the critics in a review by Eric Keown:

No doubt by this plan some of the finer moments are diminished, but in the lightness of the production we gain a sort of surface plausibility, and laughter is the kindest anaesthetic against the increasing outrage of the plot. Bertram behaves abominably to Helena, while she pursues him without any shame whatever.[3]

As happens so often in criticism of *All's Well*, the reviewer reveals his personal prejudice against the play. To accept the gimmicks, we must believe that Bertram behaves abominably to Helena and Helena shamelessly to him. We must believe that the plot becomes outrageous before we accept the need for anaesthetic laughter. Moreover, we must believe with Mr. Benthall that the play is unpleasant and unnecessarily bawdy before we accept the need for his alterations in text and tone.[4]

1. *Shakespeare at the Old Vic*, p. 58.
2. Audrey Williamson, *Old Vic Drama 2*, London, 1957, p. 141.
3. *Punch*, p. 416.
4. Besides sharp cuts in the serious scenes of the play, Mr. Benthall omitted scenes, transposed lines, and reassigned dialogue. He dropped bawdy phrases.

Sir Laurence Olivier as Parolles in the 1927 Birmingham Repertory Theatre production

My objections to Mr. Benthall's production are not directed against the insertion of extensive stage business by the director. But when the stage business obviously distorts a meaning, a character, a mood inherent in the original text, then we can object that the director is fashioning a new play. Audrey Williamson objected that '*All's Well that Ends Well*, bitter comedy, remained unplayed'.[1] We might object that *All's Well that Ends Well*, Shakespearian comedy, remained unplayed. For, the addition of Maudlin makes Lafeu a different character from that drawn by Shakespeare, even if one allows a certain touch of meddlesome old age in the original. A charming insincerity in Helena makes ridiculous the affection of the Countess and of others for the heroine, as Mr. Derek Monsey pointed out in his review.[2] Shakespeare obviously intended this affection as justification for Helena since it is his addition to his source. Commenting upon this production, Professor Harbage wrote, 'No sane observer has ever mistaken . . . the King of France for a buffoon'.[3] To make the King a buffoon is to weaken his authority over Bertram, to rob Helena's cure of any dramatic value, to damage Helena's cause since it is dependent upon a fool, to undermine the entire trial scene, and to make hopelessly absurd Bertram's final acceptance of Helena. Keown may conclude, 'Among the recruits to sheer farce none is better than Mr. Laurence Hardy's fairy-tale King', but his is a recruit serving under the banner of Mr. Benthall rather than Shakespeare.[4]

Both productions in 1953 demonstrated that *All's Well that Ends Well*, with shaping, could be produced successfully on the modern stage. Both drew large and receptive audiences; both were reviewed favourably by the majority of the critics. In both cases, credit for the successes was ascribed primarily to the directors: the touch of Mr. Guthrie had shown *All's Well* to be 'a great and beautiful play'; the touch of Mr. Benthall had given 'a coherent, convincing, and . . . new view to Shakespeare's play'. The touch of each man was felt most heavily in the addition of farcical stage business. But the search for unity, the experimentation in finding a thematic thread, was not complete. If the fairy-tale approach of Mr. Benthall suggested to Mr. David that the comedy was a forerunner of *The Winter's Tale*,[5] the bulk of twentieth-century criticism had linked it with the 'bitter' plays, *Measure for Measure* and *Troilus and Cressida*. It was in this spirit that *All's Well* was next produced.

On 26 April 1955, the play was again produced at Stratford on Avon. The comedy had not been presented there for twenty years,

1. *Old Vic Drama 2*, p. 145.   2. *The Spectator*, cxci (25 Sept. 1953), 322.
3. See n. 2, p. 175.   4. See n. 3, pp. 175–6.   5. p. 136.

and it appears that the motive for this production was none other than a sense of duty to the Shakespearian canon. The virtues brought out in the 1953 productions were ignored entirely, and critical comment reverted to traditional judgement. Mr. Noel Willman, in his first assignment at Stratford, directed the play as a dark comedy. Helena dominated the stage, not with her vivacity, nor indeed emotional variety, but by a moral earnestness which prompted frequent appeals to heaven. Her righteousness was conveyed by a distracting chanting of her lines; the 'dark designs' of her plot to win back her husband were slurred over in rapid speech as if to conceal their significance from the audience and preserve the reputation of the heroine. Throughout, she behaved 'like some ghastly Shavian woman . . . [demonstrating] a pertinacity worthy of the Royal North-West Mounted Police'.[1] Mr. Willman did repeat one innovation of Mr. Benthall's; he made Lavache an oddly deformed hunchback, a cripple. The pathos made even more sombre the mood of the play.

But Mr. Willman complicated his approach by his sets, his stage business, and his interpretations of Bertram and Parolles. He placed the play in the late seventeenth century against ponderous scenery and sumptuous costumes. The heavy representative sets robbed the stage of a starkness better suited to the mood; the prettiness of the costumes conflicted with the darkness of the theme. With the director's controlling idea, there was even less justification for elaborate stage business. Yet the walls of Florence were constructed before the eyes of the audience; a complete crew of citizens 'with hurdy-gurdy and incidental pastimes' were assembled for Helena's initial meeting with the Widow of Florence; much time was spent packing Helena's trunk on the front porch of the Widow's house; and throughout there was much pompous bowing and parading.[2] The costume alone so stamped Bertram as a young dandy that he could not be taken seriously as a partner in this 'dark comedy'. He emerged not as a man whose strong desires struggled against the moral force of Helena but 'as the end of the tennis club'.[3] The sinister potentialities of Parolles were ignored as well; Mr. Worsley regretted that the part was placed 'in the hands of a natural romantic juvenile', Mr. Keith Mitchell.[4]

Mr. Willman's failure to develop his theme consistently doomed the production. But the very application of the 'dark comedy' interpretation to the stage seemed to justify the traditional condemnation

1. Peter Fleming, 'All's Well that Ends Well', *The Spectator*, cxciv (6 May 1955), 586.
2. Alan Downer, 'A Comparison of Two Stagings: Stratford-upon-Avon and London', *SQ*, vi (Autumn 1955), 430–1.   3. *Sunday Times*, 11 May 1955.
4. T. C. Worsley, 'The Dark Not Dark Enough', *The New Statesman and Nation*, n.s. xlix (30 April 1956), 611.

of the play. Critics were disgusted anew with the characters and the plot. Mr. Brown suggested that once again the play could be stored away at Stratford 'and the emphasis restored to work in which Shakespeare was himself again'.[1] Mr. Fleming was even more harsh:

The main ingredients of the plot are sex, snobbery and deceit; the principal characters are cads or gulls or bitches; and the whole thing is dished up in a cold, perfunctory, take-it-or-leave-it way which suggests an inefficient or temporarily distracted fishmonger displaying his left-overs on a slab.[2]

For Mr. Worsley, who had enjoyed the Helena of Claire Bloom in the Benthall production, the evening was tedious:

What a ridiculous, badly written, ill-constructed play *All's Well that Ends Well* is! So one comes away thinking from a production that has misfired. Only piety keeps it in the repertoire, and that piety is surely mis-placed. If Shakespeare were not semi-sacred, and if every production of his plays didn't borrow weight from the whole corpus, no audience of sensible people would solemnly tolerate such rubbish. And, indeed, if we can detach ourselves from the aura which surrounds 'Shakespeare', it is the best laugh of the evening that thousands should assemble—and pay!— to pretend not to be bored by it. . . . Personally, I think it is acceptable only as the lightest of light tales, impertinently lighthearted rather than solemn, rattling along with a certain uninhibited salacity, not dragging in a stately measure.

Mr. Alan Downer concluded: 'The conventional director can only attempt to smother it in verisimilitude and trust that the audience will accept its conventional edified boredom as a cultural experience.'[3]

At Stratford, Ontario, in 1953, Mr. Guthrie had demonstrated that he was not a conventional director of *All's Well*, and his audience reacted not to a cultural experience but to delightful theatrical entertainment. On 21 April 1959, at Stratford on Avon, he demon-strated the same unconventionality in his second production of the play. The audience reacted with the same delight. His unconven-tionality, however, split the critics into much the same camps as did Mr. Benthall's unrestricted means to a theatrical end.

Basically, the production employed the same contrivances as the Ontario revival. Again, the costumes and settings were Edwardian. The same freedom with time and place was taken in assigning the war scenes to a World War II locale in the North African desert. As before, these scenes were turned to farce; but the farce was even more extreme:

1. Ivor Brown, *Shakespeare Memorial Theatre: 1954–56*, London, 1956, p. 7.
2. *The Spectator*, cxciv (6 May 1955), 586.
3. 'A Comparison of Two Stagings', p. 431.

The comic soldiers in baggy shorts, black socks and berets are lined up under a blazing sky by the side of a ruined desert viaduct. The Duke of Florence, a goateed parody of General Smuts, dodders along the line with his officers falling over him every time he halts to peer at a mysterious medal. When he turns suddenly his sword becomes entangled between the legs of his staff officer. When he tries to make a speech from the top of an observation tower, the microphone gets a fit of metallic coughing. When he attempts to salute the flag, it slides slowly down the post again. Meanwhile every man on the stage is improvising some ludicrous pranks such as few amateur entertainers at a Stag Night at the Sergeants' Mess could hope to equal.[1]

Diana suffered more grievously, for Mr. Guthrie robbed her not only of dignity but, by implication, of chastity too. Despite Bertram's admission that Diana is 'honest', Alan Brien reported that she was played 'as a wartime factory tart who sits on the doorstep in nightgown and housecoat, with a turban on her head and a lollipop in her mouth, giggling the lines in coffee-bar cockney'.[2] Her mother, the Widow of Florence, received much the same treatment. A strong strain of vulgarity ran through her speech, the cheap beads and dress of her costume, and her emphatic movements; she drew her greatest laugh as she waddled across the stage in search of Helena at the trial scene.

Despite the farcical additions through stage business and character changes, Mr. Guthrie still sought the spirit of high romance which he had attempted in his first production. To achieve this, he focused the serious elements of the play, through character, plot, and sets, upon Helena. If he intended that Diana and the Widow should be painted in broad splashy sweeps, Helena was to be etched in fine, precious lines. He was fortunate in his actress. Miss Zoe Caldwell received critical acclaim for the beauty of her portrayal. She played the role as a young girl whose determination sprang entirely from the zeal of youthful love. The Countess, the King, and Lafeu reacted to her accordingly. When the needs of the play demanded a maturity in action, Mr. Guthrie enhanced the loveliness of her innocence with the stateliness of his sets. The dramatic suspense in her choice of a husband was heightened by staging the scene as a formal ball. At the rear of the stage, a small orchestra played. Helena danced with the King on a spacious stage overhung with chandeliers against a background of gowns and dress suits. The regal elegance which she shared with the King strengthened the horror of Bertram's impulsive rejection most dramatically. So too, in the opinion of several critics, the final scene achieved the emotional effect which was intended by

1. Alan Brien, 'All's Well that Ends Well', *The Spectator*, ccii (24 April 1959), 579.
2. Ibid., 578.

Shakespeare. Mr. Guthrie had prepared for the difficulties of the reconciliation by managing Bertram as a youth guilty of insipid faults rather than strong vice. As Helena was ecstatic in girlish love, Bertram was callous in boyish indifference. Such pliable traits were moulded more easily under the swift strokes of the last scene. The indifference whitened to desperate anxiety; the anxiety melted to relief and reform at the feet of his ardent saviour. To many, the reconciliation was credible. Mr. Harold Hobson declared, 'It is not often that we come away from the comedy with this conviction'.[1]

The 1959 production at Stratford on Avon revealed in every aspect the strong hand of the director. *All's Well*, quite literally, was shaped by Mr. Guthrie to blend high romance with burlesque. Critical reaction to this shaping split into three views: the first insisted that the farcical stage business was essential to the success of this defective Shakespearian play;[2] the second admitted the value of the original play and thought that the stage business worked with that value— 'the production . . . is about as perfect as we are likely to see. . . . By some miracle Elizabethan braggadocio becomes common or garden bull, and the jokes, for perhaps the first time since Shakespeare's day, are jokes';[3] the third view condemned the business as absurd intrusions. For the *Spectator*'s critic, Mr. Guthrie had turned a 'mediocre play' into 'bad pantomime.' Mr. Kenneth Tynan was 'beguiled and fascinated' for the first half of the evening 'until Mr. Guthrie's love of horseplay obtrudes'.[4] In speaking of the omission of the Clown, 'who has some of the most haunting prose in Shakespeare', Mr. Tynan concluded, 'to cut a play yet make what remains last longer than the whole must argue, I suppose, a kind of dotty genius'.

An issue in this production, as in other highly interpretive approaches to Shakespeare, is whether Mr. Guthrie has worked with or against the text. The issue is complicated by the relatively little investigation which Shakespearian scholars have made into the nature of *All's Well*. Opponents of Mr. Guthrie argue that the vulgarity of Diana cheapened Helena's cause as much as the buffoonery of the King had weakened it in the Benthall production. The excesses of the military scenes undercut an obvious Shakespearian device to make impressive the military qualities of Bertram. The waddle of the Widow was as damaging to the last scene as the stage presence of the pathetically ugly Maudlin. By the final scene, the farcical contrivances had made any interest in Helena impossible. In effect, high romance could not be blended with farce.

1. *Sunday Times*, 26 April 1959. 2. See n. 4, p. 176.
3. A. Alverez, 'My Fair Helena', *The New Statesman*, N.S. lvii (25 April 1959), 573.
4. *New Yorker*, xxxv (26 Sept. 1959), 119.

The best defence of the production and an invaluable document in the critical history of *All's Well* is a long review written by Miss Muriel St. Clare Byrne for the *Shakespeare Quarterly*.[1] Much of the review is an interpretation of the play and consequently is treated later in this study. Of pertinence to the stage history, however, are the dramatic insights which she ascribes to the direction of Mr. Guthrie and the additions to the theatrical traditions of the play. Through his relatively modern setting, the director has made credible the long-maligned characters of *All's Well*. Bertram comes to life as the handsome, self-conceited, athletic under-graduate who is 'too normal to be basically unlikeable: one simply has to wait for him to grow up'. Parolles is perfectly comprehensible in his twentieth-century world: 'in our time he has again become the propper-up of bar counters. He pushes in with his betters. . . . He must sing for his supper whatever tune they call, unless he has a Bertram in tow.' So too, the warmth and robustness of the Guthrie characterizations add credibility to Shakespeare's Florentine women. Rather than working against the dramatist's intention, the contrast between the earthy Diana and the noble Helena points out the reason for Bertram's immature choice. This is not to say that Miss Caldwell's Helena lacked passion, for Mr. Guthrie relied upon her vitality repeatedly to break the mood which he had set. Thus, in the first scene, the audience feels that the vitality of Helena's love will dispel the tone of mourning which broods over Rousillon. In the final scene, it is her intensity which breaks the strain and growing ill-humour of the trial:

I saw nothing but Helena and what she did, heard nothing but what she had said, accepted the gesture of contrition and perhaps of the beginnings of love with which he knelt and clung to her. It was her moment: her words and the stage picture had said all there was to say. And from Dame Edith down, every single member of the cast *acted* that moment: you did not watch them, you felt them feeling its impact. There was no need for Bertram to speak, and if his words had been adequate they would have been out of character. (Actually, of course, the 'impossible' couplet was spoken simply and firmly. The literary eye is often deceived until the ears gain theatrical experience.)

Whether the Stratford on Avon production accomplished all of these effects is controversial. For some critics, the burlesque had made impossible the emotional impact ascribed by Miss Byrne to the last scene. Certainly, her defence of the farcical additions does not come to grips with their effect upon the nature of the play. To justify the

1. 'The Shakespeare Season at the Old Vic, 1958–59 and Stratford-upon-Avon, 1959', *SQ*, x (Autumn 1959), 556–67.

military burlesque upon the grounds that it places Bertram in the world of men is only a defence of Shakespeare's military scenes, not of the burlesque, not of a 'glorious stag party'. Such a justification assumes that the tone of the wars is 'mock-heroic and deflationary of military honour and glory'. But the mood of the wars, darkened by the moralizing of the young lords, the reported death of Helena, the intense seduction of Diana, and Bertram's reaction to the exposure of Parolles, is scarcely that of a carefree stag party. Still if Mr. Guthrie did not accomplish all the effects suggested by Miss Byrne, there is little doubt that many of his insights belong to the 'ideal' production of *All's Well*. Even opposing criticisms of the production are moderated in the provocative summary of Mr. Patrick Gibbs:

As a result, it was often an hilarious but hardly a completely satisfying interpretation. One was left with a lingering curiosity about this rare play and a feeling that were its problems to be solved rather than glossed over, as here, something almost as rewarding as *The Winter's Tale* might emerge.[1]

1. *New York Times*, 22 April 1959. See also his review in the London *Daily Telegraph*, 22 April 1959.

4

ALL'S WELL IN AMERICA AND IN THE MINOR THEATRES
(1799-1964)

THE stage history of *All's Well that Ends Well* in America is astonishingly brief. In the 'New Cambridge Edition' of the play published in 1929, Harold Child reported: 'I have found no record of its ever having been staged in the United States of America.'[1] In 1939, Mr. Alfred Westfall concluded that five Shakespearian plays, *All's Well*, the three parts of *Henry VI*, and *Pericles*, had 'rarely if ever been given on the American professional stage'.[2] In 1936, in the publication of an address before the City Historic Society of Philadelphia, Mr. John Haney included *Troilus and Cressida* with these five as Shakespearian plays which had not been recorded as produced. 'Although', he continued, 'visitors to the Chicago Fair during the summer of 1935 had an opportunity to see an abbreviated version of *All's Well that Ends Well* excellently played in the Elizabethan manner.'[3] The version was certainly abbreviated and can hardly be classified as a production of Shakespeare's play. The acting time was forty minutes. It was one of a number of abbreviated revivals of Shakespeare's plays acted in a reconstructed Globe Theatre as a fair attraction at the 'Century of Progress'. Surprisingly in such a form, the director, Thomas Stevens, retained all the characters and kept the virginity scene! In the introduction to the published text of this condensation, Stevens made the claim that this was the first professional production of *All's Well* in America.[4] A much earlier claim had been submitted by William Winter, who recorded a performance in New York on 3(?) October 1789. He was mistaken in assuming that it was Shakespeare's play. Seilhamer lists an *All's Well that Ends Well* written 'by a citizen of the United States' for the John Street Theatre, New York, and produced on 1 October 1789; 'it was never heard of afterwards'.[5]

1. 'The Stage History', *All's Well that Ends Well*, ed. Sir Arthur Quiller-Couch and Dover Wilson, Cambridge, England, 1929, p. 189.
2. *American Shakespearean Criticism: 1607–1865*, New York, 1939, p. 61.
3. 'Shakespeare and Philadelphia', *An Address Delivered before the City Historic Society of Philadelphia, November 28, 1934*, Philadelphia, 1936, p. 58.
4. *Shakespeare's All's Well that Ends Well as Produced in Brief at the Globe Theatre, Century of Progress, Chicago*, New York, 1934, n. 3.
5. William Winter, *Shakespeare on the Stage*, New York, 1911, p. 24 and George O. Seilhamer, *History of the American Theatre During the Revolution and After*, Philadelphia, 1889, ii. 269. Odell is silent on this play.

The first American production of *All's Well* took place on 8 March 1799 at the Federal Street Theatre, Boston. It is not surprising that the acting version employed was Kemble's since Helena was acted by Mrs. Elizabeth Kemble-Whitlock, sister to the Kembles. An advertisement in *J. Russell's Gazette* on 7 March announced the performance as a benefit for Mr. Whitlock and noted:

The comedy . . . is one of the few very celebrated pieces of Shakespeare, which have not been represented on our stage; and we are the more surprised at this omission of our theatric managers, as it is universally allowed to possess as much diversity of character, variety of incident, interest of fable, and poetic beauty, as most of the productions of that immortal author. . . . The underplot is chiefly founded on the whimsical character and adventures of 'Parolles'.[1]

There are no reviews of the production, but a description of Mrs. Whitlock by a Boston critic promises little for Helena. 'Her defects were her person, which was short and undignified, and her heavy, thick voice; but she had the family face, and a genuine passion, which could hold the sympathies.'[2] With an uninspiring heroine and the Kemble text, the production is significant to the stage history only in fixing the date of the first American performance.

An intriguing problem involves the Elizabethan revivals of Augustin Daly, nineteenth-century producer. Again, it is William Winter who states that *All's Well* was produced, this time by Daly between 1887 and 1899. The assertion is repeated by Hazleton Spencer in *The Art and Life of William Shakespeare* published in 1940.[3] But again Winter is in error, although here he certainly should have known the facts. Augustin Daly printed a number of the acting versions of his Shakespearian revivals; in each case he listed himself as the adapter on the title page. Actually, all the adaptations were done by Winter, who sold the versions to Daly. There is no published version of a Daly *All's Well*, but on 27 November 1882, Winter wrote to Daly:

Here are the other acts of 'All's Well.' I will, if you like, pass a day with you shortly, & we will discuss the piece, scene by scene. You will observe that I have cut the text very freely, & made several transpositions, etc.: but I have not added more than ten lines, altogether. The scenic part will be easy & not expensive. We can have a fine military pageant, & a beautiful moonlight view of Florence.[4]

1. See n. 1, p. 176.
2. See H. I. Jackson's manuscript history of the Federal Street Theatre, Boston, 1794–1803(?), p. 15A, in the Harvard Theatre Collection.
3. See p. 50 of Winter's *Shakespeare on the Stage*, New York, 1911 and p. 295 of Spencer's study, New York, 1940.
4. Marvin Felheim, *The Theatre of Augustin Daly*, Cambridge, Massachusetts, 1956, p. 226.

In a second letter dated 21 June 1883, Winter acknowledged payment from Daly for his acting version.[1] Perhaps the most significant characteristic of the text is that Winter considered the play more in need of expurgation than the English Victorians did. Not only did he omit the virginity scene, the condition of the child, and the bed-trick, but he removed all dialogue which touched in any way upon sex. In the margin adjacent to the Clown's 'O Lord, sir!' scene with the Countess, Winter jotted, 'This will be a frank scene'; then he crossed out such words as 'buttocks' and 'cuckold'. In Act v, the Clown's 'fortune's displeasure is but sluttish' was changed to 'is sorely decayed'. In all, Winter cut just short of 400 lines from the original. The emphasis of the resultant text, as in the 'Kemble Edition', was upon Helena, and to her was given the epilogue.

Yet the play was never produced. The reason can only be conjectured, for Daly's continued interest in a revival of *All's Well* is demonstrable in a second alteration apparently prepared by Daly himself. On the inside cover of this unpublished prompt-book is a handwritten note by Winter dated 14 May 1911: 'The hand-writing of this re-arrangement of the Comedy is, throughout, that of my old friend Augustine Daly. Take good care of this book, for it is valuable.'[2] The text is considerably different from the earlier Winter version and is akin to, but by no means identical with, the 'Kemble Edition'. It contains detailed stage directions and elaborate set descriptions.[3] The wording of Winter's note does not make clear whether Daly is the author of the alteration. There is nothing, however, in the Winter–Daly correspondence to indicate a second commission to Winter, nor is this second prompt-book merely a reworking of the first for publication in the series of Daly prompt-books. Indeed, this second alteration is still a working copy in that items are crossed out and marginal notes inserted. My supposition is that Daly made his own adaptation, incorporating ideas of both Winter and Kemble. He had an extraordinary interest in reviving the plays of Shakespeare. Ada Rehan, his leading actress, shared this interest; she was 'devotedly fond of Shakespeare, and all the Shakespearean characters allotted to her were studied and acted by her with eager interest and sympathy'.[4] We would imagine that Daly planned a distinguished production with an ideal Helena. Yet, despite the money paid to Winter, the details of stage sets and business in the prompt-

1. Ibid.

2. Both texts are in the Folger Shakespeare Library collection. The first is entitled 'Augustin Daly production of AW with Notes by Winter. 2 vols.' and bears the catalogue number 'Promptbook, #946'. Daly's is entitled 'All's Well that Ends Well. Shakespeare's Comedy. Rearranged by Augustin Daly' and is catalogued as 'Promptbook, Folger ms.'

3. See n. 2, p. 176.   4. William Winter, *Ada Rehan*, New York, 1898, p. 35.

books, the existence of a second alteration, and the assertion by Winter that the play had been performed, *All's Well* was not produced.

The fact in itself could be ascribed to a variety of reasons ranging from Daly's dissatisfaction with both alterations to production difficulties. It may be, however, another of the ironies of the stage history of *All's Well* that musty superstitions frightened Daly from producing a play which had consumed so much of his time. Daly had been strongly affected by his interest in Peg Woffington, whose biography he had written. 'One suspects that Daly consciously modeled Miss Rehan's repertoire on Peg's. . . . This identification of the two actresses who played so many of the same roles was so prominent in Daly's mind that he seemed constantly to have confused one with the other.'[1] Peg Woffington had played Helena in the 1742 Drury Lane revival. It was this production which suffered so many mishaps, including Mrs. Woffington's fainting in the first act, that earned for the play its epithet, 'the unfortunate comedy'. It may be that Daly, despite the attractiveness of the role for his protégé, simply could not assign to Ada Rehan a part which had been a failure for Peg Woffington. Whatever his reason, *All's Well* lost its only opportunity for professional production in nineteenth-century America.

One of the surprising revelations of the stage history, then, is that the first significant performance of *All's Well* in America is the Canadian production of Tyrone Guthrie in 1953. Indeed, its unfamiliarity contributed to its selection as the companion piece to *Richard III* for the premier season of the Stratford, Ontario Festival. Since the cast was comprised of Canadian and British actors, Mr. Guthrie hoped to improve 'team-feeling' with a play equally new to both.[2] His plan succeeded, for the critical reviews of the cast were overwhelmingly favourable. Eleanor Stuart was praised for her portrayal of the Countess as 'the Aristocratic Old Lady of High Comedy . . . [who] ruled the stage without imperiousness . . . a quality of spirit rather than of mannerism'.[3] Alec Guinness 'played a polished King of France in a quilted dressing gown from a wheel-chair'.[4] Douglas Campbell combined the farce and pathos of Parolles so well that Walter Kerr concluded: 'You come away with that rare feeling that you don't particularly care whether you ever see another actor in the role or not.'[5] And, for the first time in the stage history of *All's Well*,

1. Felheim, pp. 40–41.
2. Tyrone Guthrie, *A Life in the Theatre*, New York, 1959, p. 320.
3. Robertson Davies, 'The Players', *Renown at Stratford: A Record of the Shakespeare Festival in Canada, 1953*, Toronto, 1953, p. 50. Tyrone Guthrie is listed as the principal author of this book; Mr. Davies gives a general review of the performers.
4. Arnold Edinborough, 'A New Stratford Festival', *SQ*, v (January 1954), 49.
5. *New York Herald Tribune*, 19 July 1953.

critics agreed that an actress had fulfilled the potentialities of Helena. If Mr. Guthrie's intention was to shape a high comedy combining the unbelievable machinations of the plot with credible motivation for the characters, his intention was executed largely through the performance of Miss Helen Worth. She was the determined woman, but there was no offence in the blithe, smiling innocence of a girl who believes that 'nothing could be more reasonable than her simple request'.[1] She turned 'the nasty business of her amorous pursuit into a sweetly logical wifely manoeuvre'.[2] Her disconcerting simplicity was so effective that Mr. Kerr commented: 'Helena is, if anything, a rather more dangerous character to have around than Richard III. By an act of conscienceless sorcery, Miss Worth has made her endearing.' Mr. Guthrie had made the play a box-office success.

As I have noted earlier, the approach with even more comic stage business was repeated at Stratford, England in 1959. It is an interesting conclusion to this stage history of major productions that, at the same time Mr. Guthrie was broadening the farce within the play, Mr. John Houseman was moulding a tragi-comedy out of its serious scenes. From the first revival in 1741, interpretations had fluctuated between farce and melodrama; in 1959 both extremes were produced in the theatre. On 1 August 1959, Mr. Houseman directed the American Shakespeare Festival Theatre production of *All's Well* at Stratford, Connecticut. Surprisingly, the reception by critics and audiences was almost as enthusiastic as that won by the Guthrie revival. The direction was called one of Mr. Houseman's 'finest achievements' and the play the most encouraging work yet done by the Connecticut group.[3]

As in the nineteenth-century melodramatic approaches to *All's Well*, Helena was the centre of the play to the exclusion of all other characters. Miss Nancy Wickwire played the heroine with intensity. In the first scene, she suffered visibly at the departure of Bertram, who kissed her lightly on the brow and waved pleasantly as he made his exit. Alone on stage, she appeared much older and more mature than the brash youth who had just departed for the adventures of court. After a humourless scene with Parolles, she walked about the stage, sobbed, pondered, and finally elaborated her scheme to win Bertram through the cure of the King. Throughout the first act, her dominant quality was a force, a determined strength. Although she displayed tenderness with the Countess, still it was her enthusiasm which aroused the Countess to agree with her plan.

1. *Renown at Stratford*, p. 50.   2. Edinborough, p. 49.
3. See Claire McGlinchee, 'Stratford, Connecticut, Shakespeare Festival, 1959', *SQ*.x (Autumn 1959), 575 and Henry Hewes, the *Saturday Review*, xlii (22 Aug. 1959), 23.

In Helena's introductory scene with the King, the audience became aware that this intense woman had more in her favour than Lafeu's intercession. There was the suggestion of divine assistance in her cause. The King, in halting tones spoken from his cot, agreed to see Lafeu's 'Doctor She'. Helena *descended* a staircase as if heaven-sent. The entire scene was played slowly, quietly, with great stress upon the 'help of heaven'. At the end of the scene, Helena helped the King gently from his bed as if his consent to the miracle had already begun the process of the cure. Thereafter, the force of her character assumed a tragic intensity with Bertram's rejection of her. Her horror at the thought that she was responsible for Bertram's flight to war and at the potential danger which the war threatened to him suggested that the 'dark comedy' was in fact a very dark tragedy. The mood was sustained in Helena's arrival at Florence as a haggard pilgrim. Only the last lines of the play which record Bertram's surrender saved Helena from being added to the ranks of Shakespeare's tragic heroines.

Mr. Houseman made several points in his direction to prevent Bertram from emerging as the tragic villain. His kiss and wave to Helena in the first scene suggested a pleasantry about him that won sympathy. His conduct at his presentation to the King was dignified as were the actions of the young lords who surrounded the King. This kind of stage business was even more effective after the marriage when Bertram sent his bride back to Rousillon. He was not unkind to her. Somewhat overwhelmed by the force of her passion, he turned to say something to her, some kind word, but she had already begun her exit. He checked himself, showed dismay at hurting her, then recovered quickly and shouted his youthful boast. In Florence, there was no sport between Bertram and Diana. He was not prompted by a soldier's lust nor the waywardness of youth but by a passionate response to her. Both played the scene seriously. This distorted Diana's motivation, but their embrace and final kiss seemed an attempt to justify Bertram's conduct now and his earlier rejection of Helena. His sincerity made more difficult his lies in the trial scene and more confused Diana's delays. But the difficulty did not lose much sympathy for him as he lied; he was obviously anxious, troubled, almost overpowered by his accumulation of evidence which endangered his newly won favour. The realistic approach to the play won credibility for Bertram.[1]

---

1. It is fair to note, however, that Miss McGlinchee does not share my impression that Bertram made attempts at kindness to Helena. She thought that he 'masked his hatred for Helena poorly and left the playgoer puzzled as to what could have made him so attractive to the foolish heroine' (Ibid., n. 73, p. 576).

Mr. Houseman's direction of *All's Well* was bold. He accepted the loss of the comic potential of the play. He ignored the cuts and altera-tions of the nineteenth century which resulted in merely sentimental romance. For in preserving the text, he accepted the unsentimental determination of Helena, the unromantic deceit of the bed-trick, and the 'offensive' dialogue. The result was a dark comedy, but not a bitter comedy. The dramatic treatment of the story of Helena and Bertram could not avoid a somewhat melodramatic conclusion, but most critics expressed views similar to Mr. Hewes, who wrote in the *Saturday Review* that the production had 'made this unpopular play work by filling it with genuine passion, and allowing the characters to be naively unaware—except for brief moments—of the horror of their behavior'. Mr. Houseman, however, paid a heavy price for his tragi-comedy. The infusion of passion changed Parolles from the braggart-soldier to a coward-villain who failed to draw his first real laugh from the audience until his capture. Even then, the turnabout of his exposure was pathetic as he was knocked about by each of the departing lords in what became a repugnant scene.

The Guthrie and Houseman productions are the only major American theatre productions of *All's Well that Ends Well*. They represent relatively extreme approaches to the play. Shakespeare has not yet been exhausted in either the work of scholarship or the theatre when a play from his mature period has only recently received the attention and experimentation of the theatrical world in America.

In the twentieth century, the play has had a number of minor productions in Great Britain and the United States, minor in status, though frequently not in quality.[1] Undoubtedly, the directors and performers in these productions have seen dramatic effects which would be invaluable to this history. Even a necessarily brief and incomplete survey, however, justifies two conclusions. The play has been made entertaining theatre, not simply a curious Shakespearian failure, for the modern audience. As a result, the number of minor presentations of *All's Well* is growing. A second conclusion is that the entertainment has resulted *usually* from a light approach in inter-pretation. The Shakespeare Festival Company at Ashland, Oregon, produced the play in both 1955 and 1960. Under the direction of Robert Loper, the first production turned the play 'into a delightful comedy' in which the vices of the characters were minimized in order to make the theme one of forgiveness'.[2] In 1961, 'Ashland's most dis-tinctive triumph was again affirmed in the notoriously ignored or scorned *All's Well*. Like others of the barely tolerated plays in the

1. See n. 3, pp. 176–7.
2. Horace W. Robinson, 'Shakespeare, Ashland, Oregon', *SQ*, vi (Autumn 1955), 451.

canon, the outdoor performance on an Elizabethan stage blossomed into a work of delightful verve and flash.'[1] 'A general liveliness and a successful emphasis on the comedy' were noted in the Cambridge University Marlowe Society's production in 1950; that long-maligned clown, Lavache, came off particularly well.[2] The Clown was given an excellent representation as the eternal low comedian in a performance at William and Mary College, Virginia, 1959. Mr. Howard Scammon, the director, achieved an interesting effect by placing the Clown on an upper porch throughout the trial scene. Lavache's obvious and natural delight over the discomfiture of Parolles, the entrapment of Bertram, and the confused consternation wrought by Diana's ambiguities lightened the tone of the entire scene and suggested a reaction to the audience. A range in experimentation may be noted in the contrast between the Merton College, Oxford, production directed by Nevill Coghill in which the stage was bare and the actors sat by the sides in full view of the audience and a production at Wellesley College, Massachusetts, which noted in its press release:

We hope to offer to our audience a love story, the fascination of a suspenseful intrigue plot, engaging character studies, wit and bawdy humor, the colorful pageantry of a royal court and a military campaign, together with much exquisite poetry.[3]

A 1956 production at Antioch College contributed an interesting effect with its Parolles. In his review, Judson Jerome notes that Parolles became hysterical in the exposure scene; the officers strained to revenge themselves on this 'babbling ape'; the lords and Bertram were shamed in the vileness of the man; Bertram hurled himself off stage 'with a desperate need to reform'. The treatment, 'in this surprisingly quick-paced yarn', produced this effect:

This emphasis upon Parolles in the central and hilarious scene of his capture and questioning does a great deal to remove the problem of unity in the play. Beat the scapegoat, and the rest of the play is somewhat absolved of its mood of undefined evil. Reveal to Bertram the depths of Parolles' character, and he is motivated to begin his shuffling repentance.[4]

In a production at Bryn Mawr College in 1963, Bertram's conduct became surprisingly plausible as he balanced a natural affection for

1. R. D. Horn, 'Shakespeare and Ben Jonson-Ashland, 1961', *SQ*, xii (Autumn 1961), 415.
2. *The Stage*, 1950.
3. For Mr. Coghill's production, see *SQ*, vi (Winter 1955), 70. Mr. Paul Barstow was kind enough to send me the press release and a full account of his Wellesley College performance.
4. 'Shakespeare at Antioch', *SQ*, vii (Autumn 1956), 412.

his childhood companion and an equally natural revulsion at the prospect of marrying her.

Perhaps the most amusing fact in the stage history of the play in the minor theatres is its popularity as a burlesque in American vaudeville. If Augustin Daly hesitated to produce *All's Well* as drama for nineteenth-century America, the minstrels did not hesitate to present travesties of it. Three such were actually submitted for copyright; one was published under the title *The Serenade* and was also known as 'All's Well that Ends Well' and 'Nip and Tuck'.[1] Some of the more severe critics of the play might be willing indeed to substitute for the denouement of the original the ending of this version which 'depends for its working out on the discharging of firecrackers to frighten the actors off the stage'.

At the beginning of Chapter 3, I reviewed the stresses which the previous centuries had placed upon their interpretations of *All's Well*. I discussed those elements of the play which had delighted particular audiences. I suggested that the task which the theatre of the twentieth century assumed in producing the play was the discovery of a principle of unity which could blend the 'brilliant parts'. This task was placed in the hands of the director. Throughout the past sixty years, the director has commonly shaped the play to a Procrustean bed by stretching the comic or the serious. In my final chapter, I shall draw heavily from the stage history of *All's Well* for an analysis of the problems of the play and provocative solutions which the theatre offers. But there are a few general points which I think the reader may profitably keep in mind as he examines the scholarly criticism of the comedy.

Throughout its stage history, *All's Well* has rarely been presented as Shakespeare wrote it. In the midst of its popularity in the eighteenth century, the play with an emphasis upon farce was produced as altered by Garrick. In the nineteenth century, the Kemble version was dominant until an even worse text was prepared by the Irving Dramatic Club in 1895. In the twentieth century, the play has been altered occasionally; more often, it has reflected the intention of the director rather than of the original play. I am not concluding that the text itself will prove *All's Well* a great play upon the stage. I am concluding that, on the stage, there have been few attempts to trust to Shakespeare for the dramatic functions of each character, each scene. I am concluding that, in the scholarship of the play, very few

1. Ray B. Browne, 'Shakespeare in American Vaudeville and Negro Minstrelsy', *American Quarterly*, xii (Fall 1960), 385.

of the critics have ever seen a performance of *All's Well* in any form. Both of these disturbing facts have left their marks on the criticism of the play.

A second point is one that has been apparent throughout the stage history—there is a strain within *All's Well* resulting from the seeming discord of romance and realism, of the serious and the comic. The problem of romance and realism springs up in many issues but perhaps most obviously in these two: the love of the noble Helena for the ignoble Bertram, and the realistic trap of the substitution of one woman in the seduction of another, which follows a fairy-like miraculous cure of the King. One answer to the first problem which rings most effectively throughout the stage history is an emphasis upon the clear vision of Helena which sees a nobility in the still boyish Bertram. To the second, the stage history replies that both the cure and the bed-trick must be unreal. Neither must be examined closely; both spring from the distracting loveliness of the heroine, from a fairy-tale treatment of the entire plot, or from the supernatural assistance given the heroine in justification of her goal. The problem of the serious and the comic has been more swiftly but perhaps less satisfactorily solved. There is nothing unusual in the mixture of the grave and the humorous in drama. But here the problem is just what should be serious and what should be comic. Are Parolles, the Clown, and Lafeu really funny? Are they satiric? Are they bitter portrayals of human society? Nowhere is the problem better illustrated than in the exposure of Parolles. Is he to be played comically or tragically or at some mid point? The theatrical history of *All's Well* shows that the decision on this point will usually determine whether the production is to reveal a 'light' or 'dark' comedy. And the productions of the past are about equally divided on this touchstone of interpretation.

The third point to be remembered in the examination of the critical history is really a conclusion from the first two. No really satisfying production of *All's Well* has yet been accomplished in a major theatre. Is such a production possible? Certainly, the challenge is there for both critic and director. In his review of the 1959 Guthrie revival, the drama critic of the *London Times* wrote:

> The key needed to unlock the full meaning of this difficult comedy has yet to be found. Commentators have so far given theatrical producers little help. Professor Wilson Knight recently has striven prodigiously to fashion a key that might work, but his essay obviously came too late for it to have any influence on Mr. Guthrie's present production. We shall have to wait—probably for a long time—to see Helena brought to the stage as Shakespeare's supreme expression of a woman's love, a humble

medium for divine power which out of a contention on equal terms of male and female values achieves a mystical union between them.[1]

Whether the key is Professor Knight's or one with simpler notches, the excitement of opening a Shakespearian lock, long rusted, is there. Perhaps, to quote Mr. Patrick Gibbs again, 'something almost as rewarding as "The Winter's Tale" might emerge'.[2]

1. 22 April 1959.   2. *New York Times,* 22 April 1959.

PART II

The Critical History of
All's Well that Ends Well

5

THE SPIRIT OF FANTASY:
FARCE AND ROMANCE
(1655–1840)

THE stage history of *All's Well that Ends Well* has run along a straight course; it has reflected the tastes of each age with few surprises. When a play is infrequently produced, a performance generally reveals the prevalent attitude toward that play. Only with a very popular play do we usually see a wide range in interpretation within a generation; the frequency of production challenges directors and performers to distinguish their presentations from those of their competitors. Because literary criticism is so much more personal, so individual, because it is bound by neither the practicalities of the theatre nor the immediate applause of an audience, we may expect considerably more variation in the critical interpretations of *All's Well*. And the variation is there in eddies, undercurrents, and branches of the main-stream; nevertheless, the course of the critical history roughly parallels the stage history. Both demonstrate the comic delight of the eighteenth century, the ethical norms and sentimental inclinations of the late eighteenth and early nineteenth centuries, the concern for the heroine and melodrama throughout much of the nineteenth century. Near the end of the century, both record the increasingly realistic reaction against this melodramatic approach. In the twentieth century, the studied theatrical experiments of the directors are matched in the critical history by extensive conjecture upon the 'inherent failure' of *All's Well*. Both histories terminate, in the limit of this study, in the recent attempts to illustrate the value of Shakespeare's play.

There is no real criticism of *All's Well that Ends Well* in the seventeenth century. The few references have only historical significance in pointing up the probable unpopularity of the play. The *Shakespeare Allusion-Book* lists merely eight allusions to *All's Well* before 1700 and none earlier than 1655.[1] Three of the eight are quotations included in Cotgrave's *Treasury* under the heading, 'Of Authority'. After the first entry is a note in a seventeenth-century hand which denies that *All's Well* was written by Shakespeare—a rather foreboding beginning for the critical history. Mr. Gerald Bentley discovered

1. See n. 1, p. 177.

two additional allusions, but both of them are again from Cotgrave.[1] Among the other allusions is a curious item in Edward Archer's *An Exact and Perfect Catalogue of all the Plaies that were ever printed* . . . dated 1656. Archer classifies *All's Well* as an 'Interlude', the only such classification among the plays which he ascribes to Shakespeare. In 1671, however, Kirkman listed it as a comedy; in 1691 Langbaine called it a comedy and gave Boccaccio as its source. But throughout the century, the only recorded gleam of interest is the indication by Charles I that the play should have been entitled 'Monsieur Parolles'.[2]

The few references to *All's Well* constitute evidence that the play was not highly regarded, but we cannot conclude that its neglect was based upon critical principle. If such were the case, then the negative evidence of the seventeenth century would assume an importance in our estimation of the play. Other Shakespearian comedies, however, suffered the same disregard. From his study of the reputations of Shakespeare and Jonson in the seventeenth century, Mr. Bentley inferred that romantic comedy had little appeal for the age. Furthermore, there was no interest in the heroines of Shakespeare's plays:

> Only Desdemona and Ophelia seem to have made any impression worth mentioning. Lady Macbeth and Cleopatra, Beatrice, Portia, Rosalind, Miranda, Viola, Perdita, Imogen, and Cordelia are mentioned so seldom as to seem unknown. . . . Whatever the reasons for the situation, it is clear that the popularity of Shakespeare's characters in the seventeenth century is not due to the appeal of his heroines. They did not charm the writers of the seventeenth century as they have so many of the nineteenth and twentieth.[3]

Mr. Bentley's observation is ample explanation for the neglect of a play whose protagonist is a woman, whose hero is underdeveloped, and whose plot turns upon romantic devices.

As the stage history of *All's Well* has its beginnings in the eighteenth century, so too has the critical history. As the productions of the era emphasized Parolles, so too did the commentaries. Critical delight with Parolles is first expressed by Nicholas Rowe in his 1709 edition of Shakespeare's plays; he declared that 'the Parasite and the Vain-glorious in *Parolles*, in *All's Well that ends Well*, is as good as any thing of that kind in Plautus or Terence'.[4] In 1710, Charles Gildon concurred; Parolles was 'preferable to all in that kind, except his own

---

1. *Shakespeare & Jonson: Their Reputations in the Seventeenth Century Compared*, Chicago, 1945, ii. 3.
2. See above, p. 6.
3. Bentley, i. 128–9.
4. *Some Account of the Life of Mr. William Shakespeare (1709)*, The Augustan Reprint Society, Extra Series no. 1, #17, 1948, p. xix.

Falstaff'.[1] In the cast of characters for the 1714 edition, Rowe described Parolles as 'a Parasitical Follower of Bertram, a Coward, but Vain, and a great Pretender of Valour,'[2] a description which has been retained in many later editions. Praise for Parolles increased as the century progressed. In 1765, when Woodward had so successfully identified himself with the role, Dr. Johnson wrote in his edition:

> *Parolles* has many of the lineaments of *Falstaff*, and seems to be the character which *Shakespeare* delighted to draw, a fellow that had more wit than virtue. . . . *Parolles* is a boaster and a coward, such as has always been the sport of the stage, but perhaps never raised more laughter or contempt than in the hands of *Shakespeare*.[3]

Francis Gentleman, obviously influenced by Woodward's management of the part, prefaced the 1774 'Bell Acting Edition' with the note that Parolles was 'inimitably drawn' and Shakespeare's 'chief delight, and inducement to undertake this piece'.[4]

Comparisons to Falstaff were so common that they produced the first offshoot from the general acclaim which Parolles enjoyed. Maurice Morgann in his famous defence of Falstaff in 1777 would not allow an equality between the two characters. The magnitude of Falstaff simply overwhelmed the petty Parolles in Morgann's view. Parolles falls 'by the first shaft of ridicule, but *Falstaff* is a butt on which we empty the whole quiver'.[5] He interprets the exposure of Parolles as an annihilation of his character and, in justification, notes that the Clown and Lafeu do not 'readily recollect his person'. The significance of this interpretation lies in its being the first hint of Parolles as a figure of pathos, or worse, a symbol of human degradation. But, it must be remembered, that Morgann is defending Falstaff; Parolles becomes much less of a rival to the great swashbuckler if he is utterly 'crushed by a plot'. The popular concept of Parolles, however, remained unchanged. Dr. Johnson had seen no annihilation of character and had paraphrased the text to demonstrate his final impression: 'though justice required that he should be detected and exposed, yet his vices *sit so fit in him* that he is not at

---

1. The criticism, *An Essay on the Art, Rise, and Progress of the Stage in Greece, Rome, and England and Remarks on the Plays of Shakespeare*, was published separately in 1714, but it first appeared in the supposed seventh volume of Rowe's edition, published by Edmund Curll in 1710.

2. A copy of this edition is bound with a number of plays in the Folger Shakespeare Library in *Williams Collection of Plays* (PR 1241/W53/Cage). *All's Well* is in volume ii of the Collection, pp. 363–443, although all the plays retain the pagination of the original editions. See p. 364 for the cast of characters.

3. Samuel Johnson (ed.), *The Plays of William Shakespeare* . . . , London, 1765, iii. 384 and 399.   4. i. 297.

5. 'An Essay on the Dramatic Character of Sir John Falstaff', *Eighteenth Century Essays on Shakespeare*, ed. D. Nichol Smith, Glasgow, 1903, pp. 216–303. For the quotations in my text, see pp. 295–9.

last suffered to starve'.[1] Francis Gentleman thought that the exposure scene gave 'great scope for comic merit' and 'excellent food for mirth'.[2] And after Morgann's attack, Thomas Davies, in 1783, expressed the still dominant view:

> In all our comic writers, I know not where to meet with such an odd compound of cowardice, folly, ignorance, pertness, and effrontery, with certain semblances of courage, sense, knowledge, adroitness, and wit, as Parolles. He is, I think, inferior only to the great master of stage gaiety and mirth, Sir John Falstaff.[3]

The satisfaction and delight which the eighteenth century experienced in Parolles did not extend to other elements in the play. Throughout the period, commentators expressed displeasure with the plot, the hero, and the heroine. As early as 1710, Gildon objected to the irregularity of the plot on the usual criterion of the era that the play violated unity of place. More important, he protested against its unreality: 'The Story itself is out of a Possibility almost, at least so far out of the way of Custom and Experience, that it can't be call'd natural.' But incredulity toward romantic probability was diminishing. Shakespeare's management of the plot, rather than the story itself, became the target of critical attack. In 1753, Mrs. Charlotte Lennox compared the play most unfavourably with its source.[4] She considered Shakespeare's additions to be useless and disagreeable; the contrivances were inferior to Boccaccio; Shakespeare mangled the characters as he took them from his source; the supposed death of Helena produced dull ambiguities; and the playwright 'violated all the Rules of poetical Jusice' in granting a happy ending to a couple who 'merited nothing but Punishment'. Dr. Johnson, in milder tones, objected to the dramatist's haste in the last act, especially to the King's ready forgiveness of Bertram:

> *Shakespeare* is now hastening to the end of the play, finds his matter sufficient to fill up his remaining scenes, and therefore, as on other such occasions, contracts his dialogue and precipitates his action. . . . *Shakespeare* wanted to conclude his play.[5]

Dr. Johnson suggested a practical reason as well for the long speech of Diana's accusation against Bertram and her toying with the King: 'It was much easier than to make a pathetical interview between *Helen* and her husband, her mother, and the king.'[6] Gentleman considered the entire play a hasty composition and the plot a 'flimsy

---

1. *The Plays of William Shakespeare*, iii. 384.
2. 'Bell Acting Edition', i. 345.   3. *Dramatic Miscellanies*, London, 1783, ii. 40.
4. *Shakespear Illustrated: or the Novels and Histories, on which the Plays of Shakespear are Founded*, London, 1753, i. 189–95.
5. *The Plays of William Shakespeare*, iii. 386.   6. Ibid., p. 397.

plan: as it is, this piece can hardly live on the stage'.[1] Thomas Davies, in 1783, made the single defence of Shakespeare's treatment. He admitted that the plot was 'strange and unpromising', but he thought that the dramatist's genius had triumphed over its material.[2] The triumph was accomplished through the 'abundance of mirth' raised through the interaction of character and plot. He cited especially the 'admirable contrasts' of Parolles and Lafeu, 'from the collision of whose humours perpetual laughter is produced'.

Inevitably, attacks on the plot of *All's Well* directed critical attention to Helena and Bertram. Mrs. Lennox was vehement in her condemnation of both. In no other instance in the critical history does Helena suffer a stronger indictment. Since the charges against Helena throughout three centuries of criticism are contained in some form here, I quote Mrs. Lennox's long list of grievances:

Shakespear shows her oppressed with Despair at the Absence of the Count, incapable of either Advice or Consolation; giving unnecessary Pain to the good Countess her Mother-in-law . . . by alarming her with a pretended Design of killing herself, and by some Means or other, which we are not acquainted with, gets the Rector of the Place, to whom she had vowed a Pilgrimage (which by the Way she does not perform) to confirm the Report of her Death.

After having accomplished her Design of bedding with her Husband and procuring the Ring, she rides Post to *Marseilles* with the Widow and her Daughter, on Purpose to expose her beloved Husband to the King's Resentment, and the Contempt of all the Courtiers who were present; by making *Diana* complain to the King of the Count's having debauched her under a Promise of Marriage when his Wife was dead.

After she has thus exposed the Frailties of her Husband, she has the Cruelty to suffer him to be accused of having murdered her, and in Consequence of that Accusation, seized and imprisoned by the King's Order. . . .

After having made him endure so much Shame and Affliction, she haughtily demands his Affection as a Prize she had lawfully won.

In *Boccace* she kneels, she weeps, she persuades; and if she demands, she demands with Humility.

In Shakespear she is cruel, artful, and insolent, and ready to make Use of the King's Authority to force her Husband to do her Justice.

Here we have, then, the compilation of later accusations: the resoluteness, the aggressiveness, the cunning, the deceit, the lies, the sordidness, the insolence, the very evil of Helena. Accept each; group them as Mrs. Lennox has done, and the result is a vengeful Medea, rather than the heroine of a romantic comedy.

Bertram fares no better in the critical hands of Mrs. Lennox.

1. 'Bell Acting Edition', i. 297.   2. *Dramatic Miscellanies*, ii. 6–7.

Employing the same method of plot analysis, she concludes that he is coarse, mean, dishonest, lecherous, boastful, cruel, and intolerably weak. Indeed, we turn with some relief to the famous judgement which Dr. Johnson passed upon the hero:

I cannot reconcile my heart to Bertram; a man noble without generosity, and young without truth; who marries *Helena* as a coward, and leaves her as a profligate: when she is dead by his unkindness, sneaks home to a second marriage, is accused by a woman whom he has wronged, defends himself by falsehood, and is dismissed to happiness.[1]

The verdict of Mrs. Lennox upon Helena has rarely been seconded by later critics; the judgement of Dr. Johnson upon Bertram has been paraphrased throughout the critical history of the play. Yet surprisingly, Bertram found a defender in the very year of Dr. Johnson's attack. In 1765, W. Kenrick published a rather scurrilous critique, *A Review of Doctor Johnson's New Edition of Shakespeare: In Which the Ignorance, Or Inattention, of that Editor is Exposed, and the Poet Defended from the Persecution of His Commentators*. Despite the nature of the book and the motives of its author, Kenrick was a forerunner in offering extenuation for Bertram's conduct:

For it will hardly be admitted, by any person in his right senses, that the paternal authority of the King ought to have carried him so far as to degrade the heir apparent [?] to his crown, by marrying him to the daughter of a quack, merely because she had had the good luck, by one of her father's nostrums, to cure his majesty of a *fistula in ano*.

This circumstance considered also, I think it should have obtained some little favour for the character of Bertram in general, as well as from our editor, as from the very ingenious authoress [Mrs. Lennox] of *Shakespeare Illustrated*; for though he be on the whole a loose, unprincipled fellow, yet I think the absurdity and cruelty of this forced marriage affords a great palliation of his crimes.[2]

More indicative of forthcoming critical attitudes to Bertram and Helena are the remarks of Francis Gentleman. His realistic explanation of the hero is one that has been adopted by many later critics. Gentleman argues that Shakespeare intended to draw human nature, not perfection, in the depiction of the youth. The dramatist succeeded, for Bertram 'well represents many modern unprincipled gallants'. Helena, on the other hand, remains a romantic heroine despite the ungracious methods of her wooing; she 'confesses her love in terms of the most modest, pleasing sensibility'.[3] Gentleman's praise for the 'beauties' of her character foreshadows the idealization which would elevate her in the criticism of succeeding decades. For,

1. *The Plays of William Shakespeare*, iii. 399.   2. London, 1765, pp. 128–9.
3. 'Bell Acting Edition', i. 321, 355, and 310.

upon the application of a new critical criterion toward the latter part of the eighteenth century, interest in *All's Well* shifted from the comedy of Parolles to the nobility of Helena. Delicacy, both in morality and sensibility, dictated a re-evaluation of the play. In that process, Parolles suffered. Even among those critics who defended him as a comic negation of sensibility, there was disgust for his unprincipled conduct and offensive dialogue. Although Helena shared in the frank dialogue of the virginity scene, her innate goodness and humility, her spirit of innocence and self-sacrifice, justified her as an ideal heroine in sense and sensibility. The romantic inclination of Gentleman was given full expression in the appraisal of Davies in 1783: 'It appears, throughout the whole play, that the passion of this sweet girl is of the noblest kind'.[1] Eighteenth-century criticism had begun with praise for Parolles, had admitted the difficulties of the plot, had disputed about the characters of the hero and heroine, and ended with admiration for Helena. In this century, the streams of stage history and criticism flowed side by side.

It is not pertinent to my study to describe the textual investigations or lineal illuminations of eighteenth-century editors; these have been incorporated into later editions and are easily available to the reader. Nor is it necessary here to trace the long and still unresolved argument concerning the date of *All's Well*, the possibility of its being a revised play either by Shakespeare or others, and the relationship of the play, if any, to the puzzling 'Love's Labour's Won'. G. K. Hunter has reviewed the history and the evidence of opposing theories in the 'New Arden Edition'.[2] But there is a number of annotations which are significant both to the reader and the director of *All's Well*. Dr. Johnson, for example, underlined the importance of Lafeu's comment to the Countess, 'your son was misled with a snipp'd-taffeta fellow there', in its indication that Parolles is to be played as 'an affected follower of the fashion' and in its insistence that Parolles dominates Bertram.[3] Concerning a still disputed passage which ultimately affects every interpretation and production of the play, Dr. Johnson insisted that Lafeu and Parolles were talking at some distance from the King, Helena, and the young Lords as Helena chooses her husband. Thus, Lafeu misinterprets the action and mistakenly asks, 'Do they all deny her?' (II. iii. 86). Theobald, on the contrary, maintained that Lafeu's remarks show us the hostility of all the young lords to the marriage.[4] The lords' eagerness or lack of it shifts sympathy between Helena and Bertram accordingly.

1. *Dramatic Miscellanies*, ii. 27.
2. See n. 2, p. 177.   3. *The Plays of Shakespeare*, iii. 376.
4. Ibid., p. 321 and Lewis Theobald, *The Works of Shakespeare*, London, 1773, iii. 37.

Theobald thought, too, that Bertram should make a show of haste as he observes his wife lingering fondly after her dismissal.[1] In his commentary, Thomas Davies has at least two notes worthy of attention. In the first, he stresses the strength and importance of the tradition of wardship with its demand of complete obedience from Bertram. Aware of that tradition, Shakespeare would scarcely intend the slightest buffoonery:

> No prerogative of the crown, in the time of the feudal system, was esteemed more honourable, or was indeed more profitable, than that of wardship; nor was any part of kingly power more subject to fraudulent abuse, to tyranny and oppression. So cruelly had King John, and some of his predecessors, exerted an undue influence over their wards, that the fourth, fifth, sixth, seventh, forty-third, and forty-fourth, articles of the great charter, are all expressly written with an intention to restrain the power of the crown within proper limits respecting wardships.[2]

The King may be played with historical justification as honourable or tyrannical, but hardly as comical. In this second note, Davies draws two conclusions from Helena's ready acceptance of Parolles' vices:

> Her tenderness in discussing of his vices is a strong, though delicate, confession of her love to Bertram. . . . There is such a relative charm, in that which in any manner appertains to the person we love, let it be never so insignificant and worthless, that we are sure to be pleased with it, because it calls to mind the object of our affections. Helena's remark, that the slight and worthless, provided they have talents to excite gaiety and cheerfulness, are often preferred to the meritorious, but less pliable in temper, is equally just.[3]

The actress, then, must use the lines not merely as an introduction of Parolles to the audience, but as a demonstration of her love for Bertram and an analysis of Parolles's own appeal. For Parolles to enter and incite anything but the audience's affection is a contradiction of this introduction.

Nineteenth-century English Romantic criticism of *All's Well* blossomed into a panegyric to Helena. But before its influence had spread, A. W. Schlegel, in Germany in 1808, presented a more comprehensive interpretation of the play.[4] Schlegel's view is romantic, but his comments range over the entire play and are less extreme in judgement than those of the English Romantics. Consequently, he offers an analysis which differs from both eighteenth-century criticism and the work of his English contemporaries. In anticipation of W. W.

---

1. *The Works of Shakespeare*, iii. 48.
2. *Dramatic Miscellanies*, ii, 31.   3. Ibid., pp. 12–13.
4. *Lectures on Dramatic Art and Literature*, trans. John Black, London, 1883, pp. 384–6.

Lawrence, Schlegel linked the play to the Griselda legend and other old fabliaux in which woman's patience triumphs over man's abuse of his superior power. Despite the romantic source material, Helena is not entirely the lovely heroine of fairy-tale. Her wooing against the inclinations of Bertram is a fault which carries guilt. Only her patient suffering in the Griselda manner, especially her self-accusation that she is the persecutor of her husband before she flees Rousillon, converts that error of love to the virtue of love. Helena emerges as the ideal heroine only after a purification of her fault. The romance of the play is checked further, according to Schlegel, by the realistic depiction of Bertram, who is painted in 'the true way of the world, which never makes much of man's injustice to woman, if so-called family honour is preserved'. But he accuses Dr. Johnson of missing the point of Bertram's realism. It is just that realistic abuse of power which is necessary as the obstacle to the romance of the Griselda legends. At any time when the contempt of Bertram threatens to make intolerable the humiliation of Helena, Parolles steps in as comic relief.

Schlegel is among the first critics to mark the contrast between youth and age in the play. Just as the balance between the romantic Helena and the realistic Bertram is necessary for the plot, so the contrast of one generation and another has a dramatic function in that 'the plain honesty of the King, the good-natured impetuosity of old Lafeu, the maternal indulgence of the Countess' vie with each other 'to overcome the arrogance of the young Count'. If the play is imbalanced at all, it is because Parolles outsteps his function as comic relief. Yet the comedy is worth the imbalance, and Schlegel echoes earlier criticism:

> The mystification by which his pretended valour and his shameless slanders are unmasked must be ranked among the most comic scenes that ever were invented: they contain matter enough for an excellent comedy, if Shakespeare were not always rich even to profusion. Falstaff has thrown Parolles into the shade, otherwise among the poet's comic characters he would have been still more famous.

Schlegel's commendation of *All's Well* is based upon the delineation of a romantic heroine with a natural fault, the dramatic function of the older characters, and the comic genius apparent in Parolles. His English contemporaries praised the play for its sentimental heroine, for the delicate and tender touches among the older characters, and only occasionally for its comedy. Of the three interests, the sentimental heroine was by far the play's greatest allurement, and it was she who evoked rapturous tributes from the early nineteenth-century critics. Hazlitt saw nothing but perfection in her:

> The character of Helena is one of great sweetness and delicacy . . . the most scrupulous nicety of female modesty is not once violated. There is not one thought or action that ought to bring a blush into her cheeks, or that for a moment lessens her in our esteem.[1]

Charles Lamb declared that Shakespeare had handled the unusual case of a woman wooing 'with such exquisite address' that 'delicacy dispenses her laws in her [Helena's] favour, and Nature in her single case seems content to suffer a sweet violation'.[2] Perhaps no one is more representative of the excesses of such subjective criticism than Nathan Drake; no one is more extreme in the expression of romantic sensibilities:

> Helen, the romantic, the love-dejected Helen, must excite in every feeling bosom a high degree of sympathy; patient suffering in the female sex, expecially when resulting from ill-acquitted attachment, and united with modesty and beauty, cannot but be an object of interest and commiseration. . . .
>
> If in the infancy of her passion the error of indiscretion be attributable to Helen, how is it atoned for by the most engaging humility, by the most bewitching tenderness of heart. . . .
>
> But when the wife of Bertram, with a resignation and self-devotedness worthy of the highest praise, she deserts the house of her mother-in-law, knowing that whilst she is sheltered there her husband will not return, how does she, becoming thus an unprotected wanderer, a pilgrim *barefoot plodding the cold ground* for him who has contemned her, rise to the tone of exalted truth and heroism![3]

Would the eighteenth century recognize such a delineation of Shakespeare's heroine? Or would Mrs. Lennox be able to restrain her indignation at Mrs. Jameson's claim in 1832: 'There never was, perhaps, a more beautiful picture of a woman's love. . . . Her love is like a religion, pure, holy, and deep.'[4]

Most quoted of the Romantic tributes to Helena is Coleridge's 'loveliest character', although it is rarely noted in its full context, 'Shall we say here that Shakespeare has unnecessarily made his loveliest character utter a lie [III. v. 48–51]?' Nor is it ever coupled with his later admission, in 1833:

> Indeed, it must be confessed that her character is not very delicate, and

---

1. William Hazlitt, *Characters of Shakespeare's Plays & Lectures on English Poets*, Macmillan Library of English Classics, London, 1920, pp. 177–8.
2. *Specimens of English Dramatic Poets*, Bohn's Standard Library, London, 1901, p. 298.
3. *Shakespeare and His Times*, London, 1817, ii. 423–4.
4. Anna Brownell Jameson, *Characteristics of Women, Moral, Poetical, and Historical*, New York, [18–?], p. 80. The study was first published in London in 1832.

it required all Shakespeare's consummate skill to interest us for her; and he does this chiefly by the operation of the other characters.[1]

But if Coleridge's admiration for Helena lessened, his appreciation of romantic potentialities in *All's Well* did not. In fact, his harsh analysis of the heroine was prompted by a romantic assessment of Bertram:

> I cannot agree with the solemn abuse which the critics have poured out upon Bertram in 'All's Well that Ends Well.' He was a young nobleman in feudal times, just bursting into manhood, with all the feelings of pride of birth and appetite for pleasure and liberty natural to such a character so circumstanced.[2]

Romantic potentialities in the play were uncovered by early nineteenth-century critics in the sensibilities of the older characters and in the melodrama of the plot. The virtue of both the Countess and Lafeu was especially pleasing. Coleridge spoke of the 'beautiful precepts' of the Countess. Hazlitt praised the 'honesty and uprightness of the good old lord Lafeu'. To Mrs. Jameson, the Countess was 'like one of Titian's old women, who still, amid their wrinkles, remind us of that soul of beauty and sensibility, which must have animated them when young'. Drake felt that 'Shakespeare seems to have drawn this portrait [of the Countess] *con amore*'. The plot lent itself to the colouring of the popular sentimental novels of the day, and, through this association, won favour. Hazlitt judged the play 'one of the most pleasing of our author's comedies'. Mrs. Jameson might well have been describing a current novel in her summary of the plot:

> The situation of Helena is the most painful and degrading in which a woman can be placed. She is poor and lowly; she loves a man who is far her superior in rank, who repays her love with indifference, and rejects her hand with scorn. . . . All the circumstances and details with which Helena is surrounded, are shocking to our feelings and wounding to our delicacy: and yet the beauty of the character is made to triumph over all.

George Daniel chided 'the distorted medium of a theatre' for its forgetting 'a drama possessing so much variety of character, such delightful scenes of sentiment and humour'.[3]

Comic scenes were the third source of commendation for *All's Well* among Romantic critics. Only among the lesser critics, however, was the praise as lavish as it had been in the eighteenth century. Drake

---

1. Thomas Middleton Raysor (ed.), *Coleridge's Shakespearean Criticism*, London, 1930, ii. Coleridge's first judgement (p. 113) appeared in 'Literary Remains' in 1818; his second (p. 357) in 'Table Talk', 1 July 1833.
2. Ibid., p. 356.
3. 'Cumberland Acting Edition', p. 5.

repeated the opinion that Parolles was second only to Falstaff and he surpassed earlier commentators in declaring that the Clown was the rival of Touchstone. Daniel equated Parolles with Falstaff and admired the 'rich humour' of the Clown. But few of the major writers expressed interest in the comic elements. What enjoyment they derived from the scenes was based upon the moral lessons inherent in the situations. The incident of the drum and the exposure of Parolles were sugar-coated moral pills, pleasing in their humour and pleasing in their defence of virtue. Hazlitt wrote that the adventure of the drum had 'become proverbial as a satire on all ridiculous and blustering undertakings which the person never means to perform'. The same double pleasure was realized in the exposure, for Parolles was not pressed to the depths of humiliation. His reputation was lost, but 'he is by no means squeamish about the loss of pretensions, to which he had sense enough to know he had no real claim'.[1] The burlesque, the farce, which induced guffaws from the audiences of the eighteenth century was tempered to ridiculous folly which brought complacent smiles to the faces of the nineteenth century.

Despite the obvious differences in interpretation of *All's Well* in the two periods, the Romantic critics shared one view with their predecessors. The play was a comedy and its mood was light. Whether the emphasis was upon farcical comedy or romantic comedy, *All's Well* was not a problem play, a 'dark' or 'bitter' drama. Even the interest in a melodramatic plot and a 'love-dejected' Helena did not quiet the spirit of fantasy which whispered throughout that virtue will triumph and 'all's well that ends well'. Whether as a consequence of that spirit or not, the weight of critical opinion in both ages tipped in favour of the play.

1. Op. cit. (n. 30), p. 178.

6

PSYCHOLOGICAL REALISM:
ANALYSIS OF FAILURE
(1840–1940)

FANTASY gave way to tragi-comedy in the interpretations of *All's Well that Ends Well* which characterize mid century criticism. The plot was no longer a tender love story; it was the basis for didactic drama. Helena assumed motives and qualities unnecessary for the heroine of sentimental comedy. Justification for Bertram's role as hero was sought in psychological realism. The exposure of Parolles served as severe warning against unchecked vice.

In 1847, Verplanck argued that Shakespeare had revised an earlier comedy to fashion an *All's Well* of a 'sterner and more meditative cast . . . of a gray and sober hue'.[1] With his spiritual and reflective faculty more active than his poetic fancy, the dramatist attempted 'to impose on the reader' his conviction that moral and intellectual worth is the only ground for distinction among men. In the following year in the United States, H. N. Hudson wrote in agreement that the 'intrinsic beauty' of the lesson justified 'the freedom from merely poetical attraction, . . . that the quiet sagelike wisdom, and the sweet sad spirit of humanity, which pervade it, are far more precious than all the riches which even his transcendent imagination could display'.[2] The interpretation required a heroine of great spiritual strength, and Helena became the personification of moral and intellectual esteem. To both critics, her love and her motives are selfless. Acting on 'a mysterious, supernatural impulse' to redeem Bertram, Helena 'goes to work, more for his sake than for her own, to make a conquest within him'.[3] Rather than the long-suffering heroine of melodrama, Helena was seen as the active agent whose moral superiority determined the movement and the worth of the play.[4] Tragi-comedy, however, complicated the problem of Bertram

1. Gulian Verplanck (ed.), *The Illustrated Shakespeare*, New York, 1847, ii. 5–7. As noted in my preface, page references throughout the critical history indicate the entire argument of the critic rather than particular quotations, unless clarity demands otherwise, as in the case of an extensive treatment of *All's Well*.

2. *Lectures on Shakespeare*, New York, 1848, i. 257–74.   3. Ibid., p. 264.

4. Charles Knight, *Studies of Shakespeare*, London, 1849, pp. 129–38. The force of Helena's personality, 'refreshingly strong and frank', was seen by an American critic as fulfilling Shakespeare's condemnation of the 'social etiquette of his age and of all secluded circles'. See John Weiss, *Wit, Humour, and Shakespeare*, Boston, 1876, pp. 328–39.

as fantasy need not. In a serious drama, Bertram must exhibit, in some way, a personality which justifies Helena's love for him. So too, only a credible and convincing reconciliation satisfies the argument of the plot. For Verplanck, neither was accomplished and the play was defective. In degrading the character of Bertram, Shakespeare had sacrificed the dramatic function of the hero to emphasize the moral tone. But other critics found credibility in the psychological validity of the portrayal:

> All that we have then to ask is, whether the character is natural, and consistent with the circumstances amidst which he moves? We have no desire to reconcile our hearts to Bertram; all that we demand is, that he should not move our indignation beyond the point in which his qualities shall consist with our sympathy for Helena in her love for him. And in this view the poet, as it appears to us, has drawn Bertram's character most skilfully. Without his defects the dramatic action could not have proceeded; without his merits the dramatic sentiment could not have been maintained.[1]

If the attraction of Bertram can be recognized in an earlier environment, his present conduct is easily defended. Beginning with the hero's outraged feelings over the forced marriage, Halliwell-Phillips excuses Bertram's intended seduction of Diana because 'natural impatience and impetuosity' were 'both stimulated to excess'; Bertram became a 'victim of passion' because of the 'unsettled state of mind in which he is when at Florence'.[2] Similarly, his lies in the last scene result not from depravity but from 'the perplexing situation in which he is placed'. When this is relieved by Helena's love, quite naturally 'he yields himself a willing captive to her romantic affection'.

The moral stamp placed upon the comic scenes by Hazlitt and others received a stronger impress at mid century. Although Hudson expresses delight over 'that prince of braggarts, that valiant word-gun, that *pronoun* of a man', his enjoyment of the character is derived from the lesson of Parolles's humiliation:

> Though the joke is pushed upon Parolles to the farthest extreme, we never feel like crying out to his persecutors, hold, enough! as in the case of Malvolio: we make all possible reprisals upon him without the least compunction; for the mere fact of his being such a self-conscious and self-satisfied 'lump of counterfeit ore' is an offence for which infinite shame and ridicule are hardly a sufficient indemnification.

Charles Knight admits that the exposure and humiliation of Parolles

---

1. Ibid., p. 135.

2. J. Q. Halliwell-Phillips (ed.), *Memoranda on All's Well that Ends Well, etc.*, Brighton, 1879, pp. 21–22. The criticism was written in 1857 and reflects the mid century view.

'constitute the richness of the comedy', but he decries the comparison of 'this crawling, empty, vapouring, cowardly representative of the off-scourings of social life' to the witty and inimitable Falstaff. He places Parolles in 'the school of which Moliere is the head' rather than the school of Shakespeare. He takes a similar view of the Clown, who serves not as a vehicle for comedy but 'for some biting satire'. Only Halliwell-Phillips expresses an interest in the comedy for its own sake. He praises Parolles and ranks the Clown with Touchstone and Feste 'for humour and equivocating wit'.[1]

With the old school of German critics in somewhat low esteem today because of the narrow limits of their investigations, it is surprising that two commentators have given us comprehensive and interesting views of *All's Well*. Schlegel's modified romanticism at the beginning of the century is matched by Gervinus's moderate interpretation of the play as tragi-comedy. The interpretation is comprehensive in that it qualifies the romantic elements emphasized in the early nineteenth century, accepts the dramatic points stressed at mid century, and hints at the realistic analyses written in the later nineteenth century. In effect, Gervinus concludes that Shakespeare treated a romantic tale realistically.

In his commentaries written in 1862, Gervinus argues that *All's Well* is a reworking of 'Love's Labour's Won'.[2] Although the original comedy was a sequel to *Love's Labour's Lost*, Shakespeare revised it as a deliberate contrast to the mood of the early comedies. He omitted all sentimentality, affectation, and unnaturalness. The result is a serious play based upon a romantic source. Realistic motives give credulity to the characters as they perform romantic deeds. Helena's actions are fabulous, but they spring from a psychologically consistent personality, 'With this self-mastering, self-renouncing, modest nature, she is prudent, clever, and apt—qualities which in reality are so often united in superior women'. Even when the plot forces her to take seemingly masculine steps, Shakespeare preserves her feminity. Gervinus insists so strongly on the womanly nature of the heroine that he sees the dramatist deliberately tempering the 'too great heroism' of her self-exile by revealing an 'affectionate weakness; . . . she takes the way through Florence, that she may once more see him'. Bertram's errors are common youthful faults; the nobility of a fine nature is innate. Both the errors and the nobility are exposed, then reconciled:

1. J. Q. Halliwell-Phillips (ed.), *The Complete Works of Shakespeare*, London, 1850, i. 538.

2. G. G. Gervinus, *Shakespeare Commentaries*, trans. F. E. Bunnett, London, 1883, pp. 174–86.

No inner mental life has yet penetrated his years of churlishness. . . .
This rough, abrupt, uncourtly vein bursts forth into ebullitions of defiance
when he is excited. Full of youthful zeal, his whole soul is given to action
and fame; . . . at the turning point of the play we see him in a whirlpool of
activity, in utter confusion both of mind and manner. . . . This humiliation
of soul is to follow his outward abasement stroke by stroke; he is to learn
thoroughly to mortify his arrogance and to suspect his pride. . . . He, in his
laconic way, compresses all repentance, all contrition, all gratitude and
love into the words: 'Both, both; O pardon!'

The interpretation of Gervinus is interesting because, unlike much
fragmentary criticism of *All's Well*, it has a coherence demonstrable
upon the stage.[1] And in fact, he admits that illustration of his
analysis could be had only in the theatre, for 'few readers, and still
fewer female readers, will believe in Helena's womanly nature'. Nor
were readers of his day 'free enough from sentimentality' to see that
Bertram has a heart, a good heart, which is capable of loving
Helena. But given a great actress and a good actor, the play reveals
its artistry. This is not an unreasonable demand, for Gervinus is the
first critic to note what has been apparent in this study of the
theatrical and critical history: 'In few plays do we feel, so much as in
All's Well that Ends Well, what excessive scope the poet leaves open
to the actor's art.' He sees in that scope what few actors or actresses
have seen—the opportunity to create a great Shakespearian role.
With Bertram, he grants the difficulties apparent on the printed
page, but he insists:

The case is entirely different when, in the *acted* Bertram, they *see* the
noble nature, the ruin of his character at Florence, and the contrition
which his sins and his simplicity call forth; when, from the whole bearing
of the brusque man, they perceive what the one word 'pardon' signified in
his mouth, when they see his breast heave at the last appearance of
Helena bringing ease to his conscience. . . . Seldom has a task so indepen-
dent as the character of Bertram been left to the art of the actor; but still
more seldom is the actor to be found who knows how to execute it. To
Richard Burbage this part must have been a dainty feast.

Gervinus accuses the reader of failing to understand the realism in
characterization because of sentimentality. Yet it was realistic, not
sentimental, criticism which now launched a prolonged attack on
All's Well. The generally favourable, though slanted, estimate of the
play throughout the first sixty years gave way to hostile appraisals in
the latter part of the nineteenth century. *All's Well* failed as a play
because of its aggressive heroine, its incongruous structure, and its
bitter comedy. Arguing the inconsistency of realistic characters

1. Note the resemblances to the Stratford, Connecticut, production in 1959; see above
pp. 66–68.

in a romantic plot, Thomas Kenny called the play 'one of the least graceful and least interesting of all the comedies of Shakespeare'.[1] He condemns Helena's trespasses, her use of stratagem, her indifference to 'rigid, unequivocating truth'. Her very love for Bertram is a fault, for his 'unamiable character' is without attraction and 'seems to constitute the great defect of this drama'. Swinburne shared Kenny's distaste. In noting his agreement with Dr. Johnson's censure of Bertram, he adds: 'And I, unworthy as I may be to second or support on the score of morality the finding of so great a moralist, cannot reconcile my instincts to Helena.'[2] In an article published in the United States in 1892, Andrew Lang rejects Hazlitt's romantic evaluation of the heroine and insists that she violates modesty constantly.[3] In a typical interpretation of the time, he charges Helena with indelicacy 'as estimated by the taste of any age' in her virginity repartee, with lust in her pursuit of Bertram, and with 'a stain of violent self-will on the ermine of her passion' in her use of the bed-trick. He is willing, however, to apply the newly formulated principles of psychology in a realistic assessment of her duologue with Parolles: 'We might explain Helena's mirth as a hysterical kind of reaction from her melancholy.' It was a logical step in Shakespearian criticism to progress from the subconscious of a character to a psychoanalysis of its creator. For if Helena with her uncontrolled passion and resolute will was formed from human experience, then surely there were deep-seated causes within the dramatist for this realistic portrayal. In 1895, Barrett Wendell, in anticipation of much twentieth-century criticism, explained Shakespeare's harsh treatment of his heroine by imputing to him a cynical irony and an increasing contempt for women:

From *All's Well that Ends Well* to *Antony and Cleopatra*, there is a sense of something in the relations between men and women at once widely different from the ideal, romantic fascination expressed by the comedies, and yet just what should normally follow from such beginning. Trouble first, then vacillating doubt, then the certainty that woman may be damningly evil, succeed one another in the growth of this mood which so inextricably mingles with the ironical.[4]

Helena, then, is the first in a line of heroines who do cause harm to the men at their commands despite the ironic judgement of the Clown.

1. *The Life and Genius of Shakespeare*, London, 1864, pp. 202–8.
2. Charles Algernon Swinburne, *A Study of Shakespeare*, London, 1895, p. 147. The comment first appeared in the *Fortnightly Review*, May 1875.
3. 'All's Well that Ends Well', *Harper's Magazine*, lxxxv (July 1892), 213–27. For his analysis of Helena, see pp. 216–20.
4. *William Shakespeare*, New York, 1895, p. 339. For his interpretation of *All's Well*, see pp. 246–50.

The impetus of psychological realism struck at Shakespeare's technique in both characterization and structure. For it was in a psychological context that F. S. Boas coined his enduring phrase, 'Shakespeare's problem plays', for *All's Well, Measure for Measure, Troilus and Cressida,* and *Hamlet*:

All these dramas introduce us into highly artificial societies, whose civilization is ripe unto rottenness. Amidst such media abnormal conditions of brain and emotion are generated, and intricate cases of conscience demand a solution by unprecedented methods. Thus throughout these plays we move along dim untrodden paths, and at the close our feeling is neither of simple joy nor pain; we are excited, fascinated, perplexed, for the issues raised preclude a completely satisfactory outcome.[1]

In *All's Well*, the highly artificial society is medieval, and the intricate case of conscience is Helena's. Shakespeare's structural problem was a reconciliation of the two in terms which would be credible for his plot and pleasing for his heroine. To do this, he had to turn Boccaccio's heroine who 'is merely an adventuress into an ideal of feminine strength and devotion, capable of saving the man she loves from the consequences of a nature at once stubborn and volatile'. Shakespeare substituted for the adventuress a poor dependent characterized by servility and womanly self-abasement in the medieval sense. In the play, she acts forcefully when the needs of her mission, to serve and save her master, demand it but she withdraws immediately after into a feudal dependency. Although the characterization motivated the plot, Shakespeare's choice was wrong, for abject devotion makes a dull heroine. Because she has 'all the virtues of the missionary type', she is denied that romantic charm, that 'superb air of distinction', which wins not only admiration but love for other Shakespearian heroines. As a consequence, she fails to excite dramatic interest, and the reconciliation of plot and heroine is unsatisfying.

Critics at this time attacked the incongruities of the plot. Kenny insisted that Shakespeare had given unnecessarily repulsive vices to Bertram, vices which were 'essentially undramatic' and inappropriate in a 'romantic episode'. Lang, on the other hand, objected to the plot because Bertram is 'shamefully and cruelly wronged'.[2] Brandes blamed the faulty composition upon negligence and failing skill; 'the time was past when Shakespeare's chief strength lay in his humour'.[3] He thought the addition of Lafeu's daughter 'extraordinary' and the lies of Bertram at the trial 'an indisputable dramatic

1. Frederick S. Boas, *Shakspere and his Predecessors*, New York, 1896, pp. 344–56.
2. *Harper's Magazine*, pp. 220–2.
3. George Brandes, *William Shakespeare: A Critical Study*, New York, 1898, ii. 60–69.

mistake'. Wendell agreed that the play was carelessly written though he saw the playwright's growing cynicism as the cause:

Restless one feels this mood, unsettled, unserene, unbeautiful. There is no other work of Shakespeare's which in conception and in temper seems quite so corrupt as this . . . none less pleasing, none on which one cares less to dwell. . . . Under the mood of *All's Well that Ends Well* lies the miserable mystery of earthly love.

In an article written in 1887, Robert Boyle blamed the inconguities of the structure on the dramatist's inability to revise an earlier work.[1] The play appeared first as 'Love's Labour's Won', but the 'younger Shakespeare' had not adapted 'this husband-hunting Helen' to his dramatic necessities. In the revision, the 'elder Shakespeare' was incapable of recapturing the spirit of the original. Among the discrepancies is a haphazard differentiation between Parolles and the clown. In the earlier play, Bertram did not meet the braggart-soldier until his arrival at court. It was Lavache in typical clown fashion who debates virginity with Helena, and it was Lavache who accompanies his young master to court. Shakespeare's indifference not only impaired the plot but also destroyed the humour.

Boyle's distaste for the humour of *All's Well* was shared by his contemporaries. Parolles and the Clown fared poorly in the judgements of the late nineteenth-century critics. Brandes concurred with the view that Parolles had undergone an unpleasant transformation. What had been a gay and farcical figure, 'the first slight sketch for Falstaff', now faded before the moral lesson of the exposure. In the rewriting, the 'attempt at gaiety missed fire. The poet is at pains to impress on us the lesson we ought to learn from Parolles' self-stultification and the shame that attends on his misdeeds'. Wendell regarded the braggart as 'a curious combination of Pistol and Falstaff'. Boas considered him more akin to Pistol and the vilest of all Shakespeare's French creations: 'The exposure is so over-whelming in its merciless completeness that laughter is stifled at its source by the sting of shame at the spectacle of humanity wallowing in such a slough of mud.' Lang praised Parolles in traditional terms, but he disparaged many of the comic scenes.[2] He regarded Lavache as the worst clown in Shakespeare and his frivolities as 'coarse and stupid, even beyond the ordinary stupidity of Elizabethan horse-play. We read them with fatigue and surprise'. Brandes attributed wit to Lavache but regretted the loss of that 'serene gaiety' found in the clowns of earlier comedies. To Boas, Lavache was the 'most insipid'

1. 'All's Well that Ends Well and Love's Labour's Won', *Englische Studien*, xiv (1890), 408–21. See particularly pp. 416–20 for his argument concerning characterization.
2. *Harper's Magazine*; see pp. 222–4 for his discussion of Parolles and p. 214 for his view of Lavache.

of jesters whose crudities were 'scarcely suitable to the ears of the stately and virtuous Countess'.

At the turn of the twentieth century, critical opinion generally condemned *All's Well* as a failure. Its heroine lacked nobility; its characters lacked consistency; its plot lacked coherence; its comedy lacked humour. These defects were explained by the negligence, or artistic incapability, or neurotic obsessions of the playwright. Critical tools from the expanding sciences of nineteenth-century psychology and sociology were applied to the problems of the play. A virtuous Helena does not banter about virginity with a rogue unless she is reacting to an emotional shock. A defiant Bertram is in no sense blameworthy for a revolt against a tyrannical society and a *bourgeois* wife. A compulsive Shakespeare manifests an unhealthy cynicism about sexual passion and a subconscious hatred of women. I am not suggesting that any one critic would approve of such a critical compilation. But the compilation is not unfair in that it records attitudes which mark a new approach to Shakespeare and his comedy. Nor is it a parody of views in this particular age; it contains the germ of much twentieth-century criticism which would probe the weaknesses of *All's Well*. It does not consider, however, the few dissident voices which sang of the good things in the play. There were the romantic voices of Dowden and Swinburne; a more clamorous voice belonged to that arch-realist of the theatre, Shaw.

Dowden praised the strength of Helena's love as a romantic expansion of the human spirit. It was this which attracted Shakespeare to the story: 'This one thing is the energy, the leap-up, the direct advance of the *will* of Helena, her prompt, unerroneous tendency towards the right and efficient *deed.* . . . Her entire force of character is concentrated in what she does.'[1] Those plot elements found distasteful by other critics, such as the bed-trick, are justified by the practicality of Helena's virtuous nature. She strives for the truly miraculous, that which successfully unites the romantic and the actual. Her courage is proclaimed in the title of the play, 'like an utterance of the heart of Helena'. Although Swinburne liked neither Helena nor Bertram, he expressed his affection for the other characters most touchingly:

Parolles is even better than Bobadil, as Bobadil is even better than Bessus; and Lafeu is one of the very best old men in all the range of comic art. But the whole charm and beauty of the play, the quality which raised it above the rank of its fellows by making it loveable as well as admirable,

1. Edward Dowden, *Shakespere: His Mind and Art*, New York, 1881, pp. 76–80. The book was first published in London in 1875. Dowden's analysis of the will of Helena brings to mind A. C. Bradley's interpretation of Iago.

we find only in the 'sweet, serene, skylike' sanctity and attraction of adorable old age, made more than ever near and dear to us in the comparable [sic] figure of the old Countess of Rousillion. At the close of the play, Fletcher would inevitably have married her to Lafeu—or rather possibly, to the King.[1]

Such a marriage would surely have eliminated the dispute over romance and realism in the interpretation of the comedy!

Swinburne's tribute to 'adorable old age' was echoed twenty years later in Shaw's famous description of the Countess, 'the most beautiful old woman's part ever written'.[2] But Shaw defended the entire play, and on those very grounds which were the bases for the critical attacks of his contemporaries. The play succeeds because of its realism. Helena is 'an enlightened lady doctor' who prefigures Nora in Ibsen's *A Doll's House*;[3] Bertram is a 'perfectly ordinary young man [of] unimaginative prejudices and selfish conventionality'.[4] Parolles is 'a capital study of the adventurous yarn-spinner society-struck coward', a familiar figure in 'modern fiction'. If the play has been a failure, the blame falls, not on internal defects, but on the romantic, narrow outlook of audiences dating from Shakespeare's age. When the 'inconsistencies' of the characters are regarded as the inconsistencies of life, the merit of *All's Well* is apparent.

In the midst of attacks, Shaw's defence served notice that the play had potential appeal to realistic critics. Shaw may have analysed the comedy with the distorted vision of his own philosophy, but his colleagues had revealed attitudes as subjective. The primary value of the criticism in the 1890s, whether hostile or friendly, was in its provocation. The extremities of the opinions prompted a restudy of the play; later twentieth-century criticism has been engaged in that restudy. In the early years of the century, however, *All's Well* was attacked more harshly than at any other time in its critical history. What little favourable criticism appeared was reactionary. Thus, Frank Sharp in the United States echoed earlier English Romantic views in describing Helena as 'one of the most perfect of Shakespeare's characters'; Albert Tolman echoed Dowden in admiring the 'desperate venture of the indomitable Helena'; Walter Raleigh echoed Shaw in blaming hostility to Helena upon the sentimental prejudices of the critics.[5] But the late nineteenth-century indictment of the heroine and the plot could not be dismissed by such limited

1. Swinburne, p. 147.
2. John F. Matthews (ed.), *Shaw's Dramatic Criticism (1895–98)*, New York, 1959, p. 17. The review appeared originally in the *Saturday Review*, 2 Feb. 1895.
3. George Bernard Shaw, *Our Theatres in the Nineties*, London, 1932, iii. 2.
4. *Shaw's Dramatic Criticism*, p. 15.
5. see n. 1, pp. 177–8.

defences. Applying uncompromisingly realistic criteria, the commentators passed even sterner judgements upon the play.

Thomas Lounsbury's analysis of Helena in 1901 is perhaps as fine an example of critical realism as Drake's ecstatic eulogy in 1817 is of romanticism.[1] He charges Helena with inexcusable conduct in her pursuit of a man who does not want her. Of this 'essentially unwomanly act', he writes:

> In real life we know how we should all think and feel in such a case. Our sympathies would not go out to the successful schemer, but to the hunted man who is compelled to have associated with him in the closest relation of life a woman for whom he feels dislike. . . . Nothing but misery will be the fate of a couple where the consciousness of the difference of station would add to the estrangement produced by difference of character, and where fraud has been the only agency to bring about the consummation of a union which could never have been effected in the first place save by force.

Masefield too looked realistically beyond the play and saw no hope for a happy marriage between Bertram and the ruthless Helena, but, to Masefield, this was Shakespeare's cynical intention:

> Shakespeare saw her more clearly than any man who has ever lived. He saw her as a woman who practices a borrowed art, not for art's sake, nor for charity, but, woman fashion, for a selfish end. He saw her put a man into a position of ignominy quite unbearable, and then plot with other women to keep him in that position. Lastly, he saw her beloved all the time by the conventionally minded of both sexes.[2]

Frank Harris sees a closer relationship between creator and character; she is coarse and sensual, 'the mouthpiece of young Shakespeare's crude opinions'.[3] He insists: 'One might as well take the miaullings of a midnight cat for eloquence as this for the dramatic presentation of a maiden's character.' So, Brander Matthews regards her challenge to the young lords to marry her as degrading and her conversation with Parolles 'reeking with vulgarity and quite impossible to a modest-minded girl'.[4] Allowing no romantic quarter, he concludes that we despise both Bertram and Helena.

In echoes of late nineteenth-century criticism, the plot fared no better than the heroine. Matthews objects to the offensive story with its distasteful marriage, the despicable bed-trick, and the quibbling indecencies which 'tickled the groundlings'. Structurally, the play is 'a straggling sequence of episodes of mere narrative badly presented

1. *Shakespeare as a Dramatic Artist*, New York, 1901, pp. 388–91.
2. John Masefield, *William Shakespeare*, New York, 1911, pp. 144–9.
3. *The Women of Shakespeare*, New York, 1912, p. 141. See pp. 134–8 for his discussion of Lord Herbert and Mary Fitton which is mentioned below.
4. *Shakespeare as a Playwright*, New York, 1913, pp. 222–6.

in dialogue'; among Shakespearian plays it is 'the feeblest of the lot, dramaturgically and psychologically'. Masefield thought the drama uneven and attributed this defect to the alterations which Shakespeare had made upon an earlier version while in the 'ruthless mood that gave birth to *Measure for Measure*'. This mood, realistically explained by 'perhaps some trick of health', produced a pitiless view of human obsessions. Harris searched much deeper into the personal life of the dramatist to account for the failure in construction. Because of his frustrated love for the 'excessively sensual, bold, and free-spoken' Mary Fitton, Shakespeare was less interested in dramatic structure and plot motivation than in passing final judgement upon Lord Herbert and Mary Fitton.

The comic elements were spared such extreme interpretations. At the worst, George Krapp, in his study of Parolles published in 1916, merely poses the possibility of autobiographical touches in the braggart-opportunist.[1] Is there not, he asks, a parallel to Parolles in the number of young adventurers who were hoisting themselves regardless of education and birth, men like Marlowe, Nashe, and Greene? Does Shakespeare avoid a condemnation of Parolles because the dramatist, too, is rising in his world merely by his wit? But Shakespeare does justify the fate of Parolles by stressing the parasite's lack of principle; does he justify the fate of Marlowe for the same reason? Such rhetorical questions may be dismissed as groundless conjecture, but they do illustrate the serious view which Krapp took of this traditionally comic character. His analysis of Parolles is an attempt to justify the braggart since 'the critics are at one in finding "All's Well" one of the least agreeable of Shakspere's plays, and Parolles one of the least agreeable of the persons in the play'. This judgement, however, is usually founded upon an unfair comparison between Parolles and Falstaff. The braggart-soldier is not intended to be the witty practitioner of pranks; he is the victim of pranks justified with a 'formally constructed play in which royalty and high nobility occupy the chief places and in which the unsympathetic portrayal of an ignoble, unpretentious character was an almost necessary consequence'. In addition to the contrast, Parolles's topical humour as a contemporary caricature, Krapp cautiously asserts, explains Shakespeare's intentions. But Matthews had written a more representative analysis three years prior. Like so many of his colleagues, he condemned Parolles as a failure along with the other elements of *All's Well*:

He is a diminished replica of Falstaff done without gusto or unction. The episodes in which he appears lack spontaneity; they suggest fatigue

1. See n. 2, p. 178.

of invention; and such humour as they have is largely mechanical and often perfunctory. The protracted scene in which Parolles is convicted of cowardice has flashes of fun now and again, but it is only an example of that most primitive form of humor, the practical joke.

The criticism of the early years of the twentieth century was often baseless conjecture, often indefensible attack. A re-examination of the play, more objective in principle and temperate in judgement, was necessary to disprove the conception of Helena as a debased, sensual woman, of the plot as an intimate expression of Shakespeare's frustrated and bitter love, of Parolles as a humourless, mechanical imitation of Falstaff. From 1920 to 1940, prominent Shakespearian scholars attempted such a re-examination. Their studies were foreshadowed in the restrained evaluations of *All's Well* by two of its editors in the beginning of the century. In 1904, W. Osborne Brigstocke had raised an admittedly qualified defence:

> Everyone who reads this play is at first shocked and perplexed by the revolting idea which underlies the plot. It *is* revolting, there is no doubt about it; and it leaves so unpleasant a flavour with some people that it is not tasted again. I hold that the taste for *All's Well that Ends Well* is an acquired taste: and when the taste has been once acquired, one wonders how the revolting side of the plot could ever have hidden the manifold, and in certain respects unique, interest of the play.[1]

Among the unique elements, Brigstocke lists the blending of various Shakespearian styles, the 'brightness' of Helena, and the gleams of irony from the dark tragedies, particularly the characterization of Parolles: 'all the terrible possibilities which lie in a man like Parolles if he happens to be not "a great way fool" were developed in Iago, a terrible incarnation of malice.'[2] So too, Lowes, in his 1912 edition, admitted 'a certain distaste which the play inspires in the minds of most of its readers'.[3] The distaste is caused by a discord which resulted from Shakespeare's attempt to shift the motivation from sensual gratification in Boccaccio to purity and strength. Despite the discord, the play has a 'permanent appeal' through the 'character of Helena, as set off and softened by the grave sweetness and dignity of the Countess and the King'.

Succeeding critics were willing to grant to both editors that the play had interesting elements, but their major interest was absorbed in the discord, the dramatic failure of *All's Well*. What causes the 'unpleasant flavour', the 'certain distaste' in the minds of the

1. *All's Well that Ends Well*, The Arden Edition, London, 1904, p. xv.
2. Ibid., p. xxxvii.
3. John Livingstone Lowes (ed.), *All's Well that Ends Well*, The Tudor Shakespeare, New York, 1912, pp. xiii–xiv.

readers? From 1920 to 1940, three reasons in particular were advanced: inconsistency in the character of Helena, the demands upon the audience, and the ineptness of Shakespeare's dramatic powers at the time of composition. The reasons were not new, but the evidence offered in support provided fresh insights into the play. Nor are the reasons mutually exclusive; the last certainly can include the first two. The divisions are useful, however, because they reveal the emphasis of individual critics and they illustrate the more systematic, more comprehensive, more scholarly analyses of the play which characterize the work of this period.

In *Shakespeare's Treatment of Love and Marriage and Other Essays*, published in 1921, C. H. Herford considers the inconsistency in the character of Helena the result of a revised version.[1] Shakespeare's problem was a refinement of that spirit which manifested itself in the original Helena as uninhibited aggression. In the revision, he added a number of restraints: Helena links herself to the chaste goddess, Diana; she does nothing without the permission of the Countess; she goes to court only 'with all proper convoy'; she chooses Bertram as a life-long service, rather than a prize. But the great decision for Shakespeare, and for Helena, occurs after she is deserted by her husband. Should she follow Bertram as in Boccaccio's narrative, or should she yield him up? In Hereford's opinion, Shakespeare could not decide and the character of the heroine is split. He first gives to Helena an eloquent speech of renunciation, but then refuses to answer our suspicion that her pilgrimage is merely a ruse for 'resolute pursuit'. She is torn between the desire to pursue and the desire to yield. The dramatist has failed 'to fit a character based upon a nobler type of love into a plot based upon a grosser'. In 1922, Schücking explained 'the lack of agreement between the character of the heroine and the action of the play' as a vacillation between strength and weakness.[2] On the one hand, Helena shows energy and will power in winning Bertram twice; on the other, she frequently reveals sentimental traits, as in her conversations with the Countess. 'And she would hardly go about weeping in such a manner that even the steward becomes an involuntary witness of her love complaints.' In a more impressionistic and harsher judgement, Miss Ellen Terry implies this same duality; she protests against both self-abasement and aggression in the heroine:

Helena in *All's Well that Ends Well*, and Julia in *Two Gentlemen of Verona* belong to the 'doormat' type. They bear any amount of humiliation from the men they love, seem almost to enjoy being maltreated and scorned by

1. London, 1921, pp. 31–35.
2. Levin L. Schücking, *Character Problems in Shakespeare's Plays*, New York, 1922, p. 196.

them, and hunt them down in the most undignified way when they are trying to escape. The fraud with which Helena captures Bertram, who has left his home and country to get away from her, is really despicable.[1]

More romantically, two critics admitted the inconsistency in characterization but came to Helena's defence. John Bailey acknowledges the 'odious stratagem' of the plot and the amazement with which the reader responds to Helena's discussion of virginity with 'such a piece of underbred riff-raff as Parolles', but he insists that she emerges 'a living, moving, very human and lovable woman' with more attraction than Isabella in *Measure for Measure*.[2] Unless we accept Helena, 'the play is nothing at all'. And as an aid to our acceptance, Bailey offers as one instance of merit:

> Except the end of *Othello*, there is in all Shakespeare no passage between man and wife more signally marked with the genius of truth than the 'Something; and scarce so much' with which she asks the only thing she ever asked of that poor creature her husband. . . . She is the play.

E. E. Stoll, in *Shakespeare's Young Lovers*, published in 1937, makes a similar plea for the attractiveness of Helena, although he does not see in her the warm vitality praised by Bailey.[3] He concedes the inconsistency in character—'incredible, ineffable Helena. . . . She does not fit into society as we know it, and still less into the Elizabethan.' Her justification, however, is not in reality, but in fantasy. She exists 'where speech is song and the real gives place to the ideal'. Stoll grants the necessity of allowance for medieval convention in the plot; he sees the problem of Bertram as an unworthy object of Helena's love; but 'her purity and delicacy and unfaltering devotion' is 'a plain case of Shakespeare's poetry in the treatment of character'.

Whether the reader condemned *All's Well* because of the 'inconsistency' of Helena's characterization or whether he yielded to her charm in spite of it very probably depended upon his inclination rather than upon the text itself. For, throughout the long history of the play, the decision of critics has frequently been based upon subjective responses. The fact that the play drew such an abundance of impressionistic criticism, the fact that it had such devoted defenders and severe antagonists, directed the investigation of the twentieth century to another course. The failure of the comedy perhaps lay not entirely within the text but without. If *All's Well* inspired contradictory verdicts among its audience, then the difference rested in the audience. There had been hints of this conclusion in earlier commentaries. Numerous critics had written that Shakespeare composed the

---

1. *Four Lectures on Shakespeare*, ed. Christopher St. John, London, 1932, p. 151.
2. *Shakespeare*, New York, 1929, pp. 163–5.   3. Toronto, 1937, pp. 82–83.

'offensive' passages for the groundlings of his own audience. Lowes had annotated the virginity dialogue with the comment that many editors had regarded the passage as an interpolation, 'but that many things are distasteful to us' that were not to the Elizabethans.[1] Several critics had accused their colleagues of sentimental blindness in their indictments of the play. The first thorough analysis of the audience and the comedy, however, was made by W. W. Lawrence.[2]

In the past, critic and reader had objected to the masculine resoluteness of Helena, to the despicable bed-trick, and to the incredible cure of the King. Lawrence sought to dispel these protests by linking all three to literary tradition and by demonstrating the total acceptance of such conventions by the Elizabethan audience. The first two involve the major complications of the plot, the conception of a child and the possession of a ring. According to Lawrence, both belong to the 'fulfillment of tasks' in the history of literature. He found parallels and analogues in Boccaccio, an Indian tale, a Turkish story, a Norwegian ballad, an episode in *Magussaga*, the prose romance, *Le Livre du Tres Chevalereux Comte d'Artois et de sa Femme*, and of course, Shakespeare's own *Measure for Measure*. The stories exalt the cleverness and devotion of the woman; the husband has neglected his duty to his wife; the husband amends his attitude in the face of his wife's demonstration of courage and love. In the light of these stories and many other legends, Lawrence concludes that Helena's 'resoluteness' was regarded by the Elizabethans as the womanly courage common in 'fulfillment of tasks' literature. The charge that her use of the bed-trick is immodest would have been incredible by the norms of Shakespeare's age. 'The answer would have been: she is lying with her husband, as any chaste wife has a right to do.' Furthermore, the ending of *All's Well* fulfils the whole point of the 'Faithful Wife' theme.

Lawrence traces the third element, the cure of the King, to the 'clever wench' stories in Oriental fables, in Campbell's *Popular Tales of the West Highlands*, and in the *Gesta Romanorum*. In Boccaccio, the 'cleverness' of the 'wench' assumed greater importance as a proof of Giletta's worthiness to marry above her rank. In Shakespeare's time, the narrowing gap between nobility and middle class caused the dramatist to shift the unworthiness on to the hero with his snobbery. Shakespeare, then, used the cure of the King as evidence of Helena's love through the power of her virtue rather than as demonstration of her worth through the traditional cleverness:

1. Lowes, p. 132.
2. W. W. Lawrence, *Shakespeare's Problem Comedies*, New York, 1931. The original article appeared in *PMLA*, xxxvii (Sept. 1922), 418–69.

Shakespeare's formula is, then: a noble girl loves a self-willed fellow incapable of feeling her worth, though above her in station; she puts her life in jeopardy to win him, and he repulses her through false pride and stubbornness. With all this before them, and with the Clever Wench tradition of the popular tales in their consciousness, the audience cannot but sympathize with Helena, and the main theme of the drama, the Fulfillment of the Tasks, may proceed.'[1]

Lawrence's defence of *All's Well* is limited to these elements; he does not justify Shakespeare's dramatic manipulation of his sources. Thus, the defects within the play are not the determination of Helena, the use of the bed-trick, and the cure of the King. If audiences have termed the play unpleasant because of these, the error has been theirs in the loss of traditional conventions and in the shifting of tastes. If critics have sought a cynical, or ironical, or frustrated Shakespeare because of these, the fault has been theirs in the neglect of the Elizabethan framework. But, Lawrence asserts, that very framework of literary tradition hampered the dramatist's treatment of these elements. If Shakespeare expected his audience to understand the intended effects of his folk-lore sources, he was not free to alter those parts of his story which had become fixed in legend. In his attempt to infuse traditional, unrealistic plot elements with psychological motivation, Shakespeare succeeds only with Bertram, Parolles, and Lavache. With other characters, the motivation is neither psychologically true nor dramatically useful:

To realize the total lack of plausibility consider especially the part played by Diana. The obscure Florentine maiden becomes an expert stage-manager, keeping everyone in the dark as to her real purpose, boldly bandying words with the king, driving Bertram into a tight corner, and finally producing Helena, as a grand coup de theatre.[2]

Even though the value of his study lies in his analysis of audience and convention, Lawrence's final assessment of the play differs little from his contemporaries. '*All's Well* is artificial in effect; almost entertainment provided according to formula. The technique of transforming narrative into drama is in good order, but the imagination of the dramatist has seldom been kindled, or his sensibilities aroused.' Lawrence has gone to great lengths to prove that the plot is essentially romantic, based upon fable; yet he objects that the actions required of the characters are not natural to them. He implies what the Elizabethan audience perhaps did not assume, that the play must be realistic drama. The implication is openly expressed in his preference for *Measure for Measure* to *All's Well* in that the treatment of folk-lore in that play can be traced to real life.[3]

1. Ibid., pp. 61–62.   2. Ibid., p. 75.   3. Ibid., pp. 78–84.

Among the critics who held the audience responsible for the failure, Shaw was most uncomprising. In 1928, he insisted that the part of Helena was 'still too genuine and beautiful and modern for the public'.[1] More commonly, commentators developed Lawrence's theory that many of the defects disappear if we share the vision of the Elizabethans. Oliver Elton points out a textual basis for realizing that view: 'The trick by which she gains Bertram is applauded by the worthy persons in the drama,—and therefore, we may divine, by the poet, although the modern reader blenches.'[2] Stoll comments that the modern audience accepts the convention of love at first sight, yet objects to hasty marriages. But in Shakespeare's comedies, arbitrary reconciliations are common; 'he or his audience or both together suffer from an insatiable craving to see every Jack have his Jill, without the justification of Moliere.'[3] In 1931, Alwin Thaler defended the merit of the play particularly for the Elizabethan stage, but he also saw value in it for any responsive audience.[4] In Shakespeare's theatre the machinations of the plot would have been recognized immediately as devices of traditional folk-lore. The audience would have accepted the character of the heroine, for they were accustomed to the patient women of the plays, Imogen, Hero, Mariana, and Helena. The character of Bertram presented no problem, for they made great allowances for the young men in the comedies, Proteus, Claudio, Angelo, and Bertram. Nor would the reconciliation be shocking: 'if the license of the men and the patience of the women in these plays did not far exceed the standards of the Elizabethan code, then the endings, too, are not altogether irrational.' But beyond these conventions, Thaler argues that many of the 'problems' are issues only in the scholar's study, not on the stage of any age. As an example of creating difficulties foreign to the plays, he points to Coleridge's charge than Angelo and Claudio are as morally guilty as if their actions had had tragic consequences. The audience is much too busy 'to propound ethics in a vacuum', and its uproarious laughter over comic figures such as Lucio, Dogberry, and Parolles allows no intrusive speculation on the tragic potentialities of the other characters. Much near-villainy, which stands out in the imagination of the reader, is forgotten by an engrossed audience or is nullified by the later emphasis of a talented actor. Similarly, a

---

1. Although this comment is quoted in my Chapter 3, its pertinence here justifies the repetition. E. J. West (ed.), 'How to Lecture on Ibsen', *Shaw on Theatre*, New York, 1958, p. 56.
   2. *The English Muse*, London, 1933, p. 167.
   3. *Shakespeare's Young Lovers*, pp. 98–99.
   4. *Shakspere's Silences*, Cambridge, Massachusetts, 1929, pp. 83–86. See pp. 57–59 for his discussion of Lafeu's daughter noted below.

curiosity such as the mention of Lafeu's daughter as an earlier object of Bertram's affection produces irritations for the reader and fruitless investigation for the scholar. It may have been added by the dramatist as an afterthought 'in order to strike something off the score against Bertram for the moment', and it may accomplish just that theatrical effect.

Certainly, Thaler's central point that the play was written for an absorbed audience rather than a discriminating reader provides balance to the criticism of those commentators who ascribed the failure of *All's Well* to Shakespeare's dramatic artistry. Perhaps balance is nowhere more urgently needed than in the unfortunate attack upon the comedy in the 1929 'New Cambridge Edition'.[1] Both the introduction by Sir Arthur Quiller-Couch and the notes by John Dover Wilson did great damage to the reputation of *All's Well*. In the introduction, Quiller-Couch grants that the play and the comic elements may have been popular in Shakespeare's day, but this is his single concession. His indictment is sweeping:

> Shakespeare ignores or slurs over [his source] in hopeless skrimble-skramble. . . . We conceive Parolles to be on the whole, with all his concern in this play, about the inanest of all Shakespeare's inventions. . . . Out with Parolles might well go Lafeu, who surely has no business in the story, save (1) as usher, and (2) to tell Parolles what we already think of him. . . . The Clown Lavache again is, for furtherance of the action, nothing to any purpose. . . . Lavache in this play is a poor thin fellow, and we find ourselves throughout impatiently echoing his mistress's first inquiry, 'What does this knave here?' . . . This Bertram is just such a stage puppet as Shakespeare inartistically makes him. . . . The whole of the concluding scene is clearly bad playwright's work, being at once spun-out and scamped.   (pp. xxiv–xxxi)

Such value judgements are, of course, the right of the critic, but Quiller-Couch ignores any obligation to validate these judgements. The comments which I have quoted above are interspersed not with evidence but with what appears to be a petulant contradiction of earlier critics. Quiller-Couch calls for justice for Bertram, 'a high-bred, brave and spirited lad' (p. xxvi). What defects the hero has were caused by his upbringing 'among solicitous women without fatherly counsel or correction' (p. xxvi). This leads us some distance from the text, but we are pushed much farther by the charge that 'if one may make a guess, Helena herself has had her share in spoiling him' (p. xxvi). Shakespeare's *All's Well* is ignored entirely in the ensuing discussion of Bertram as a type which Shakespeare 'admired,

1. Sir Arthur Quiller-Couch and John Dover Wilson (eds.), *All's Well that Ends Well*, Cambridge, England, 1929.

aspired towards, was possibly indebted to' (p. xxvii). The subjectivity of the interpretation is patent in a judgement upon Helena which the editor admits might have been a fanciful after-thought, 'nastily suggested by a nasty play' (p. xxxi). He argues that, since Helena alone among all Shakespearian heroines lacks royal or noble blood, since her 'quarry on which Venus so ruthlessly attaches herself is a prey with two heads', she becomes 'a heroine of the pushing, calculating sort . . . and if affection help advancement, so much the better!' (p. xxxi). The principal motive of the heroine, then, is social or class advancement; Quiller-Couch has added to the history of the play a new allegation against the character of Helena. These charges lead him to conclude, 'In fine we hold this play to be one of Shakespeare's worst' (p. xxxv).

Whether John Dover Wilson agreed with all the opinions of his co-editor is not apparent, but he was not content to attribute all the mistakes in this play to Shakespeare. In his accompanying analysis of the comedy's prose, he discovers a second author, a rather nasty one at that:

> Indeed, once the presence of a collaborator or reviser, with a passion for sententious couplets and a mind running on sexual disease, be admitted, his handiwork becomes evident all over the play, and we begin to ask ourselves how Shakespeare can ever have been credited with some of the prose it contains, so poor is its quality, so empty its meaning.   (p. 110)

Not only is there the hand of a collaborator, but the entire play is 'a Jacobean revision of an Elizabethan play perhaps by Shakespeare but if so probably containing pre-Shakespearian elements' (p. 113). The failure of *All's Well* is essentially the failure of the collaborator.

Few contemporaries of the 'Cambridge' editors heeded the warning expressed in the review of the edition which appeared in the *Times Literary Supplement*:

> From beginning to end we, today, keep stumbling over ethical substance where the play's contemporaries saw probably nothing but familiar characters and familiar theatrical situations in which they could be pleasantly interested. . . . It is conceivable that [Bertram's lies] were theatrically intended and happily received by the audience as somewhat comical. . . . Literary judgments have their useful and necessary part to play in an edition of Shakespeare, but it is time that they yielded the pride of place to the dramatic and the theatrical.[1]

The majority of the critics saw only defects which resulted from the suspension of Shakespeare's creative genius. Logan Pearsall Smith agreed with the conclusions of W. W. Lawrence and John Bailey:

1. 24 Oct. 1929.

All's Well reads 'like hack-work'.[1] In his study of Shakespeare published in 1936, J. M. Murry writes that the failure of the comedy is simply in the dramatist's 'inability to deal further with the situation before him' in the final scene.[2] And Shakespeare admits the failure:

He throws in his hand with a laugh. The gods would have it so. All's well that ends well. It is not quite 'the supremely cynical title' for which I once argued; but it is cynical, in a good-humoured way. The difference is that the object of the good-humoured cynicism is not humanity in general, but Shakespeare's own impossible job as a playwright.

A more unpleasant cynicism weakened by inartistic indifference, was attributed to Shakespeare by Una Ellis-Fermor in *The Jacobean Drama*, published in 1936.[3] In tracing the dramatist's development, she notes: 'With *All's Well*, . . . the "twilight of deliberation" has deepened. The conclusion is as cynical as that of *Troilus*; more so, perhaps in its implications. It is huddled up hastily, the reactions of the main characters perfunctorily indicated.' H. B. Charlton denies that cynicism is the cause of the defects.[4] The source offers far greater potential for cynicism than is found in the play; furthermore, the benign presentation of the serene older characters makes absurd the term 'dark comedy'. Working with a unique chronology for the plays, Charlton explains the defects as natural steps in an artistic progression that leads from *Troilus and Cressida, Measure for Measure,* and *All's Well* to *Twelfth Night, Much Ado,* and *As You Like It!* Shakespeare was travelling along a road that stretched from the misleading comedy of Falstaff with 'joy in self' to the great comedy of natural goodness with joy for others. The progression is made through woman, and Helena just falls short of ideal characterization. Clearly however, Parolles is the significant refutation of Falstaff and 'his infectious and rapturous denial of the spiritual life'.[5]

In 1939 Mark Van Doren wrote that *All's Well* 'has failed, but it is one of Shakespeare's most interesting failures'.[6] The fault lay not in the mood of the playwright but in the form dictated by the material; our interest is incited by the inability of the dramatist's imagination to cope with that form. For the story of the comedy is essentially narrative, to be told 'briefly and abstractly, as a fable is told'. In this form, the story and its analogues had been told throughout the world 'before Shakespeare undertook to give it locality, detail, and atmosphere'. The undertaking 'attempted to make drama out of anecdote, to pad a dry skeleton with living flesh, to

1. *On Reading Shakespeare*, London, 1933, p. 58 n. Smith includes in his indictment *The Taming of the Shrew* and *The Merry Wives*.
2. John Middleton Murry, *Shakespeare*, New York, 1936, pp. 248–53.
3. London, 1936, p. 260.   4. *Shakesperian Comedy*, London, 1938, pp. 230–2.
5. Ibid., p. 263.   6. *Shakespeare*, New York, 1939, pp. 209–16.

force upon the imagination what only wit can credit'. The inherent difficulty in form, the dramatization of what had to remain simple narrative, was beyond the genius of Shakespeare's imagination, which, 'sensibly perhaps, stopped working'. The dramatist lost interest in his characters and setting. Bertram leaves for Paris as an interesting young man who has been crushed at Rousillon under the weight of death and generations, but Shakespeare makes nothing of his hero because he could see no reality in a young man responsive to the demands of the legend. The devices of the fairy-tale rob Helena of our pity; her pursuit becomes mechanical; 'her life has been maneuvered into nothingness'. Parolles 'must make the best of his presence in what is after all a mirthless play'. The Countess has no life; 'the blood is half frozen in her veins, as it is in the veins of the play she somehow dominates'. Of Lavache, Mr. Van Doren says: 'This clown is as bleak and bitter as the air that blows through his old mistress's room.' And Lafeu is the 'old lord who haunts' Rousillon with the Countess. What atmosphere the dramatist supplies is 'one of darkness, old age, disease, sadness, and death; and of superannuated people who nevertheless hold on to the chill edges of their former styles'. Such a mood suppressed Shakespeare's poetic interests as well as his dramatic. There are no bright flashes of poetry; there are only superficial injections of irony. Not in characterization nor in atmosphere nor in language could the creative genius of the playwright inflate the thin story of fable into the rousing vitality of drama.

The criticism of *All's Well* from 1920 to 1940 is characterized by the appraisal of the play as a failure and by the threefold explanation of that failure—inconsistency in characterization, demands upon the audience, and incapability of its author. As always, there were dissenting opinions and special investigations which are valuable for their insights. Perhaps Oliver Elton, in 1936, presented the most challenging minority view in his interpretation of Helena.[1] It was challenging to his contemporaries in that it denied an inconsistency in her character and deficiency in her creator. It was challenging to later critics in that it suggested a new approach to her personality. Elton believes that the play had been revised but that the revision had produced not confusion but a marvellous variety in the heroine:

The complex Helena in *All's Well*, the only thinker amongst Shakespeare's women, the self-analyst, has many and divers tones. . . . A creature of reason and will, she concentrates both on a purpose that is deeper rooted than reason; and the smallest acquaintance with life forbids us to marvel at her choice of a Bertram. Yet she holds her feeling, as if at arm's length, and watches it, even in public.

1. 'Style in Shakespeare', *Essays and Addresses*, London, 1939, pp. 22–23.

Helena is a philosopher, but she is motivated by a force deeper than reason; the unworthy Bertram is her choice, but life makes such choices common; Helena is in love, but she can examine her love objectively. The examination is in language grave and simple, but it is the language of poetry:

> Please it your majesty, I have done already.
> The blushes in my cheeks thus whisper me:
> 'We blush that thou should'st choose; but, be refused,
> Let the white death sit on thy cheek for ever,
> We'll ne'er come there again.'   (II. iii. 68–72)

In these lines, Elton sees the love, the complexity, and the objectivity of the heroine:

Simple the language is, but not so the idea; the blushes, which are real enough and honest, have voices; and we think how, at moments of tension, Shakespeare ever loves to personify. His vision of Helena's introspective nature dictates the peculiar figure. The climactic image,

> Let the white death sit on thy cheek for ever,

with its rise and fall of sound and hardly definable image, projects that image, before her as in a mirror. The three emphatic words in the centre of it form, in Browning's phrase, not a fourth word, but a star. Here again is the effect, if not the result, of studious art.

E. E. Stoll made a limited defence of Helena in *Shakespeare's Young Lovers* in 1936, but his justification of her conduct was not expounded fully until 1944.[1] In the earlier year, he praised the determination, the forceful will, of Shakespeare's heroines because it is just that which makes them romantic. Caroline Spurgeon touched upon the images and a trace of 'symbolic thought' in the play, but her conclusion remained tentative until developed by later critics: 'It may be pure chance, but many of Helena's sayings and images increase and carry on the suggestion or idea of stars and heavenly bodies moving in the firmament.'[2]

Other special studies of the period include Chambers's discussion of the text, the date on the basis of internal and external evidence, and the possibility of multiple authorship.[3] One conclusion rejects a common argument: the rhyme gives indication of early composition; Chambers insists that it resembles the neighbouring verse and consequently is used deliberately for dramatic effect. W. J. Lawrence made an interesting discovery, whether formulaic or accidental on

---

1. *Shakespeare's Young Lovers*, p. 51.
2. *Shakespeare's Imagery And What It Tells Us*, New York, 1935, pp. 273–5.
3. E. K. Chambers, *William Shakespeare*, Oxford, 1930, i. 449–52.

Shakespeare's part.[1] He observes that Bertram disappears from the play from Act IV, scene iv to Act V, scene iii, or during four short scenes. Both Hamlet and Macbeth have similar withdrawals:

> Bertram, in *All's Well that Ends Well*, has no amiable characteristics, and one is apt to wonder why Shakespeare bestowed upon him the distinction which he usually reserved for men and women of a nobler or finer type.

Of greater significance for a stage production is Arthur Case's resolution of the double stage direction for Parolles's entrance in the final scene.[2] The First Folio directs Parolles to enter with Diana and the Widow at line 156; but his entrance is also marked at line 232. Most editors, including Mr. Hunter in the recent 'New Arden Edition', dismiss the first entrance. Case argues that both are correct and that an intervening exit has been omitted:

> Parolles has been led to enter the audience-chamber on the heels of Diana, out of curiosity, but in his new-born spirit of humility he remains on the fringe of the crowd near one of the entrances. When he hears Diana name him as a witness he realizes his awkward predicament and slips hastily out of the door, unobserved by the characters on the stage, but not by the audience. The situation affords one of the few opportunities for laughter in the course of the sordid exposure of Bertram's baseness.

Since an entrance must be dropped or an exit added, the editor must alter the text. Mr. Case has at least theatrical justification for his proposal. In the last twenty years, criticism of *All's Well* has sought more frequently such justification.

---

1. *Speeding Up Shakespeare*, London, 1937, p. 45.
2. Arthur E. Case, 'Some Stage-Directions in *All's Well that Ends Well*', *MLN*, xlii, no. 2 (Feb. 1927), 82–83.

7

THE REAPPRAISAL:
A PATTERN OF UNITY
(1940–1964)

THE year 1940 offers a convenient and not entirely arbitrary division between the criticism which dismissed *All's Well that Ends Well* as a failure and the criticism of the last twenty-four years. There was neither a sudden nor sharp reversal of opinion; a number of studies continued to probe the defective nature of the play. But, since 1940, there has been a gradual reappraisal which balances weaknesses with merits. Recent criticism may be characterized by its new interest in *All's Well*, a consideration of the play in its own right; in effect, by a restoration of the play to moderate respectability in the Shakespearian canon. Perhaps this interest must be attributed initially to the contemporary enthusiasm for Shakespeare generally both in scholarship and in the theatre.[1] But if that enthusiasm has endangered objective assessments of other plays, it has produced a more valid criticism of *All's Well*. If the light upon Shakespeare in our age is dazzling, such light has long been needed to illumine the neglected 'dark' comedy. The unprecedented number of theatrical performances and special studies of the play have uncovered virtues buried by the categorical and violent censures of earlier critics.

Among those critics who continued to emphasize the weakness of *All's Well*, blame was placed upon the mood or the imagination of the dramatist as had been done in preceding studies. In 1949, Parrott wrote that Shakespeare had no interest in comedy when he composed the play.[2] In the original 'Love's Labours Won', the playwright had taken a serious domestic drama from Boccaccio and added a flavour of bitter comedy. In the revised play, he created Lavache for Robert Armin, heightened the satiric comedy of Parolles, and 'let it go at that'. In his haste to return to the composition of *Othello*, he made Lavache 'a poor specimen of the Fool', was indifferent to the potentially interesting characterization of Helena, and treated Bertram contemptuously. In Donald Stauffer's view, *All's Well* was written by 'a shrewd knave and an unhappy', whose

---

1. No further evidence of that enthusiasm is needed than Gordon Ross Smith's *A Classified Shakespeare Bibliography, 1936–1958*, 1963, with its list of 25,000 items.
2. Thomas Marc Parrott, *Shakespearean Comedy*, New York, 1949, pp. 347–54.

principal interest in the story was probably 'the theme of despised love' with Helena its mouthpiece.[1] In 1954, Lorentz Eckhoff placed the play in Shakespeare's gloomy period with its 'curiously bitter' humour, but he decided that the dramatist's interest had been stimulated by the 'striking resemblance' between Helena and Brutus.[2]

A more objective analysis of the 'dark comedy' theory has been presented by Clifford Leech in that his study is based upon the text of the play and assumes no personal mood in the playwright.[3] Mr. Leech does assert that the treatment of material reveals a more contemplative, a more questioning Shakespeare, but considers this only a new critical spirit in his artistic development. It is this critical spirit which is at the root of the 'aesthetic problem—the problem of the dramatist's failure in imagination'.[4] It establishes unresolved contrasts throughout; it creates ambivalent responses in the audience. The critical spirit insists upon a realistic atmosphere at Rousillon and at Court, but this atmosphere makes incredible the half-magical cure of the King. It distorts the Christian ritualistic verse of Helena as she persuades the King by giving to it the artificial accent of the Player-Queen in *Hamlet*. So too it pushes the serious advice which the Countess addresses to her son into the idiom and sentiment of Polonius. It makes the words and deeds of the elders rebound as ironic judgements upon themselves. The King's promise at the end of the play to find a husband for Diana only reflects Shakespeare's judgement upon the folly of the King throughout. The major evidence for this new attitude in Shakespeare's artistic development, however, is the characterization of Helena. *All's Well* is not simply a love story; it is an analysis of love in the heroine. The play is a probing into the ambivalent attitude which the Elizabethans had toward love: on the one hand, the fineness of courtly love; on the other hand, the disease of love. The noble sentiments of Helena's love are offset by the impurities in it, the deceptions, the fraud, the sexuality. The extent of her love as a disease is shown in the bed-trick which, in this play, was no more acceptable to the Elizabethans than to any other audience. What prompts Helena to resolve the conflict in her love is her ambition. 'The dramatist's attitude is made plainer if we . . . see ambition as the force that turns Helena from a passive love-sickness to active planning.'[5] And Shakespeare's attitude is clear when, most ironically, he makes the unworthy Bertram the object of her love. 'Here the satiric element of *All's Well*

1. *Shakespeare's World of Images*, New York, 1949, pp. 118–23.
2. *Shakespeare: Spokesman of the Third Estate*, Oslo, 1954, pp. 129–33.
3. 'The Theme of Ambition in *All's Well that Ends Well*', *ELH*, xxi (March 1954), 17–29.   4. Ibid., p. 29.   5. Ibid., p. 27.

is important, for we are made to see the value of Helena's prize.' By focusing upon the vanity of such ambition, Shakespeare has failed to resolve the dual nature of her love and 'the effect of the play as we have it is blurred'.[1] Mr. Leech concludes: 'But we should not be too surprised that sometimes the magic [of Shakespeare's imagination] would not work.'

Mr. Leech's interpretation is the most coherent treatment of the play as satire. With evidence drawn only from the text and Elizabethan background, it proposes a carefully reasoned approach. I believe that the interpretation may be argued point by point, but there is such refreshing consistency in Mr. Leech's theory that any refutation must be 'point by point'.

Two critics have related the failure of *All's Well* to dramatic form. Miss Muriel Bradbrook maintains that Shakespeare had set out to write a moral play, 'a grave discussion of the question of what constituted true nobility, and the relation to birth to merit'.[2] The form paralleled that of the old moralities and moral histories. Bertram represented high birth; Helena native merit; Parolles the Lie Incarnate, 'the chief danger of noble youth'.[3] But the social or moral problem which was the original theme became bisected by the human problem of unrequited love. As a consequence, the resultant play presents an insoluble conflict between a personal and an impersonal theme. The characters remain merely human; they fail to develop as symbols as do characters in *Measure for Measure*. *All's Well* remains 'of its age rather than for all times'.[4] In an article published in 1960, Robert Y. Turner likewise argues for a morality pattern which involves the prodigal son and Griselda formulas, but he sees Shakespeare influenced by a new dramatic form, an adaptation of the structure of Jonsonian comedy to traditional romantic stories.[5] After emphasizing purgation by trial and the problem of Bertram's reform, he falls back upon the traditional judgement that we cannot accept fully the aggressive heroine and the snobbish hero: '*All's Well* seems to have been endowed with conventions that have lost their savor.'

It seems somewhat unfair to include Mr. G. K. Hunter in that backflow of contemporary criticism which has continued to stress the failure of *All's Well that Ends Well*. For, surely, his recent 'New

1. Ibid., p. 29.

2. Miss Bradbrook's criticism is contained in two works: 'Virtue is the True Nobility', *RES*, n.s. i, no. 4 (Oct. 1950), 289–301, and *Shakespeare and Elizabethan Poetry*, London, 1951. For this reference, see *Shakespeare and Elizabethan Poetry*, p. 162.

3. 'Virtue is the True Nobility', pp. 291–3. See also p. 301.

4. *Shakespeare and Elizabethan Poetry*, p. 169.

5. 'Dramatic Conventions in *All's Well that Ends Well*', *PMLA*, lxxv (Dec. 1960), 497–502.

Arden Edition' does much to enhance the play.[1] But within the critical introduction, the reader is disappointed by the reply which Mr. Hunter gives to his own challenge: 'Criticism of *All's Well* has failed, for it has failed to provide a context within which the genuine virtues of the play can be appreciated.'[2] The context which the editor provides once again analyses the failure; it does little to justify the dramatic potential of the play. The comedy assumes significance only as a developmental step to the later romances:

> Much of the perversity of the denouement disappears if we see it as an attempt at the effects gradually mastered in the intervening comedies, and triumphantly achieved in *The Winter's Tale*, an attempt foiled in *All's Well* by stylistic and constructional methods inappropriate to the genre. The same theory explains much else that is perverse in the play.[3]

Mr. Hunter's position, then, is a restatement of the charge that Shakespeare's creative talent could not cope with the materials which the playwright had selected. In the editor's opinion, the structure is built upon three bases: the roles of Helena, Parolles, and Lavache. There is a deliberate dichotomy in the delineation of Helena which serves as a structural division. In the first half of the play, Helena is active and causes the movement of the plot. In the second half, Helena is passive; as the title implies, forces simply work out the consequences of the earlier activity. This change preserves our sympathy for the heroine. 'Helena is a "clever wench" only in the sense in which Griselda is—clever enough to be virtuous, pious, and patient till Destiny and Justice work things out for her.'[4] As a second structural base, the sub-plot of Parolles is made a parody of the major plot. Third, the action is accompanied by a commentary, 'of which the principal agent is the clown'. Through Lavache, the pretensions of both the good and the wicked are exposed. Woven into the structure is a complexity of themes: the contrast between youth and age, social consequences in a new world of opportunism, a series of intellectual dilemmas, such as rank as an impediment to marriage, concepts of virtue and honour, virginity in pursuit of marriage. Under the weight of such issues, the play totters. Shakespeare has juxtaposed extreme romantic conventions against satiric and critical realism. As a result, there is the problem of the bed-trick, which mixes a realistic device with romantic motivation; the character of Bertram, which cannot sustain the role of natural man redeemed by Grace; the inflexibility of Helena, which cannot rise from reality to symbol; the humour of Parolles, whose Jonsonian success does not fit the play; and the inept verse, which fails to establish a tone for the disparate

1. *All's Well that Ends Well*, The New Arden Edition, London, 1959.
2. Ibid., p. xxix.   3. Ibid., p. lv.   4. Ibid., p. xxxii.

elements. Mr. Hunter has not given us a context in which the virtues of the comedy can be appreciated. He himself concludes:

> There are two or three great speeches . . . in which there emerges a complex and bitter music, the identification and appreciation of which is probably, on one level, the last reward of a study of *All's Well that Ends Well*.[1]

The emphasis which Mr. Hunter places upon the discordant elements in the play is characteristic of criticism prior to 1940 rather than of recent scholarship. More indicative of the contemporary reappraisal is Hazleton Spencer's *The Art and Life of William Shakespeare* published in 1940, a book which both in chronology and analysis may serve as a bridge between the two periods.[2] In his examination of the play's problems, Mr. Spencer agrees substantially with earlier critical views; in his defence of the merits of *All's Well*, he anticipates later criticism. He agrees with W. W. Lawrence that more problems exist for the modern audience than did for the Elizabethan. In discussing problems within the text, he agrees with those critics who blame the playwright's neglect. Since the play was written in 1602, Shakespeare was absorbed in the tragedies and wrote hastily, perhaps 'in response to the company's need of a new comedy'. Consequently the plot is thin with merely a 'quasi-realistic handling of the romantic story'. The realism is due to neglect; he agrees with Charlton that 'there is no trace of irony and skepticism'. He admits with Mr. Van Doren that the play lacks poetry, that there is no 'romantic haze or fairy mist'. Instead of an Illyrian shore and a languishing Duke, *All's Well* has merely an ambitious boy aristocrat.

Yet despite the problems, the play is a successful romance, and here Mr. Spencer departs from the criticism of his colleagues. Shifting tastes, not the text, deny romance to the play. He insists: 'It was in a later age, when the old romances were no longer human nature's daily food, that it occurred to anyone to question whether the ending is really a happy one.' Shakespeare skilfully guides Helena between coquetry and aggressiveness. Her competence does not depend on feminine artifice, on lures or enchantments, nor is it in any sense a demonstration of ignoble self-will. It depends upon a boldness long characteristic of the heroines of old romance, 'more intellectual than temperamental'. So too, the character of Bertram is not to be taken realistically. Critical reaction to Bertram is an excellent demonstration of shifting taste and criteria, for it denies romance to a character who is simply unsentimental:

1. Ibid., p. lix.   2. New York, 1940, pp. 292–8.

He takes to war as to his native element; and he assumes, like any young blood without a poetic side, that one learns what women are by commencing rake. Compared with the young gentlemen of the eighteenth century novel, Bertram is, save of course for a deficiency of sensibility, almost a model youth. It is perhaps regrettable that Shakespeare failed to invent a scene in which the recreant husband might help an old lady across the street or throw his purse to a deserving beggar or perform some other good turn that would prove him the owner of a heart of gold at least the equal of Tom Jones's. Aptitude for war, however, went a long way toward establishing a romantic hero. He is, moreover, a count and a protege of the King of France. He does the right thing in the end. The play's title clinches the argument against its detractors.

Mr. Spencer's defence of romantic characterization includes Parolles as well. 'However he marches to the wars in the column that stretches back through the *commedia dell'arte* to the ancient comedy of Rome', he is unique, a character so fashioned that 'his first entrance doubtless raised a mighty laugh'. But the braggart-soldier should not dominate the play. *All's Well* is neither farce nor satire: it is a serious romance: 'Its tone, while not gay, is not depressing; on the contrary, it is lofty and exhilarating.'

In effect, Mr. Spencer weighs the defects and merits of *All's Well* in his critical scale and, unlike his contemporaries, concludes that the play has value in itself. His method and judgement characterize recent criticism. Since 1940, the play has been defended on three counts: it is high romance; it is good theatre; it is a revelation of a significant Shakespearian theme. As always with such categories, the counts are not mutually exclusive, but each suggests the approach of particular critics. Underlying each defence is the discovery of an artistic unity or, at least, an unrealized principle of structural unity. Where a unity has been claimed, *All's Well* has been labelled a success. Where only the principle of unity and not the artistic execution is claimed, *All's Well* has been labelled an interesting experiment. In either case, critics would rescue the play from the oblivion to which less discerning ages have cast it, just as modern producers have rescued it from the darkened theatre.

In 1944, E. E. Stoll defended the play and its heroine on much the same grounds as Spencer.[1] He doubted the necessity of searching through medieval legend, as W. W. Lawrence had done, to justify a fable appealing to the Elizabethans in its obvious romantic quality. A robust audience would have enjoyed the contrast of the refined and delicate heroine to so indelicate a situation. Typical of that situation and illustrative of the romantic effect is the virginity

1. *From Shakespeare to Joyce*, New York, 1944, pp. 241–9.

scene: 'This is Gothic art. . . . Coming after one heartfelt soliloquy and before another, the colloquy is both indecent and comical, both pathetical and ironical, as they talk of virginity, the defending of it or the losing of it "to one's own liking." ' Helena needs no more defence than other Shakespearian heroines who act against the dictates of decorum; in fact, she is no different from the heroines in Italian and Spanish *novelle* and comedies, in Ariosto, Spenser, and medieval romances. Even the realistic elements strengthen our impression of Helena as 'lovable and admirable'. There is one exception and this constitutes the defect in the play. The final blackening of Bertram's character has been done for 'stagy excitement. . . . Bertram is made more plausible (but less acceptable), by Helena's being made less plausible and less acceptable'.

Similar analyses have been proposed by Professors Hardin Craig and Alfred Harbage.[1] Mr. Craig believes that the play was undoubtedly a success before Shakespeare's audience. When viewed properly, it is a bright and active comedy with elements of danger and distress. Such 'dark' acts as Bertram's intended seduction carry little stain for a young nobleman 'in a free age and situation'. In his study of the Elizabethan audience, Mr. Harbage sees so many similarities between *All's Well* and other Shakespearian comedies that he regards it as highly improbable that either author or audience would consider the play 'bitter'. His argument may be demonstrated by his study of vice in these comedies. He links *All's Well* to other Shakespearian plays in its ending, a happy triumph of virtue over vice (Bertram's self-conceit); in the means employed by Helena to an end 'no different from that of women generally';[2] in the hasty repentance of the last scene where characteristically the dramatist does not drag out humiliation if no irreparable harm has been done— 'Bertram's act of contrition is composed of a single word and some dumb-show (though it suffices to make Lafeu weep)';[3] and finally in his making vice a mere incongruity. The Clown's defence of cuckoldry and Parolles's attack on virginity are comparable to the moral paradoxes of Falstaff: 'We are freed from the burdens of fear and disapproval. We fondle the viper [vice] and stroke the wolf. We laugh. It is Shakespeare's intention.'[4] The vices in *All's Well*, if seen in the light of similar situations in similar Shakespearian comedies, are not inconsistent with the pattern of romance.

As the unpleasantness of vice disappears in the light spirit of romance, so, in the opinion of a second group of critics, do the incon-

1. Hardin Craig, *An Interpretation of Shakespeare,* New York, 1948, pp. 221–8, and Alfred Harbage, *As They Liked It,* New York, 1947, p. xii.
2. *As They Liked It,* pp. 36–37.   3. Ibid., p. 132.   4. Ibid., pp. 78–79.

sistencies of character and mood dissolve in the absorbing fantasy of the theatre. This thesis is given its most interesting and effective explanation in an article written by Harold S. Wilson in 1950. He states:

It will be here suggested that the artifice of the play is due to Shakespeare's attempt to give depth to the simple tale he followed at his source; that this artifice consists especially in a process of varying emphasis in the conduct of the action calculated to strengthen the consistency and unity of the story as Shakespeare chose to tell it; and finally, that this artifice is more properly regarded as a virtue of the play than a defect, since it is managed competently enough with an eye to the stage.[1]

In his demonstration, Wilson dismisses the objection to the bed-trick as an objection to the story itself. He lists as the most serious attack on the play the charge of inconsistency or implausibility in the hero and heroine, especially in the final scene. In a comparison of the comedy with its source, however, he finds that these 'defects' are the very changes deliberately made by Shakespeare. He argues that the playwright accepted these 'alleged' difficulties:

in an attempt to transform a simple tale of reconciliation effected through circumstance into a study of character; and that he used a method of shifting emphasis to obscure the implausibilities resulting from the treatment of his source and calculated to give a sufficient unity of effect in stage performance.[2]

In this shifting emphasis, 'Helena works out her designs unobtrusively in the background as the audience is occupied with Diana and the Widow, Parolles and the drum, Bertram and his ordeal'.[3] In addition, the bolder actions are manipulated by Diana, an alter ego for Helena, 'while our original impression of the heroine is maintained by the attitude of the other characters toward her and what they say of her'. Helena remains consistent throughout the latter half of the play because our 'idea' of her is sustained until 'she reappears in her old role of the humble and devoted wife'. In disagreement with W. W. Lawrence and many other critics, Wilson defends Diana's activities as stage manager and the entire set of complications in the last scene on psychological grounds as well as theatrical effectiveness. If Helena had merely demanded justice of the King, the play would have been reduced to the simplicity of fairy-tale. Helena is not seeking justice; she is seeking the love of her husband. Diana, acting on the plan of the heroine, complicates the trial so that Bertram is overwhelmed emotionally, with full psychological justification.

1. Harold S. Wilson, 'Dramatic Emphasis in *All's Well that Ends Well*', *Huntington Library Quarterly*, xiii (May 1950), 219.
2. Ibid., p. 222.   3. Ibid., p. 226.

Shakespeare expects his audience to be absorbed in the barrage which crushes the hero. In the theatre, 'the necessary sense of growing pressure upon Bertram' is created.[1] The audience sees, as the reader may not, the superiority of Helena's love to the hero's arrogance. The dramatic emphasis, shifted consciously by the playwright for his effects, covers the weakness which troubles the attentive reader.

The point is stressed by Mr. Kenneth Muir in his study of Shakespeare's sources.[2] The reader may feel that the characters are not fully humanized; 'but it is a play which acts much better than it reads'. On stage, Helena in particular never loses the sympathy of the audience. The undertones and ambiguities to which the scholar objects as incongruities 'may not be evidence of failure on the part of the dramatist but a deliberate deepening of this theme'. In Mr. Muir's opinion, two alterations might have made the play more successful for both the reader and the audience: 'If the Clown were given better jokes and Bertram a better speech at the end, the play would leave us with feelings of greater satisfaction.'

The commentary of E. M. W. Tillyard falls into the third category of contemporary scholarship, that of thematic criticism; but his introduction to his analysis may serve as a bridge between the defence of *All's Well* as a stage production and the defence of the play as an intellectual proposition:

> Fail the play does, when read: but who of its judges have seen it acted? Not I at any rate; and I suspect that it acts far better than it reads. For one thing it is very well plotted; and in the usual Shakespearean manner. . . . This admirable construction, which I cannot remember to have been sufficiently praised, might be more evident on the stage than in the study and might ensure for the play a position far higher than its present one, should it ever force its way into the repertory that enjoys regular presentation. But on the only available criterion, that of reading, it remains true that in its total effect *All's Well* fails and that the failure is caused most obviously by the comparative feebleness of execution.[3]

The failure of the total effect, at least in the reading, forces Tillyard to include *All's Well* among the 'problem plays', a term made popular in the twentieth century by W. W. Lawrence after its introduction by Boas in 1896. Tillyard admits the difficulty in defining the term, for each play presents its own reasons for the categorization. For his purposes, Tillyard includes Hamlet with the more usual grouping of *All's Well, Measure for Measure,* and *Troilus and Cressida.* What links the four plays is Shakespeare's absorption with religious dogma or abstract speculation and with realistic characterization—

1. Ibid., p. 237.   2. *Shakespeare's Sources,* London, 1957, p. 101.
3. E. M. W. Tillyard, *Shakespeare's Problem Plays,* London, 1950, pp. 89–90.

even to the neglect of the overriding themes of the plays. *All's Well* is a problem play because it is schizophrenic: Shakespeare's speculation about 'the wretched insufficiency of natural man' and his realistic interest 'in the detailed workings' of the minds of his 'too sober' heroine and 'too unpleasant' hero could not be reconciled with folklore material.[1] Shakespeare has tried to inject theological principles into the fable and morality patterns into the characters. To the legend, he has added several religious themes. Helena calls upon heaven to work a miraculous cure of the king; in that cure, the king tests heaven, not Helena. The two lords discuss man's natural depravity, his need for grace, and the ultimate revelation of all crime. To the characters, Shakespeare has tried to add symbolic values. In this attempt, he very likely used the morality play and moral history as types. There are similarities between Bertram and Prince Hal, Parolles and Falstaff, Helena and the Chief Justice (both represent Honour and Justice). More directly, the dramatist made the obvious identification of character and virtue: Helena represents heavenly grace and Bertram natural, unredeemed man. Still the fable remained, and the play never acquired the moral earnestness of *Measure for Measure*. So too, the characters remained realistic under the compulsion of the dramatist and failed to assume the symbolism of *The Winter's Tale* and *The Tempest*. Shakespeare may have recognized the impossibility of a blending of romantic plot and realistic characterization in *All's Well* and so gave himself up to his own interests resorting in crises 'to the conventional, the sententious, or the hieratic'.[2]

Nevertheless, his experiment makes the play an extremely interesting one, and Tillyard's final judgement is that the 'great merits' tip the scales favourably. In addition to his praise of the characterizations, he defends the play as seminal in Shakespeare's development of thematic drama. The success of his last plays in the treatment of mercy and forgiveness has its seed in *All's Well* and *Measure for Measure*.

Much recent criticism has been devoted to a defence of *All's Well* on thematic grounds. In a comparative analysis of Shakespeare's plays and Spenser's *The Faerie Queene*, Miss Abbie Findlay Potts sees in *All's Well* and plays proximate in date of composition a common theme which was strongly influenced by Spenser's work.[3] Throughout the period, Shakespeare expresses concern for 'ethical disproportion and its attempted cure by dedicated agents'. The characters in

1. Ibid., pp. 3–5.   2. Ibid., p. 102.
3. *Shakespeare and The Faerie Queene*, Ithaca, New York, 1958, pp. 64–75. For my quotations, see pp. 67 and 65.

All's Well have recognizable Spenserian prototypes and are themselves prototypes of later Shakespearian creations. The play becomes
much 'less enigmatic when studied in the light of love's pageants
played "diuersely" in "diuerse minds" . . . throughout the Book of
Chastity' and in 'the precarious balance between Discord and Con-
cord in the Book of Friendship'. Another view of *All's Well* as a
demonstration of an intellectual proposition is elaborated by Mr.
John Arthos.[1] The play is a 'comedy of generation', which compares
the loves of parents and lovers, of possessive parents and unwanted
lovers. It compounds the comparison through the theme of ambition;
it blends all the elements ironically in forcing the lover Helena to
become a parent to win her love. The healing power of love demonstrates its strength. Stimulated by recurring images and symbols,
Mr. John F. Adams terms the play the 'paradox of procreation'.[2]
The problem of understanding right action is dramatized in terms of
three interrelated themes: the problem of the nature of honour; the
problem of heritage, that is, the responsibilities of youth to the past;
and the problem of sex and procreation. To the late Dame Edith
Sitwell, the play is one 'in which the strong force of life fights against
a thin meager living death'.[3] Helena is the symbol of the theme; 'she
is irresistible with the force of Spring, the ferment, the mounting
sap'. Of all the characters in the play, only Bertram and Parolles
show a similar vitality, and it is this which attracts the heroine to
both of them.

Approaching the comedy from its 'verbal music' rather than its
thought, Miss Ellis-Fermor arrives at the same conclusion as Tillyard.[4] *All's Well* is an interesting intellectual experiment which
Shakespeare does not complete successfully until his last plays. The
conceptual theme is supported by a musical theme, a sound distinctive in this comedy:

> In fact there is in this play a new and unfamiliar diction and music, one
> which, though impeded and sometimes silenced . . . nevertheless persists
> sometimes to the verge of achievement and always with consistency:

> > The fated sky
> > Gives us free scope; only doth backward pull
> > Our slow designs when we ourselves are dull

Here almost alone in Shakespeare's plays, we are in a world where the

---

1. 'The Comedy of Generation', *Essays in Criticism*, v (April 1955), 97–117.
2. '*All's Well that Ends Well*: The Paradox of Procreation', *SQ*, xii (Summer 1961), 261–70.
3. *A Poet's Notebook*, Boston, 1950, pp. 148–50.
4. Una Ellis-Fermor, 'Some Functions of Verbal Music in Drama', *Shakespeare Jahr-buch*, xc (1954), 40–43.

words do not 'sing and shine'; their music is that of low-toned, meditative speech, where no splendour or sudden glory of images evokes in response a memorable or poignant cadence.

She believes that this peculiar tone illustrates a dramatist experimenting with new themes and a new world where the passions have been channelled by moral purpose and dedication. Only in the last plays does Shakespeare solve the dramatic problems of the passionless drama: 'It may be that when *All's Well* was written, the time for this attempt had not yet come.'

Critics who form this third group among the defenders of *All's Well* regard the play as an experiment interesting in its intellectual theme, its symbolic characters, its passionless mood. Although they may not agree on the extent of the failure, they share the opinion that Shakespeare was not entirely successful in the execution of the experiment until his last plays. In 1958, G. Wilson Knight published an essay in which he forcefully defended a thematic interpretation of the comedy.[1] But he did not accept the widespread view that the play was a developmental exercise, for he dated it among the last plays.

Mr. Knight's essay is an important document in the critical history of *All's Well that Ends Well*. It is the play's most exhaustive defence; it is its most extreme defence. Those remarks in his analysis which circle closely and immediately about the text are stimulating insights, but too often they set into motion ever-widening commentary, which, like rippling waves, drift far from the play. Nowhere is this more evident than in his discussion of the theme. Mr. Knight proposes that Shakespeare establishes an atmosphere for *All's Well* in which the scale of values is not absolute, in which exactitudes are impossible. The atmosphere involves such a conflict in ethical ideas and personal relationships that compromise is essential. Whenever compromise is necessary, we term its criterion 'honour'. Honour is the theme of the play. The complexities of the concept are manifested in the complexities of the characters as they engage in problems of compromise. The problems are the principal issues in honour: honour in the exercise of power as in war, and honour in sexual relationships as in the preservation of chastity. The first type is basically masculine; the second basically but not exclusively feminine. The opposition of Bertram to Helena is the opposition of these different concepts of honour. On the one hand, much of the play revolves about the conflict within feminine principles of honour, the preservation of chastity. The virginity speech, the many references to virginity, Helena's plea to the goddess Diana, the symbolic

1. 'The Third Eye', *The Sovereign Flower*, New York, 1958, pp. 93–160.

substitution of the Florentine Diana for the heavenly protectress of the chaste, the argument of Bertram in his attempted seduction of Diana, all illustrate aspects of this conflict. On the other hand, Bertram's desire for the wars is his obvious impulse to masculine honour; the character of Parolles, the exposure of the drum, the comments of the young lords, all point up the conflict within the masculine concept. Bertram's wooing of Diana while he is at the wars brings together the two types of honour. The jewel of Diana's chastity and the jewel of Bertram's ancestry—his ring—become symbols of the clash between these opposing principles:

> The two honours, male and female, are fighting out their difference. The problem is, and is meant to appear, rather different as viewed from different sexual viewpoints, and we cannot assume that Bertram is here wholly repudiated: the quality of the poetry alone forbids that.[1]

At this point in his theory, Mr. Knight adds a complication beyond both the conflicts within the masculine and feminine principles and the conflict between these principles. He sees greater complexity because Helena is not contained by the female concept of honour. She is the aggressor. She '*assumes, for once, the male prerogative of action.* Helena goes out as a Saint Joan to fight for the female virtues, for the female honour, for "virginity" as a conquering power. That is her role; and it includes a miracle.'[2] The miracle adds new significance to the theme of honour. Against a supernatural background, Helena and Bertram become the representatives respectively of Church and State, of the Medieval Age and the Renaissance, of East and West, of the occult and science. But Helena is more than an agent for one side. Although involved in her own conflict, she resolves all conflicts. She rises as the essence of necessary compromise: 'She stands at the very heart of that complex of which the Clown and Parolles are the two opposing extremes [ethical absolute and ethical negation]. She alone escapes the Clown's condemnation and she alone refuses to condemn Parolles.'[3] Helena is the principle of love. As such, if Helena is the all-embracing force in the play, if she is aided by the miraculous, if her very love is miraculous, if she assumes the role of the aggressor, then the heroine is, in consequence, bisexual. Her female humility becomes a male force, dynamic and assertive. As a 'creature of bisexuality and virgin integration',[4] she aims at an ideal state where the virtues of virginity and marriage are identified. In Helena, Mr. Knight sees not only the Elizabethan concept of the Phoenix, not only autobiographical parallels to the sonnets, but a semi-divine bridge between heaven and earth: 'She

1. Ibid., p. 110.   2. Ibid., p. 112.   3. Ibid., p. 159.   4. Ibid., pp. 159–60.

functions, within the play, almost as Christ within the Christian scheme. The play is a microcosm of that scheme.'[1]

Mr. Knight has moved from the necessity of compromise through an analysis of the theme of honour, then, to the opposition of male and female virtues in war and chastity. Because of the supernatural, these virtues raise the hero and heroine to one symbolic level where they represent East and West; they elevate the heroine even higher to a bisexual plane where she corresponds somewhat to Shakespeare and functions somewhat as Christ. The rippling waves have moved far beyond the horizon of *All's Well that Ends Well*.

An interesting corollary to contemporary criticism of the comedy is the frequent defence of Bertram. In 1940, Mr. Spencer considered the hero as nothing worse than an 'ambitious boy aristocrat', far better than the heroes of eighteenth-century novels. Hardin Craig dismisses Bertram's acts as merely youthful conduct. Miss Bradbrook makes a limited plea in presenting him through the eyes of Helena and as a victim of Parolles's evil influence. She expresses the modern view that Bertram is not a thinly drawn caricature:

[Shakespeare] set out to start a discussion on the fashioning of a gentleman, and found himself impelled to draw the likeness of one whom Lafeu called an 'asse' and Hellen the god of her 'idolatrius fancie,' but whose portrait stands out clearly as something more complex than either.[2]

Tillyard denies that Helena is any more interesting or instructive than Bertram.[3] The hero is crudely immature, but not vicious. The entire plot is based upon Bertram's yielding 'to the pressure of numbers'; a division can be drawn in the structure of the play between Bertram's early attempt at self-assertion and his later cowardice when he is confronted by his mother's letter, the anger of the King, the supposed death of Helena, the exposure of Parolles, and the bewildering events of the trial. Mr. Knight regards the hero as a normal young man who simply lacks judgement and a scale of value.[4] He has no self-knowledge, and this is what he must gain. He errs both in rejecting Helena on grounds of rank and in limiting his goals to the ultimately vain honour of war, but Helena redeems him from both. A number of recent studies have stressed the equality of Bertram and Helena as dual protagonists. Miss Potts suggests this is her identification of them as Spenserian types.[5] In his book on Shakespearian comedy published in 1957, Mr. John Russell Brown asserts that Shakespeare treats the actions of both hero and heroine

---

1. Ibid., p. 146.
2. *Shakespeare and Elizabethan Poetry*, p. 170.
3. Tillyard, p. 111. See pp. 113–17 for his discussion of Bertram.
4. 'The Third Eye', p. 112.   5. *Shakespeare and The Faerie Queene*, p. 67.

as imperfect responses to love.[1] Only when these responses have been purified in each is a reconciliation possible. 'At the conclusion, under the eyes of the King, Helena and Bertram are ready to take up a new relationship in love which must be judged by the standards which they have previously violated.' Dr. Yellowlees, in a somewhat subjective and impassioned lecture, strengthens Bertram's case by a harsh attack upon Helena.[2] The hero was 'sinned against as much as sinning' by that 'designing minx', Helena, who, in the professional eyes of the doctor, was the 'Queen of Quacks'. (Helena's medical skill has been defended in a reply by Charles J. Sisson who cites a case-history from Dr. William Harvey.)[3]

In an article published in 1956, Mr. Albert Carter proposed a defence of Bertram which was more than a critical corollary.[4] He maintains that justification of the hero's cause leads to recognition that *All's Well* is a good play. Bertram's faults are necessary for and typical of comedy; they differ very little from Helena's defects which include lies and deceits. In each character there is a comic flaw: in Bertram it is a need to justify himself; in Helena it is her wit and reliance upon the past. At the end of the play, both a guilty Bertram and a guilty Helena are comically chastened. But in that chastisement, the assertion of their youth is a comic reprimand to the elders, the intrusive Countess, the intractable King, and the opinionated Lafeu. Mr. Carter's essay prompted a more cautious defence by Mr. Francis G. Schoff.[5] In reply, Mr. Schoff denies the necessity of slandering the other characters in *All's Well* in order to justify Bertram. Shakespeare has given many indications of his intention in delineating the hero. The difference in rank is a real and essential obstacle to Helena's love as she herself insists. Furthermore, Bertram is eager to be off to manly pursuits and acts of daring in war. The other characters speak harshly of him only when they are angry. Even after his desertion of her, Helena's love for him is constant. At his worst, at the very time when he is apparently seducing Diana, the young lords point out how human his conduct is (IV. iii. 68–71). Finally, Mr. Schoff asserts, one of Bertram's most severe critics, Lafeu, is willing to accept the hero for a son-in-law. He concludes: 'No, there is no problem about Bertram if we take him as Shakespeare gives him to us.'

1. *Shakespeare & His Comedies*, London, 1957, pp. 191–6.
2. Henry Yellowlees, 'Medicine and Surgery in the 1955 Season's Plays', *More Talking of Shakespeare*, ed. John Garrett, London, 1959, pp. 175–7.
3. 'Shakespeare's Helena and Dr. William Harvey: With a case-history from Harvey's practice', *Essays and Studies*, xiii (1960), 1–20.
4. 'In Defense of Bertram', *SQ*, vii (Winter 1956), 21–31.
5. 'Claudio, Bertram, and a Note on Interpretation', *SQ*, x (Winter 1959), 16–19.

Specialized studies of Shakespeare over the past twenty years have produced a number of significant references to *All's Well*. In his source study, Mr. Kenneth Muir discusses the possible influence of the controversy in England and the continent about the foundation of true nobility, rank or virtue.[1] Mr. Frederick Ness's investigation into the dramatist's use of rhyme justifies the artistry which Shakespeare displays in its management in *All's Well*.[2] Mr. Herbert Wright suggests a French translation of the *Decameron* by Antoine Le Macon as a new source for the play.[3] Among the textual annotations is a proposed solution of a long-standing problem which affects the interpretation of Helena's character. Many critics have been skeptical of Helena's pilgrimage; the shrine which she intends to visit is in Spain, and consequently, her journey to Florence is a deliberate deception to trap her husband. Mr. Mario Praz writes:

The 'Saint Jacque le Grand' to which Helena is supposed to betake herself on a pilgrimage in *All's Well*, would not be the well-known sanctuary in Spain, but San Giacomo d'Altopascio not far from Florence, and the palmers' hostel 'at the S. Francis here beside the port' (III. v. 37) would stand for the oratory of San Francesco dei Vanchetoni in the neighbourhood of Porta al Prato in Florence.[4]

In examining Parolles as a comic antagonist, E. M. Blistein explained the comic transformation: 'From artificial captain he has become a nobleman's genuine fool, and he does not mind. He is, in fact, grateful. The audience has laughed at him for pretending to be something he was not. Lafeu henceforth will laugh with him for being what he is.'[5] Mr. Ronald Watkins's comparison of the Steward and other Shakespearian servants illuminates a minor part:

A virtuous Oswald we might call him (Oswald also writes his Lady's letters), a discreet Malvolio; his name is Rinaldo, to remind us of Polonius' confidential envoy; the comparisions are not without value in helping an actor of any of these four parts to conceive his performance.[6]

Several commentaries have touched upon Lavache and his function in the comedy. Professor Harbage links him with Faulconbridge, Berowne, Jacques, Lucio, Apemantus, and Thersites as commentators who cannot be trusted:

Each of these characters has been identified at various times as Shakespeare in disguise. But they are all eccentrics with satirical tongues; their fellow characters warn us against some of them, and against satire.[7]

1. *Shakespeare's Sources*, pp. 99–100.   2. See n. 1, p. 178.
3. *Boccaccio in English*, London, 1957, p. 214.
4. 'Shakespeare's Italy', *SS*, vii (1954), 96–97.
5. E. M. Blistein, 'The Object of Scorn: An Aspect of the Comic Antagonist', *Western Humanities Review*, xiv (Spring 1960), 209–22.
6. *On Producing Shakespeare*, London, 1950, p. 152.
7. *As They Liked It*, pp. 110–11.

Mr. Bridges-Adams maintains that the Clown's function diminishes as Shakespeare strives for greater homogeneity in the construction of his plays; in *All's Well*, Lavache is only a shadow of the former Shakespearian clown.[1] Although admitting that Lavache is the least characteristic of all the playwright's fools, Mr. Robert Goldsmith sees a dramatic function in the Clown and his love as a parody of the main plot.[2] As Touchstone does in his love affair, Lavache comments ironically on the conduct of his betters. 'If his humor tastes a little sour now and then, the explanation may be that it is nourished on the unpleasant follies of Bertram and Parolles.' If he is less important than Touchstone, it is because 'he is in no way a measure of the play's meaning'. Mr. Nevill Coghill believes that the Clown's 'actual function is to be a time-sandwich', to keep a scene going in order that necessary time may elapse.[3] But Shakespeare lavishes two or three creative touches upon him 'which seem to qualify him for something better than his part and play'. Lavache, too, shares in the recent defence of *All's Well*, for Mr. Coghill declares, 'He is an extreme example of what one finds in so many of Shakespeare's creations—there is more to them than they actually need for the plays in which they appear—they spill over into life.'

With centuries of Shakespearian scholarship behind us, we have difficulty in conceiving the possibility of fresh, exciting discoveries or valid interpretations which edge us closer to the intention of the dramatist. We view each new criticism of *Hamlet, Othello*, or *King Lear* with understandable suspicion. Yet the possibility of such analyses increases as we move from the recognizably great plays of Shakespeare. Plays which have been dismissed in a few pages by critics absorbed with more easily demonstrable evidence of the playwright's genius, plays which have been neglected by directors and actors absorbed with more manageable parts moulded by stage traditions, still offer a challenge to critic and director alike. Recent theatrical experiments and recent scholarship have taken up the challenge in *All's Well that Ends Well* with the result that the most exciting innovations and interesting interpretations have come at the terminus of this history. In 1950, Tillyard could explain that the only guide for the critic of the play was his careful reading of the text. Since then, productions by the Old Vic, by the companies at Stratford on Avon, Stratford, Ontario, and Stratford, Connecticut, by numerous professional, collegiate, and amateur groups have made

1. W. Bridges-Adams, *The Irresistible Theatre*, London, 1957, i. 191.
2. *Wise Fools in Shakespeare*, East Lansing, Michigan, 1955, pp. 57–60.
3. 'Wags, Clowns and Jesters', *More Talking of Shakespeare*, ed. John Garrett, London, 1959, p. 16.

possible an answer to his question, 'Who of its judges have seen it acted?' In an exhaustive evaluation of the 1959 Guthrie production, Miss Muriel St. Clare Byrne provided an excellent answer.[1] In the stage history, I discussed her review of the performance, but her analysis of the play demands attention as well in the critical history as a stimulating defence of *All's Well*, a defence which insists upon the essential unity of the play.

Miss Byrne believes that the play is a delightful romantic comedy, well-plotted, with superior characterization. The perfectly plausible substance of the comedy, plot, and characterization is the situation of Helena:

> [She is] a heroine of unusually strong character and intelligence, with that capacity for loving (in the adult sense) that Shakespeare admires in women, who is in love not with a hero but with a handsome, aristocratic, spirited, young woodenhead—a very young and very ordinary young man. And this is an ordinary twentieth century situation.[2]

The situation is easily comprehensible—to the Elizabethans who accepted 'the categorical imperative that a woman must marry' and to the moderns who believe that woman needs and wants to marry. Helena, an orphan, sets out in the spirit of romance to win the man whom she loves with the aid only of her wits and his mother. All the plot elements unite to strengthen the dramatic effect of that search. So, Shakespeare begins the play with mourning to heighten the following vitality which we recognize in Helena's assertion of her love; he creates a similar mood of desolation for her return to Rousillon to heighten her decisiveness which we recognize in her selfless flight from the house. There is the same symmetry in dialogue. The words of Parolles which urge Helena to lose her virginity increase in significance when we consider his role as go-between for Bertram and Diana. He provides Helena the means 'for virgins to "undermine" men' in her undermining Bertram's intended seduction. There is symmetry too in that the romantic expression of Helena's love in that scene is followed by the realistic talk of virginity; in the seduction, the romantic intentions of Bertram are diverted by the realistic device of the bed-trick. Miss Byrne argues for Shakespeare's skill in plotting in that one plot detail serves many functions. An example is the Florentine war which provides an escape for Bertram, a locale for the bed-trick, and a male counterpart to the female world of Rousillon. Furthermore, the mock-heroic tone of the war and the exposure

---

1. 'The Shakespeare Season at the Old Vic, 1958–9 and Stratford-upon-Avon, 1959', *SQ*, x (Autumn 1959), 545–67. For another interesting defence at the conclusion of this critical history, see Jay L. Halio's 'All's Well that Ends Well', *SQ*, xv (Winter 1964), 33–43.   2. Ibid., p. 557.

of Parolles illustrate the irresponsibilities of this male environment lead Bertram to self-revelation.

In her interpretations of the characters, Miss Byrne attributes strength, intelligence, warmth, poise, and passion to Helena, a heroine of wonderful variety. Bertram is a very young, handsome boy, 'stiff with undergraduate-level masculine and aristocratic self-conceit', a type that is easy prey to the swagger of a Parolles.[1] Bertram has a case as a coerced young man, but the immaturity of his conduct nullifies it; 'one simply has to wait for him to grow up'. The Countess is not aged, for her son is still a minor. But her beauty is in her serenity and assurance, her graciousness and generosity of spirit. These qualities are manifest in her lovely 'benediction upon the ardor and passion of youth' in her reverie and in the 'exquisite duologue' which she has with Helena when the heroine confesses her love. The King is effective as a figure of quiet, assured dignity with a 'slightly hypochondriacal irritability'. Contrary to eighteenth-century interpretations, Miss Byrne believes that Parolles must never dominate the play, but simply record the 'truthful anatomy of the parasite's progress'. The Widow and Diana come alive with robustness if they are characterized in a 'shabby-genteel mode'. Diana gives plausibility to the plot and to the characterization of Bertram if she is a contrasting type to Helena, a girl with obvious appeal to the immature Count. Lavache is 'a privileged, outspoken, John-Brownish old retainer'.

In the opinion of Miss Byrne, *All's Well* succeeds because of its wonderfully interesting characters, its integrated plot, and the romantic appeal of its joyful ending; the comedy is another mark of the genius of Shakespeare. Miss Byrne's criticism completes a long cycle in the history of the play. 'The unfortunate comedy' has won approval from critics and popularity from theatre-goers. Whether its current favour is a return to the judgement of Shakespearian audiences, we cannot say, but there is some basis for Miss Byrne's happy comparison:

It is ironical to reflect that this so-called 'bitter comedy,' one of the least liked and least known of the plays, has now been introduced to a mass-audience, who have possibly never heard of it and almost certainly never read it, as a play written to delight and entertain in a theatre. Many thousands of these lucky people now start off with the right idea, like Bankside audiences who recognized that a play was a play and did not confuse it with the sermon at Paul's. They are not a coterie audience for plays unpleasant, any more than Shakespeare's was; they are unlikely to go looking for trouble among such bedevilments as collaborators, revisers,

1. Ibid. For a discussion of the characters, see pp. 560–2 and 566–7.

transcribers and textual layers; and would be at a loss to understand why we should be told that its 'problems' still await solution. Some of them may even agree with Bernard Shaw, who spoke of it as one of the plays 'rooted in my deeper affections;' and would be genuinely puzzled to be told that the substituted-bedfellow trick is 'disgusting' and 'degrading' and that not to be 'nauseated' by it is tantamount to a confession that one is dead to all finer feeling. Having got the idea of dramatic stock devices— mistaken identity, the dead restored to life and similar tricks—they do not confuse the substituted-bedfellow business with Elizabethan or modern morals, but recognize at sight the myth or fairy-tale solution-by-stratagem of the accomplishment of the impossible task.[1]

1. Ibid., p. 556.

PART III
Interpretation

8

A DEFENCE OF
ALL'S WELL THAT ENDS WELL

THE history of *All's Well that Ends Well* reveals a range in interpretation beyond the usual latitude found in Shakespearian criticism.
The range is due to the general critical sentiment that the play lacks
artistic unity and clarity of form. Either the parts of the play could
not be blended coherently or the dramatist failed to order the parts
to a single end. Some critics have argued that Shakespeare has not
defined the issues of the plot; others, that he has not delineated his
characters within fixed, sharp lines; a third group, that he has not
established the tone; a fourth group points to the apparently disparate clash between realism and romance or fable and satire. The
consequence of this criticism has been an attempt to impose some
principle of reconciliation to clarify theme, to minimize discord. Too
frequently, the attempt had led to an inflexible interpretation based
upon a subjective response to a particular element in *All's Well*.
That element to which the critic, the director, or the actor was
attracted dictated the dramatic form which he superimposed upon
Shakespeare's 'incongruities'. These forms have been as varied as
Polonius's famous catalogue of dramatic types: 'tragedy, comedy,
history, pastoral, pastoral-comical, historical-pastoral, tragical-
historical, tragical-comical-historical-pastoral.' The critical and
theatrical history of *All's Well* may be categorized under six major
interpretations which have emphasized single aspects: farcical
comedy, sentimental romance, romantic fable, serious drama,
cynical satire, and a thematic dramatization. The emphasis of each
illustrates the subjective response of the critic.

If *All's Well* is treated as farcical comedy, the emphasis is upon
Parolles. He dominates the scenes in which he appears and sets the
mood for the remaining scenes. Thus, in the virginity duologue,
Helena is merely a foil for his ribald bantering. At court, Bertram
shows complete dependence upon his idol and imitates every gesture,
every expression; both Bertram and the young lords are exploited
by Parolles for the amusement of the audience. In the activities at
Florence, the episode with the drum overshadows Bertram's wooing.
The laughter provoked by each lie of the cringing braggart and by
each slur upon the embarrassed lords is sustained even after the

exposure by the irrepressible Parolles; he throws off his disgrace with a shrug. The trial scene, too, bears his stamp if he is brought on stage early, allowed some silent foolery, permitted to strut as a witness, and granted some farcical tears with the sentimental Lafeu at the conclusion. The comic tone is supported by the other characters as well. Helena, although overshadowed, relishes her witty repartees with Parolles and the Clown. She displays a roguish delight in the bed-trick and in the exposure of Bertram. Bertram, in ludicrous contrast, is made a passive, bewildered dupe of Parolles, Helena, and Diana. In such an interpretation, the King may be played as a buffoon, Lafeu as either a character of humours or a gay old courtier, the Widow and Diana as comical opportunists. The absurdities of the Clown convey a flippancy in him and a levity in the Countess.

If *All's Well* is interpreted as a sentimental romance, the emphasis is upon Helena and her search for requited love. Helena, 'loveliest of heroines', is meek, patient, and devoted throughout the pathetic trials of the plot. Her beloved is a handsome young nobleman whose arrogance must be tamed by her virtue. The King, the Countess, and Lafeu are endearing representatives of wise old age whose allegiance to the heroine is a blessing of her love. Their serenity is a hint of the quiet joy which awaits the end of Helena's anguish. Everything in the play is directed to the delicate sensibility of the heroine and to the bliss of the reconciliation. Consequently, the virginity duologue is omitted and references to the bed-trick are dropped. Parolles loses influence over Bertram, is ignored by Helena, and is severely chastened in the scene of his exposure. The role of the Clown may be eliminated.

The third major interpretation regards *All's Well* as a romantic fable in which the intrigues and deceptions of the plot are stressed. In order to bring out the traditional basis for the story, the movement of the play builds to three peaks, the cure of the King, the use of the bed-trick, and the redemption of Bertram. Each is accentuated as the fulfilment of a task which will lead to the resolution of the dilemma. That resolution may be accomplished by Helena as either a bright and confident clever wench or a miracle worker who moves blithely to her goal on heavenly wings. Great emphasis is placed upon the noble parentage of Bertram to indicate the innate virtue which will blossom when the wild weeds of youth have been plucked from his soul. Since psychological motivation is relatively unimportant, the other characters fill out the play as stock figures. Parolles, in particular, loses personality; he is merely the type-villain, the braggart-soldier and corrupter of youth. Throughout the play, the atmosphere of legend is served by heraldic pomp and symbolic action.

Realistic interpretations of *All's Well* include the serious drama and the cynical satire. Considered as the basis for a serious play, the plot may expose the moral problem of birth versus merit, the social problem which explores the legitimacy of female aggression, or the domestic problem of the unwanted wife. The problem is set against meditative speeches which analyse the contrasting characteristics of virtue and vice, inherited nobility and natural virtue, chastity and desire, youth and age. Helena may be cast as a philosopher whose objective view of life shows the necessity of her means to her end. On the one hand, she may be played as the angelic redeemer who rescues her beloved from himself; on the other, she may be a very human lover who wins an unattractive husband through feminine wiles. Bertram is played as a realistic young nobleman who understandably objects to an enforced marriage. Typical of youth in any age, he is fretful under restraint, scornful of responsibility, eager for military honour, and disposed to sexual misconduct. His surrender to Helena is effected through the pressures which bear upon his pliable personality. The tone of the serious drama is maintained throughout by the grave concern of the elder characters for Helena, by the despair of Parolles at his exposure, by the critical commentary of the sharp-tongued clown.

If the play is regarded as a satire, then cynicism infects the realism. The dark mood is established in the first scene by the stress on disease, old age, and death. At court there is obvious mutual contempt between youth and age, and contempt is the keynote of the relationships among the characters. Parolles is contemptuous of Lafeu, the lords of the King, Lavache of the Countess, Bertram of Helena, Lafeu of both Parolles and the Clown. Bertram scorns authority, and Helena scorns decorum. The heroine is ruthless in the pursuit of a husband. With a leer, she reveals her indelicacy as she muses on the loss of her virginity. Her lofty expressions of love are mocked by the immodesty of the bed-trick and the gross trial by which she exposes Bertram. She places him in an intolerable situation and gains only his disdain. Bertram is a satiric depiction of romantic hero; he is a snobbish, lecherous cad. The 'lovers' are surrounded by the despicable Parolles, the bitter Clown, the greedy Widow, the saucy Diana, and the intrusive elders. Irony runs through the principal action of the play and weaves the sub-plots to it. Despite the motives voiced by the characters, it is sexual passion which links Helena to Bertram and Bertram to Diana. The 'romance' of Lavache and Isbel parodies both links. Ironically, the mean value of the heroine's goal makes absurd her elaborate schemes. The success of those schemes is parodied in an obvious parallel: the exposure of

Parolles brings complete disgrace to him and a resigned acceptance
of mere existence; the exposure of Bertram brings complete disgrace
to the Count and an enforced acceptance of Helena.

The thematic approach to *All's Well* argues a fusion of realism and
romance through symbolism. The apparent incongruity of parts is
resolved with the unfolding symbol and type-character, with the
eliciting of that theme which prompted Shakespeare to write his
play. Several thematic interpretations have been proposed in the
history of *All's Well*, but two in particular recur. In the first, the
play is seen as a morality: Helena is divine grace, Bertram unredeemed man, Parolles vice personified, the King justice. Emphasis is
placed upon the binding authority of the King and the miraculous
power of the heroine. The speeches reveal a complexity of meaning
which has pertinence to all mankind; the verse has a quality of
incantation in the recitation. In the second thematic interpretation,
honour is made the unifying theme. As Bertram is the youthful war-
rior dedicated to war, Helena is the chaste handmaid of the goddess
Diana. Bertram must cope with the concept of honour in his sphere,
and Parolles is a symbol of the dishonour which may ensnare him.
Helena must reconcile honour and passion within the sphere of love,
and the earthly Diana accomplishes this for her. Male and female
concepts are brought into opposition by the contrary goals of hero
and heroine. In order to extend the theme of honour, symbolic
extremes are set up in the amoral Parolles and the uncompromising
Lavache. In the view of one critic, Helena, through her suffering,
purifies her concept of honour and redeems Bertram. For another
critic, there is no need of purification; Shakespeare has elevated
Helena above any one code, and she resolves all conflicts in the play
as a semi-divine creature.

Such constricted interpretations of *All's Well* have achieved at times
a unity of form, but only at the expense of Shakespeare's intention,
only by the distortion of his play. For, the very recurrence of six
major approaches throughout its history suggests a complexity which
cannot legitimately be reduced to a single focus. Clearly and
paradoxically for the critic, the history shows that there are elements
of farce, fable, melodrama, realism, satire, and symbolism in the
play. Criticism generally has insisted that these elements jar, that
only by the elimination of several can an artistic unity be imposed.
But the very essence of Shakespearian comedy is variety, a blending
of seemingly jarring worlds. In no Shakespearian comedy is there
that one-dimensional sketch of life which critics have argued for in
this play. Artistic coherence does not demand identical parts; it only
requires a congruity of parts within the structural pattern. If these

various literary modes coexist in *All's Well* with dramatic justification, then the play has a structural unity and an aesthetic effect
which critics have failed to expose. In an article which has application to this point, Mr. Clifford Leech warns against the tendency
in the modern theatre to impose a 'total coherence' upon Shakespeare's plays:

> Today a director will take preliminary thought for the significance of
> the play, will see to it that his actors, his scenery- and costume-designers,
> his electricians, and all the other contributors to the total effect, are
> sufficiently imbued with the same approach, the same interpretation. . . .
> Indeed, if one is to any extent to quarrel with the directors, one must
> question also some of the scholars: it is they who have frequently offered
> a 'meaning,' directly available and easily comprehensible, which the
> directors have felt it their duty to make plain. It is my purpose to suggest
> that, in the days before total 'meaning' was so forcibly underlined, the
> theatre may have been truer to the nature of a Shakespeare play.[1]

What is the nature of *All's Well that Ends Well?* Does that nature,
justify the coexistence of these various literary modes? We have three
pieces of evidence: the text of the play, its source, and a general
knowledge of Shakespeare's artistic methods as dramatist and poet.[2]
Presumably, the text provides the final version of a play prepared for
performance on stage. Variations between the text and its source
provide clues to the intention of the playwright; deliberate changes
suggest specific effects.[3] Shakespeare's general method as a dramatist
provides the foundation for particular judgements in this play. His
methods as a poet have significance in that his artistry in imagery and
symbol, in irony and vision, may surpass the immediate comprehension of a theatrical audience. I propose, then, to examine the
nature of *All's Well* on the basis of this evidence.

The first scene of *All's Well* is excellent exposition. Mood, plot,
character, and theme are deftly sketched in lines which, characteristic of Shakespeare's economy, serve several functions. The
Countess's mourning for her late husband and her melancholy at the
departure of her son, the regretful recollections of Gerard de Narbon
and his medical skill, the despairing talk of the King's disease, and
the tears of Helena establish a sombre mood. The deaths of the two
fathers set up a parallel between hero and heroine which is extended
throughout the play as the structural basis for the plot. Bertram and

1. Clifford Leech, 'The "Capability" of Shakespeare', *SQ*, xi (Spring 1960), 123.
2. The critical history of *All's Well* includes many analyses which are based upon other
material, particularly upon biographical details and philosophical outlook of the dramatist. Even were these not conjectural, they are still subservient to the primary evidence of
play, source, and general artistic method.
3. See n. 1, p. 178.

Helena are both wards: Bertram, we are told, will find in the King a second father; Helena has already been bequeathed to the Countess's overlooking. As the plot develops, both, ironically, object to their wardships. Because of her love for Bertram and her fear of acknowledging him as brother, Helena protests against the Countess's use of the title 'mother'. Because of his contempt for Helena, Bertram protests against the father-king's arrangement of his marriage. The marriage forces Bertram to flee from King and Court as a soldier; his desertion forces Helena to flee from Countess and home as a pilgrim. Only in the final scene are the young people reconciled to an acceptable relationship: Helena's 'O my dear mother' (v. iii. 313) is uttered not to her mother-guardian, but to her mother-in-law. In addition to the structural function in the plot, references to the deceased fathers characterize the children. The Countess describes Helena in terms of inherited and acquired virtues:

> I have those hopes of her good that her education promises her dispositions she inherits—which make fair gifts fairer; for where an unclean mind carries virtuous qualities, there commendations go with pity; they are virtues and traitors too. In her they are the better for their simpleness; she derives her honesty and achieves her goodness.   (i. i. 36–42)[1]

Helena is praised for perfecting those natural qualities which she has derived from her father. This characterization, moreover, elicits from the Countess a theme of the play: inherited qualities must be nurtured before goodness is achieved. If they are ruled by an 'unclean mind', they become traitors to our characters. The dramatic elaboration of this theme is the basis for the characterization of Bertram, who fails to cultivate his inherited nobility. Thus the Countess's praise of Helena is restated as disprise of Bertram in Act iv. In a thematic judgement upon mankind generally and Bertram specifically, the Second Lord defines us as 'merely our own traitors . . . so he [Bertram] that in this action contrives against his own nobility, in his proper stream o'erflows himself' (iv. iii. 20–24). At this early moment in the play, however, we have only to realize that Bertram has yet to develop inherited qualities, that he has yet to achieve that goodness which is Helena's. The terms of his conflict are made explicit in the hopeful farewell of his mother:

> Be thou bless'd, Bertram, and succeed thy father
> In manners as in shape! Thy blood and virtue
> Contend for empire in thee, and thy goodness
> Share with thy birthright.   (i. i. 57–60)

1. In his note to this passage, Mr. Hunter maintains, 'The antithesis between *mind* and *virtuous qualities* is between inherited nature and the qualities imparted by training. *Virtuous qualities* does not mean "fine moral qualities", but "the qualities of a virtuoso, skill, capacity, technical prowess" ' (p. 5).

The talk of death and departure characterize the elders as well. In 'the most beautiful old woman's part ever written', a widow's grief and a mother's anxiety are mollified by the dignity of the Countess, a 'breeding' which, as another instance of the thematic nurturing of inherited qualities, prefigures the potential maturity of Bertram. Lafeu's concerned responses to her demonstrate his warm amiability. His role as court councillor is implicit in his description of the King's virtue and of the disease which plagues the King. The description not only introduces the King but also prepares the audience for the first major action. For, the Countess's reply, 'Would for the king's sake, he [Gerard de Narbon] were living! I think it would be the death of king's disease' (I. i. 20–22), serves the plot in two ways. It suggests to the thoughtful Helena a means of fulfilling her love; as an exclamation of faith, it makes the consequent cure of the King more plausible to the audience.

The lines of the hero and heroine in the first part of the scene do little to extend the characterizations beyond the delineations of the Countess. In her only line, Helena hints at a motive of grief which is comprehensible only in her first soliloquy. Bertram's lines have been interpreted as indications of a vicious temperament, but this premature view of his personality destroys the dramatic effect of Helena's revelation of her love. His 'Madam, I desire your holy wishes' (I. i. 55) may be a brash interruption in the discussion of grief, but, even as such, it is no worse than might be expected from an 'unseason'd courtier' (I. i. 67). In itself, the line is indifferent; the suggestion of a faulty text, the insertion of stage business, or merely the intonation of the voice obscures Shakespeare's intention. Indifferent too are his parting words to Helena, 'Be comfortable to my mother, your mistress, and make much of her' (I. i. 73–74). But surely in this case, their indifference is the very point of the lines. There is neither warmth nor scorn. From Bertram's view, the departing son bids the household dependant to assist his mother. An indifferent Bertram intensifies the effect of Helena's soliloquy.

In a brief seventy-six lines, the exposition has prepared the audience for the play's primary interest, the seemingly futile love of Helena:

> O, were that all! I think not on my father,
> And these great tears grace his remembrance more
> Than those I shed for him. What was he like?
> I have forgot him; my imagination
> Carries no favour in't but Bertram's.
> I am undone; there is no living, none,
> If Bertram be away; 'twere all one

That I should love a bright particular star
And think to wed it, he is so above me.
In his bright radiance and collateral light
Must I be comforted, not in his sphere.
Th' ambition in my love thus plagues itself:
The hind that would be mated by the lion
Must die for love. 'Twas pretty, though a plague,
To see him every hour; to sit and draw
His arched brows, his hawking eye, his curls,
In our heart's table—heart too capable
Of every line and trick of his sweet favour.
But now he's gone, and my idolatrous fancy
Must sanctify his relics.   (i. i. 77–96)

In the revelation of her love, Helena sketches such an attractive
portrait of Bertram that the attention of the audience is redirected
to the hero. The rather indifferent young man who has just left the
stage now assumes a romantic image.[1] Shakespeare makes use of this
device throughout *All's Well*. More typical of Shakespeare's dramatic
technique is the introduction of a major character, through the
speech of another, before he appears on stage. In *All's Well*, however, Helena constantly follows Bertram on stage to interpret his
conduct through her love. The reason for the device is clear: the
reaction of the audience is not to be fixed by his conduct; rather, the
conduct is to be reconsidered in the light of her love. This device, of
course, does not prevent Shakespeare from foreshadowing the actions
of Bertram. Bertram's later objection to Helena because of class distinction gains some legitimacy in this speech by Helena's admission
that the difference in social rank constitutes an apparently insuperable
obstacle to her love. This kind of foreshadowing makes more acceptable the subsequent reconsideration demanded of the audience.

The entire first scene shows a gradual shift in mood from darkness
to light. The soliloquy is pivotal in that shift. (Helena's soliloquy
initiates a change in mood which brightens as the scene progresses.)
The sombre response to death is not to be extended into the play, and
Helena's dismissal of it, 'O, were that all! . . .' leads us into the world
of comedy. With Helena, we are not to be involved in death, in the
potentially tragic circumstances of the opening lines, but in life and
love.[2] The romantic exaggeration of her loss—the departure of
Bertram outweighs death—lightens the tone. Even a serious concern
for the futility of her love is undermined by the sentimental picture

1. Clearly, the actor who plays Bertram must be physically attractive. A handsome
young hero not only explains his appeal to Helena and Diana but also compensates
somewhat for the defect in his personality.   2. See n. 2, p. 178.

which Helena draws of herself sketching Bertram's features in her heart. In the same spirit of young love is her worshipful 'my idolatrous fancy / Must sanctify his relics'. Both imagery and diction reinforce the shift in mood. Images of death and darkness yield to 'bright particular star' and 'Bright radiance and collateral light'. The Countess's 'I bury a second husband' is now vitalized in Helena's:

> The hind that would be mated by the lion
> Must die for love.

As a striking instance of Shakespearian compression, the sentence not only contributes to the mood, not only defines the distinctive quality of the love and Helena's awareness of it, but also foreshadows the plot on two levels. On the denotative level of 'die', Helena is mated to Bertram, then feigns death, and finally wins him; on the sexually connotative level of 'die', Helena is mated to Bertram, but wins him only after the 'death' of sexual union.

The soliloquy is interrupted by the entrance of Parolles, and the comic mood shines more brightly. For Parolles is colourful and alluring:

> Who comes here?
> One that goes with him; I love him for his sake,
> And yet I know him a notorious liar,
> Think him a great way fool, solely a coward;
> Yet these fix'd evils sit so fit in him
> That they take place when virtue's steely bones
> Looks bleak i' th' cold wind; withal, full oft we see
> Cold wisdom waiting on superfluous folly.
>
> (I. i. 97–103)

In a choral role, Helena, who has just delineated Bertram for the audience, now indicates the intended response to Parolles. Although he has serious faults, we are not to consider them seriously. In fact, in the world of comedy, these faults 'sit so fit' in him that the absurdity of the character dismisses any moral judgement. Other evidence supports his attractiveness. Parolles mixes freely with the other young lords at court and appears to deceive them temporarily (II. i); the First Lord attributes a seductive charm to him (III. ii. 90–91); and, even Lafeu admits the disgraced braggart into his household (v. ii. 49–51). Helena's assessment of Parolles establishes a basis for the justification of Bertram. The structural link between Bertram and Parolles is made later, but Helena's acceptance of the vices of the braggart anticipates her willingness to accept the faults of her beloved. Although Helena's motivation is love, the contributing congeniality of Parolles must surely be matched or surpassed by the external charm of Bertram. Until his defiance of the King, there is nothing in the text to support a disagreeable Bertram. He is escorted to Court by the King's chief adviser, welcomed affectionately by the King, and is adopted as a comrade by the other lords. After his defiance, he is still received warmly wherever he goes. He is commissioned general of the troop by the Duke of Florence, praised by the Widow and her neighbour, and is attractive to Diana. He is readily forgiven by the Countess, the King, and Lafeu; Lafeu's daughter is willing to marry him. Most important, his appeal is essential to Helena's love. In this speech, Shakespeare paints the broad stripes of Parolles's personality as a hint of the finer lines in Bertram.

There is little need to justify the humour of the virginity repartee which follows. It has a comic appeal for the modern audience as well as the Elizabethan, if not for the Victorian. What has been obscured in the argument over propriety, however, is the structural function of the duologue.[1] Just prior to it in her first soliloquy, Helena has expressed the futility of her love; just after it in her second soliloquy, she resolves to fulfill her love. What happens between these two speeches must account for the difference in attitude. In the interim, Parolles has engaged Helena in a typically Elizabethan wordplay upon the term virginity. How does Helena react? At first, she falls in with his banter. To his question, 'Are you meditating on virginity?' she poses a question which will feed the exchange, 'Man is enemy to virginity; how may we barricado it against him?' The question and her next few replies serve the comedy, but we note that there is little interchange thereafter. Parolles dominates the stage, delights the audience with his argument against virginity. Meanwhile, the topic has dropped Helena into a reverie which links her two soliloquies. Parolles's first exclamation, 'Away with't!' intrudes upon her thoughts and her answer reflects the first soliloquy, 'I will stand for't a little, though therefore I die a virgin.' After another exhortation, his second exclamation, 'Away with't!' intrudes again, but this revealing reply foreshadows her second soliloquy, 'How might one do, sir, to lose it to her own liking?' The singular, personal form of both lines contrasts with Helena's general applications to virgins at the beginning of the duologue.

There are several ironies in the exchange between Parolles and Helena. The couching of the discussion in military terms is natural to the braggart-soldier, but the assault of man and the barricade of woman are reversed in Bertram and Helena. It is Bertram who flees before the offer of Helena; moreover, he prefers war to a conquest of

---

1. Mr. Hunter mentions the structural function but relates it to the virginity theme; for his interpretations of the function, see pp. xli–xliii.

her virginity. It is ironic that Parolles prompts the plan that leads to his young master's flight. So too, his urging, 'Out with't! Within the year it will make itself two' is actualized in an 'increase' which brings Bertram to accept his wife. There is irony in that Parolles assists Helena in the loss of her virginity, for he acts as pander between Bertram and Diana. The duologue, although many critics have insisted to the contrary, is demonstrably not an interpolation.

Editors have generally agreed that the speech of Helena's which follows shows signs of textual corruption because of its abrupt shifts, the ambiguity in its second line, and its obscure dramatic function:

> Not my virginity; yet . . .
> There shall your master have a thousand loves,
> A mother, and a mistress, and a friend,
> A phoenix, captain, and an enemy,
> A guide, a goddess, and a sovereign,
> A counsellor, a traitress, and a dear;
> His humble ambition, proud humility,
> His jarring-concord, and his discord-dulcet,
> His faith, his sweet disaster; with a world
> Of pretty, fond, adoptious christendoms
> That blinking Cupid gossips. Now shall he—
> I know not what he shall. God send him well!
> The court's a learning-place, and he is one—
>   (I. i. 161–73)

Mr. Hunter is hesitant to concede a textual corruption and annotates the lines to suggest a pattern of continuity. Helena is 'fooling the time'; she uses abrupt transitions to conceal her deeper meanings from Parolles. The annotation, however, raises a problem for the actress who must convey these deeper meanings to the audience while she conceals them from Parolles. I believe that a restoration of the first line as it appears in the First Folio may make the speech intelligible and prompt a solution to the actress. The Folio reads, 'Not my virginity yet:'. Literally, the line is a satisfactory answer to Parolles's question, 'Will you anything with it?' If the line is delivered in the same distracted manner as I have suggested for the duologue, with a slight stress upon 'yet', it likewise reveals to the audience what has absorbed Helena—the formulation of a plan which involves an action precedent to the loss of virginity, a plan which is made explicit in the second soliloquy, the cure of the king as a remedy for her love. The vocalization of her thought before Parolles startles Helena, however, and she quickly redirects the conversation. The redirection is marked stylistically by a shift from prose to verse. With a gesture that indicates the Court, or at least the departure of Parolles and Bertram (Parolles might very well have set down baggage to which Helena points), Helena engages Parolles in courtly, fashionable talk of love and its conceits. Eager for a new line of wordplay, Parolles, amused, waits to reply. When Helena places Bertram in this love cult, however, her own feelings break over this witty patter and she cannot continue, 'Now shall he—I know not what he shall.' Her awareness that 'The court's a learning-place, and he is one—' frightens her. The recital of love titles which were meant to conceal the hint of the first line has instead built up an anxiety which strengthens her reason for action. Her anxiety is apparent even to Parolles, who responds not with banter, not with a bawdy analysis of love at court, but with unaffected questions that seek an explanation. Helena's reply is a riddle to Parolles but it conveys to the audience her desire that her love might manifest itself tangibly to Bertram. The entrance of the Page cuts off further questions and the scene falls back into prose.

The exchange adds credibility to the love of Helena and to the later developments of the plot. Helena recognizes traits in Bertram which make him easy prey for courtly fashions and courtly love. Despite these traits and the anxiety which they arouse in her, she determines to win him. Her insight and her acceptance prepare the audience for Bertram's conduct and weaken any condemnation of him.

The interruption by the Page marks a return to the bantering style at the beginning of the virginity duologue. Her quick retorts illustrate the wit and zest by which Helena easily overcomes Parolles, as she did not do when distracted by her own thoughts. Her jests underscore the braggart's cowardice which will be exposed later. As Helena knows Bertram, so she knows Parolles. In fact, it is she, not Lafeu as so many critics argue, who is the first to see through him.

The scene ends with Helena's second soliloquy in which she reveals her resolution to win Bertram and hints at the King's disease as the means. Her thoughts and images link this soliloquy closely to the first. If earlier she had sighed, 'I am undone', she now decides, 'Our remedies oft in ourselves do lie.' If she had regretted the distance which made Bertram a 'bright particular star', she now decides, 'the fated sky / Gives us free scope'. If she had blamed the ambition in her love 'which thus plagues itself', she now asks, 'What power is it that mounts my love so high?' and suggests nature as the answer. If she had decided earlier that 'the hind that would be mated by the lion / Must die for love', she now sees that only those 'who weigh their pain in sense' refuse the attempt. The hind and lion have now become 'like likes'. Is Helena now the aggressive female condemned by so many critics?

I do not think so. What has Shakespeare done, what can the actress do, to protect Helena during this transformation? First, Shakespeare has tied these soliloquies together so that the second recalls the first, and the actress can reinforce this by posture and gesture. The Helena of the second soliloquy recalls the loving maiden of whom we all approved in the first soliloquy. Second, Shakespeare has made Parolles the unwitting source of the idea; through his bawdiness, as a scapegoat, he carries away any reproach which decorum might dictate. Third, Helena's introductory association of Parolles with Bertram gives a psychological validity to her absorption in Bertram while Parolles jests about virginity. Fourth, because of that absorption, Shakespeare preserves her indecorous participation in ribaldry. While Parolles roguishly delights the audience with his wordplay, Helena indifferently serves as a foil to his wit and ponders the problem of her love. Finally, Shakespeare softens her resolution in the soliloquy by couching it in a general romantic 'truth':

> Who ever strove
> To show her merit that did miss her love?
> (I. i. 222–3)

The structure of *All's Well* displays superb craftsmanship; as so often in the plays of Shakespeare, balance is the principle of construction. The second scene creates the background for the hero's interest—military honours and the adventures of war; the third scene promotes Helena's interest—her love for Bertram. The interview at Court gains credit for Bertram through the King's eulogy of the deceased Count Rousillon. The commendation of the Countess and the tenderness of the scene at Rousillon gather sympathy for Helena. The King concludes his scene by expressing his regard for Bertram, 'My son's no dearer' (I. ii. 76); the Countess ends the third scene with full approval of her ward:

> and be sure of this,
> What I can help thee to, thou shalt not miss.
> (I. iii. 250–1)

Shakespeare has begun both scenes along lines which quite similarly introduce the sub-plots. The second scene opens with a sketchy discussion of the Florentine war. Some critics have seen in the vagueness of the reports a cynical attitude on the part of the dramatist to the war, and consequently to masculine poses of honour. Rather, the vagueness indicates to the audience its degree of concern. We are not to bother about the merits of the opposing forces, nor about the tragic potential of war, for the dramatic function of the

Florentine battle is merely setting for the involvements of Bertram and the exposure of Parolles. The third scene begins with the Clown's request for permission to marry, but this too we are not to take seriously. The request touches off the customary parody of the main plot by the Shakespearian clown. His interview with the Countess just prior to Helena's interview reminds us of the mimicry between Prince Hal and Falstaff which anticipates Hal's audience with his father in *1 Henry IV*. The effect is much the same: the comic burlesque heightens the dramatic intensity but undermines the tragic potential of the ensuing confrontation. The Clown presents his request in the form of an old proverb, 'Service is no heritage', which expresses Helena's present state. His paraphrase however, 'and I think I shall never have the blessing of God till I have issue a' my body', looks ahead to Helena's state after Bertram has decreed his conditions. We have already heard the sweet strains of Helena's love in her soliloquies; soon, that love will be strengthened by divine support. The Clown explains his love simply as the needs of his body and adds 'other holy reasons, such as they are' (i. iii. 30–31). Among these holy reasons, the Clown includes, 'I do marry that I may repent', and his words will echo in the last scene of the play when Bertram falls to his knees before Helena. The Clown's eager acceptance of his wife's 'friends' looks back to Helena's affection for Parolles and forward to the parasite's betrayal of that affection. Lavache amusingly formulates a theme of the play when he says, 'That man should be at woman's command, and yet no hurt done' (i. iii. 89–90). In its context, it is an admission that he has served under the command of the Countess and has survived through her kindness. As a theme, it announces that no harm shall come to the hero through the manipulations of the heroine. We are told, in effect, that *All's Well* is a comedy. His line is paraphrased throughout the play; in her interview with the Countess, Helena protests:

> Be not offended, for it hurts not him
> That he is lov'd of me. (i. iii. 191–2)

If the phrasing by the Clown has a sexual connotation as some editors believe, there is still significance to the main plot. If 'hurt' connotes the loss of virginity, then Bertram who 'should be at woman's command' upon the authority of the King fulfills the Clown's 'no hurt done' by his flight from Helena. If 'hurt' connotes the loss of chastity, the 'command' of Helena in substituting herself, his lawful wife, in the attempted seduction of Diana preserves both Bertram and Diana from 'hurt'.

Yet, to regard the Clown as a choral commentator upon the love of Helena and the major plot, to ascribe his cynicism to Shakespeare's philosophy, is to ignore the text and the role of the clown in the plays. Quite clearly, the Clown uses marriage as a means to sensual satisfaction; Helena uses the loss of virginity as a means to gain her 'bright particular star'. The critic who confuses the two reveals his own cynicism, not Shakespeare's. Lavache's reasons for marrying Isbel no more tarnish the love of Helena than the same reasons of Touchstone for marrying Audrey tarnish the love of Rosalind. Touchstone in *As You Like It*, Feste in *Twelfth Night*, Lucio in *Measure for Measure*, Thersites in *Troilus and Cressida*, Lavache in *All's Well*, all comment upon life with varying degrees of cynicism. To identify the Fool with the dramatist is to reduce the vision of Shakespeare to a single focus.

Particularly illustrative of the parallel development in these two scenes are the speeches of the Countess and the King. Before the entrance of Helena, the Countess comments, 'Her father bequeath'd her to me' and prepares the audience for Helena's success, 'She herself, without other advantage, may lawfully make title to as much love as she finds; there is more owing her than is paid, and more shall be paid her than she'll demand' (I. iii. 97–101). At the entrance of Bertram, the King comments, 'Youth, thou bear'st thy father's face' and prepares the audience for Bertram's conflict, 'Thy father's moral parts / Mayest thou inherit too!' (I. ii. 19–22). As the King then recalls his own youth, he describes Bertram's father as the greatest of soldiers and the humblest of men. The King has just noted the physical identification of father and son; his words now anticipate the military reputation which Bertram is to achieve as general of the troop and justify the final submission of Bertram when he fits the moral image of his father. So too, the Countess's recollection of her youth and 'love's strong passion' (I. iii. 123–31) serves as anticipation of Helena's plan and justification for her love. The confession of that love is preceded by Helena's amusing opposition to the term 'mother'; Bertram's struggle to become his father's son is lightly and ironically parodied in Helena's refusal to remain her adopted mother's daughter. As the King has prepared us for Bertram's success in battle, the Countess's response to Helena's confession prepares us for her successful cure of the King:

> Why, Helen, thou shalt have my leave and love,
> Means and attendants, and my loving greetings
> To those of mine in Court. I'll stay at home
> And pray God's blessing into thy attempt.
>   (I. iii. 246–9)

A touching similarity in the speeches of the King and Countess is their simple expression of humility and insight: Royalty realizes, 'I fill a place, I know't' (I. ii. 69), and Wisdom recalls, 'Even so it was with me when I was young' (I. iii. 123).

At the end of Act I, what did the 'first-night' audience make of *All's Well that Ends Well?* An attractive young lord departs fondly but impatiently from his charming mother. He sets out for adventure and manhood with experience and folly as companions. He arrives at Court and is greeted affectionately by his benevolent King. Meanwhile, he is loved without his knowledge by a virtuous dependant in his household. She is deeply and seemingly futilely in love with him. Despite the barrier of rank, she elects to risk all dangers to win him. She knows that she has the support of his mother and she senses the approval of heaven (I. iii. 237–41). Has not Shakespeare led his audience to three questions which excited its suspense: in terms of romance, will the beautiful and virtuous maiden win her nobleman? in terms of a morality tradition, will the noble youth be led by experience or folly? in terms of philosophical theme, can virtue be equated with nobility of birth?

That Shakespeare has intended romance at this point of his play may be demonstrated by the changes which he has made in Boccaccio's rather realistic Giletta, the source-counterpart for Helena. Giletta has not seen Beltramo for a number of years; she has come of age, is independently wealthy, and has many suitors. The report of Beltramo's comeliness, however, increases her ardour for him, and she seeks a method of escaping the surveillance of her kinsmen to pursue her love. On her arrival in Paris, she visits Beltramo before she cures the King. Although she tells the King that God will aid her in the cure, she has already diagnosed the disease as one which her father's medicine will easily cure. By eliminating the kinsfolk and wealth, Shakespeare has made his heroine more dependent upon her virtue and has heightened the romantic barrier between heroine and hero. By omitting the rival suitors and reducing Helena's age, Shakespeare has preserved the youthful innocence of her love. Giletta, capable, knowledgeable, self-sufficient, wins her husband through the force of her personality. Helena performs much the same deeds, but always with greater hesitation, greater risk, and greater humility. Helena is motivated by the irrepressible force of young love which ignores decorum as the simple directness of a child ignores it. Giletta, confident of her power, will compound medicine to heal the King; Helena, confident of her love, will call upon heaven to cure him. Boccaccio makes realistic the clever wench of fable. Shakespeare, on the contrary, fashions his heroine out of romantic aspirations and places his realism elsewhere in the play.

The second act of *All's Well* is crowded with action. As the young lords depart for battle, Bertram is denied permission to join them in the Florentine war. Helena, introduced to the King by Lafeu, convinces the King of her remedy and cures his disease. As her reward, she chooses Bertram for her husband. Bertram protests, and, in so doing, arouses the anger of his king. Under the force of that anger, Bertram yields, but plots to free himself from his 'clog'. The act ends with Bertram's preparations for Florence and Helena's dismissal to Rousillon. Shakespeare moves here with the speed and suspense which we associate with his pace in *Othello*. Yet, swift pacing does not imply careless writing as some critics have suggested about this play. Complications of plot and character are anticipated with a sure artistic touch from the opening lines of the act. In his farewell to the lords as they leave for war, the King hints at his own predisposition for cure:

> and yet my heart
> Will not confess he owes the malady
> That doth my life besiege.
>
> (II. i. 8–10)

His plea, 'be you sons / Of worthy Frenchmen' (II. i. 11–12), recalls the military skill of Bertram's father which the King has previously praised and again adds plausibility to the role which Bertram will play in the Florentine wars. The audience is forewarned about the attempted seduction of Diana in the King's jocular charge:

> Those girls of Italy, take heed of them;
> They say our French lack language to deny
> If they demand; beware of being captives
> Before you serve.   (II. i. 19–22)

The forewarning operates on several levels. Literally, the King is expressing an Elizabethan commonplace about Italian girls and so draws empathy from the audience for the young lords and indirectly for Bertram. The King's amusement mitigates the later conduct of Bertram. There is a double irony in the lines, however, on a second level. Immediately, it is not the 'girls of Italy' whom Bertram must heed, but Helena. In the encounter with the King, Bertram 'lacks language' to deny what is demanded of him. He marries Helena and so would be captive before he serves. When he flees from this servitude, ironically it is Diana who must take heed of him. It is he who now demands and demands so attractively that she 'lacks language' to refuse. It is Diana who must beware of being a captive. But once the words of the King are applied to the major plot, to Helena's conspiracy with Diana to win Bertram, they take on a satiric significance. Bertram merely imagines himself to be the aggressor, and we return to the literal level with a new aptness. Bertram fails to take heed of 'those girls of Italy' (Diana-Helena), fails to deny what Helena implicitly demands of him (fulfilment of his own conditions), and is taken captive by her. The marvellous complexity of the lines is heightened by Shakespeare's continued employment of the language of war in a discussion of love.[1] The scene acts both as a spur to the keen spirit of the hero and as a satirical tempering of that spirit.

The central incident of the act, Bertram's defiance of the King, adds new dimensions to the major characters and increases our interest in them. Bertram's faults, anticipated by the Countess in her advice to her son and feared by Helena as she had imagined Bertram at court, burst out in his proud indignation. The resolution of Helena melts away as she shyly withdraws her suit. The King, incensed, imposes a command upon Bertram which echoes the powerful voice of his youth. Lafeu reveals a deeper humanity in his pity for Helena. At this moment of crisis, the new dimension in each character stands out against the delineations of preceding scenes and draws new sympathies from the audience. The King had been sportive with the departing lords, merry with Lafeu, kind to Helena; now his anger at Bertram's defiance strikes the audience as righteous. Where Lafeu had been jovial, now his pained embarrassment at the situation of Helena is shared by the audience. Helena had spoken persuasively and determinedly to the King before his cure; now, she engages the sympathy of all with her humble plea:

> That you are well restor'd, my lord, I'm glad.
> Let the rest go. (II. iii. 147–8)

Bertram's petulant temper and ignoble conduct are strong contrasts to his yearnings for military honour. But the link between these two attitudes has been represented by his choice of Folly rather than Experience. From the beginning of Act II, Bertram has fallen under the influence of Parolles and his absurd advice.[2]

With a plot rooted in folk-lore, Shakespeare turned back for the composition of *All's Well* to an earlier tradition in the theatre, to the morality play, for patterns which might serve his plot. Bertram has an allegorical pale as he sets out for life and adventure between Lafeu and Parolles. He makes the customary morality-choice of folly and adopts Parolles as his companion. Folly is exposed in the drum scene. Bertram is redeemed at the end of the play. But too much occurs between these events, especially between the exposure of

---

1. For an interpretation of the imagery as satire, see Clifford Leech's 'The Theme of Ambition in "All's Well that Ends Well"', *ELH*, xxi (March 1954), 17–29.
2. See II. i. 47–59.

Parolles and the redemption of Bertram, for the critic to insist upon
All's Well as a morality play. The play is not an allegory in that
Shakespeare does not sustain the pattern as our major interest. The
morality pattern in *All's Well* is merely a familiar convention
designed to clarify plot and character. It works in much the same way
with Helena. Throughout her interview with the King and the
resultant cure, we are given an indefinable impression that her love
is linked with Divinity, that she is an agent for the miraculous, that
heaven assists in the cure of the King as a redemptive means for
Bertram. The effect of the incantation and the oblique references to
the help of heaven imply a supernatural force. Again, however, the
pattern is kept vague; the impression never deepens as the motif of
the play. It simply strengthens what Shakespeare wishes to establish;
the cure of the King is a prefiguration of the cure of Bertram.

To emphasize this, Shakespeare not only employs a morality pattern but also interweaves images, ideas, and deeds which have significance for both cures. As Helena paraphrased the Clown's 'no
hurt done' in her confession of love to the Countess, so in her interview with the King she pleads:

> What I can do can do no hurt to try,
> Since you set up your rest 'gainst remedy.
> (II. i. 133–4)

The conclusion to this speech describes the desperate plights of both
Helena and the King, but the hope which she offers to the King is an
expression of faith in her own love:

> Oft expectation fails, and most there
> Where most it promises, and oft it hits
> Where hope is coldest and despair most fits.
> (II. i. 141–3)

The King's first refusal of Helena's aid foreshadows Bertram's first
rejection of her love. Helena's insistence upon the help of heaven
recalls the religious imagery in her confession of love and anticipates
the redemption of Bertram (II. i. 147–57). When the King asks what
she will risk, Helena replies in terms which identify the cure of the
King with her love:

> Tax of impudence,
> A strumpet's boldness, a divulged shame,
> Traduc'd by odious ballads; my maiden's name
> Sear'd otherwise; ne worse of worst, extended
> With vildest torture, let my life be ended.
> (II. i. 169–73)

In Boccaccio, Giletta simply says, 'If I do not heale you within these

eight dayes, let me be burnt' (p. 147). Helena's reply is an admission
that the cure of the King is a means to her love. If the means fail, she
will accept her pursuit of Bertram as 'a strumpet's boldness'. Helena
is testing heaven as much as the King; the cure of the King is justification of her love. The King submits to Helena's cure when he
recognizes her merit and realizes what she is willing to risk:

> Thy life is dear, for all that life can rate
> Worth name of life in thee hath estimate:
> Youth, beauty, wisdom, courage—all
> That happiness and prime can happy call.
>   (II. i. 178–81)

Bertram must come to the same recognition of merit and realization
of what Helena has risked before he submits to her. The legitimacy
of Helena's claim to a husband as her reward is averred when she
assures the King:

> But such a one, thy vassal, whom I know
> Is free for me to ask, thee to bestow.
>   (II. i. 198–9)

The King's response is an expression of faith in Helena; nevertheless,
his conclusion is analogous to the conditions of Bertram's letter:

> If thou proceed
> As high as word, my deed shall match thy deed.
>   (II. i. 208–9)

If Helena can turn her words into action, the King's deed shall
match hers; in his letter, Bertram promises to match Helena's love,
if she can turn her vows of love into deed by the fulfilment of his
conditions.

The miraculous in this scene should be stressed in the production
of *All's Well*. Shakespeare obviously intended this: he has changed
his source to strengthen the intervention of heaven; he has suggested
the supernatural through incantation; he has linked both cures
through religious imagery. Through the miraculous in this scene, the
final reform of Bertram is more acceptable. The miraculous, however, is not our dominant interest. After the cure of the King, no
concern for it in itself remains, and we turn our attention, as Shakespeare directs it, to the quite human and psychologically intriguing
responses of Bertram and Helena to each other.

The persuasion of the King is followed by the comic conversation
between the Countess and the Clown. This brief scene has often been
dismissed as a time-server in the crowded action of Act II. It is a time-
server; it passes the time in which the cure is being effected. The
question, however, is not whether the function of the scene is the

passage of time, but why Shakespeare chose this particular form for accomplishing his effect. The scene adds depth to several elements of *All's Well*. First, it continues the interesting delineation of the Clown and supports a personality more complex than that necessary for parody. Perhaps Kittredge offered the best insight into that personality when he described the Clown as a country fellow, a handy man about the palace (IV. v. 53–56), who was the favourite of the former Count and, as such, enjoyed great freedom.[1] He is now tolerated by the Countess out of love for her husband as Parolles is tolerated by Helena. Shakespeare may well have had in mind a contrast to Touchstone as he developed Lavache. As Touchstone is the courtly jester who goes to the country, Lavache is the country clown who is sent to Court. Touchstone woos a country maiden and decides to wed her; Lavache loses interest in his country maiden and forsakes her after he has been to Court. Touchstone displays the affected skill of the rhetorician before the rustic; Lavache expounds homely moralities before the lord, Lafeu. Touchstone serves as a parody of his mistress's love; Lavache, in his falling prey to the affectations of court and in his rejection of Isbel, serves as a parody of his young master. Helena has warned, 'The court's a learning-place.'

Apart from the characterization of the Clown and, of course, the comic appeal of the scene, the dialogue between the Countess and Lavache is employed by Shakespeare as a justification of Helena. If we condemn Helena for her repartee with Parolles, we miss the point here where the venerable Countess, Helena's 'mother', jests with the Clown. As I have noted, the reasons for the tolerant attitudes of both women are the loves which they bear. The justification is clearly accentuated when the Countess agrees to the foolery, 'To be young again, if **we** could, I will be a fool in question, hoping to be the wiser by your answer' (II. ii. 37–38). In retrospect, we see that the young Helena served as a fool to the wit of Parolles and grew wiser in the pursuit of her love. That Shakespeare intended the identification is demonstrated by the verbal echoes. The Countess's 'To be young again' recalls the recollection of her youth as she mused on Helena's love. The Clown urges her to the foolery with the iterative sentiment, 'it shall do you no harm to learn' (II. ii. 35–36). The thematic implication of service likewise makes an impression upon an audience even if it misses all the ramifications of the Clown's, 'I see things may serve long, but not serve ever' (II. ii. 53). There is a structural parallel as well in that Parolles and Lavache both end their repartees with their departures for court.

1. I am indebted to Kittredge's lecture notes on the play as prepared by Professor Arthur Colby Sprague.

In the swift movement of the Elizabethan theatre, the comedy of the Clown with his single answer to all demands passes immediately to the verbosity of Lafeu and Parolles. Both these comic interludes lighten the mood in order to lessen the pain of Helena's impending sorrow. Yet again, Shakespeare accomplishes more than one effect. Out of the comic whirlwind of words emerges an important idea— the cure of the King is miraculous. Heaven has given its approval to Helena's love.[1] The legitimacy of Helena's claim is made absolute in the strong language of the King:

> Fair maid, send forth thine eye. This youthful parcel
> Of noble bachelors stand at my bestowing,
> O'er whom both sovereign power and father's voice
> I have to use. Thy frank election make;
> Thou hast power to choose, and they none to forsake.
>   (II. iii. 52–56)

There is no question of Helena's position: the Countess, the King, and Heaven have given their blessing.

Confronted with the choice, Helena hesitates to act. Her speech, 'I am a simple maid . . .' (II. iii. 66–72) with its plea, 'Please it your majesty, I have done already', expresses her reluctance with such humility and delicacy that the audience shares her fears. When the King urges her to her choice, she determines:

> Now, Dian, from thy altar do I fly,
> And to imperial Love, that god most high
> Do my sighs stream.   (II. iii. 74–76)

In two brief speeches, in two brief moments, Shakespeare has given the epitome of Helena's character and the conflict within her. We have been prepared for the terms of that conflict by the two soliloquies in Act I. In the first soliloquy and in her hesitation here, we see her virtue manifested simply and modestly. We see those qualities which win her the love of all the characters in the play. In the second soliloquy and in the speech quoted above, we see that virtue infused by the power of love. We see a strength which breaks the natural restraints of her personality. In religious imagery borrowed from the pagans (Christian images would have been unseemly), Helena subdues her modesty and flies to love.[2] To mistake Helena's resolution as aggressiveness is to ignore Shakespeare's technique and to misunderstand human nature. Helena's use of personification conveys with simplicity and beauty the emotion which is experienced by every maiden as she hesitatingly chooses the passion of love.

1. See n. 3, p. 178.
2. The imagery continues to associate Helena's love with divine approval. The cure of the King is expressed through Christian imagery; the fulfilment of love is expressed through pagan imagery.

Most critics have fallen in with Dr. Johnson's position on the reactions of the young lords to Helena's suit. The text gives but brief replies as she approaches each. More explicit comments are added by Lafeu, but these seem to contradict the dialogue between Helena and each lord. The conventional view insists that the lords are eager to marry Helena and that Lafeu, supposedly at some distance, misinterprets their replies as refusals. The lines of the young men, however, are ambiguous courtesies. On stage they may be defined by gesture and facial expressions as enthusiastic assents on the one hand or merely decorous acquiescences to a favourite of the King on the other hand. If the lords are interpreted as eager for the match, then Lafeu must misunderstand the action—but for what dramatic effect? His misunderstanding fails to build suspense since the audience hears the exchanges between Helena and the courtiers. It fails to create irony, for irony follows only if Lafeu mistakenly expects Bertram to accept the suit. In any case, Lafeu's lines sustain sympathy for Helena, but a misunderstanding of the lords' enthusiasm diminishes the need for sympathy; the need is more urgent if the youths are reluctant to marry her. Despite the authority of Dr. Johnson, I believe that there is stronger dramatic justification for reading Lafeu's lines as the stage action. Lafeu's function throughout the scene is to comment upon the action and to join the king in reinforcing Helena's position. It is not the practice of Shakespeare to allow his commentator to misinterpret the action with no indication in the text.[1] Even stranger in this approach is that the discredited Lafeu then anticipates Bertram's refusal! Dr. Johnson's interpretation demands that Lafeu err in the first instances which he is watching and yet predict the last. Both dramatic logic and dramatic effect are served if Lafeu correctly assesses the young lords' reluctance and correctly forecasts Bertram's rejection. In the first instance, Lafeu is a choral character who vocalizes our feelings for Helena; in the second instance, he tempers our shock by preparing us for Bertram's harsh refusal.

From another point of view, there is no reason why the lords should be anxious to marry Helena. Bertram, at least, has experienced her kindness, if not appreciated it. To the other youth, Helena is simply an unknown of inferior rank to whom marriage can scarcely signify advancement. To the Elizabethans, the disinclination of the courtiers would have been understandable; to modern audiences, romantic enthusiasm must be accepted as merely dramatic convention. By making the lords guardedly reluctant, Shakespeare prevents

---

1. See n. 4, p. 178.

a total imbalance in a scene heavily weighed for Helena. The reluctance of the lords gives some limited support to Bertram's case. As an additional dramatic gain, the coolness of the lords stages the dilemma which the audience sees in Helena's love and which she herself expressed in her first soliloquy. This is the source of the plot's suspense. Will Bertram accept as his wife a dependent from his own household? As the other courtiers bow graciously and relievedly away, the audience's anxiety increases—as Lafeu's words express. As he does so often, Shakespeare exposes all sides of the dilemma.

Yet, the audience is prepared for its answer to the dilemma. Sympathy is not to be divided impartially between the hero and the heroine; it is owed to Helena. Lafeu fulfills his function as commentator and choral voice when he anticipates and scorns Bertram's reaction:

There's one grape yet. I am sure thy father drunk wine; but if thou be'st not an ass, I am a youth of fourteen; I have known thee already.

(II. iii. 99–101)

To Lafeu, a nobleman, Bertram's rejection of Helena will come not because of the youth's rank but in spite of it. Bertram has not yet profited from his parentage. He will act out of foolish immaturity. So he does when he refuses Helena on the grounds of rank alone. His position is undermined by the King's immediate offer:

'Tis only title thou disdain'st in her, the which I can build up.

(II. iii. 117–18)

That the King had the right to confer nobility upon Helena was a commonplace to the Elizabethans.[1] More emphatic for Helena's cause is the sermon upon honour which the King delivers to Bertram. In the clearest terms, he expounds the principle which the audience has heard as a theme from the beginning of the play:[2]

> that is honour's scorn
> Which challenges itself as honour's born
> And is not like the sire. Honours thrive
> When rather from our acts we them derive
> Than our foregoers.   (II. iii. 133–7)

The willingness of the King to elevate Helena in rank provides a fairy-tale solution to the dilemma of the plot. Bertram's stubborn refusal to accept the solution moves the play beyond the expectations of the audience and beyond its source. In Boccaccio, the King is loath

---

1. Curtis Brown Watson, *Shakespeare and the Renaissance Concept of Honor*, Princeton, 1960, pp. 183–4. See also Joel Hurstfield's *The Queen's Wards: Wardship and Marriage Under Elizabeth I*, London, 1958.
2. See n. 5, p. 179.

to grant Beltramo to Giletta. He forces her upon Beltramo because
he will not break his promise to her, but he does not change her
social status. Beltramo's objection to her, 'Will you then (sir) give me
a Phisition to wife?', remains valid and Beltramo calls upon heaven
to witness his right, 'It is not the pleasure of God that ever I should
in that wise bestow my selfe' (p. 147). In his play Shakespeare has
already set heaven on Helena's side; here, he concludes the King's
charge to Bertram with moral sanctions:

> As thou lov'st her
> Thy love's to me religious; else, does err.
> (II. iii. 182–3)

The problem, then, in *All's Well* is no longer the conflicting claims
of the loving dependant and the indifferent master. Love and right
are now set against contempt and error. Nevertheless, what had
begun as romance and what might have been resolved as fable does
not become a simple morality play. Shakespeare fixes the resolution
of the conflict not upon an abstraction of God's mercy, but upon the
psychological collapse of a vain young man.

The new terms of the conflict are dramatized by the responses of
both Helena and Bertram. Helena's few lines are a resignation of her
claim upon Bertram, a dissolution of the earlier conflict. The King,
however, raises the issue to a higher level, 'My honour's at the stake'
(II. iii. 149), and relieves Helena of the potentially aggressive insistence of Boccaccio's Giletta. Bertram's replies grow in petulancy, 'I
cannot love her nor will strive to do't' (II. iii. 145). The audience
grown aware that it is not rank, but Bertram's character, 'Proud,
scornful boy', which has created a new dilemma. This dilemma will
be resolved only when Bertram can convert his insincere 'Pardon, my
gracious lord' (II. iii. 167) into his humble plea for pardon at the
knees of Helena (V. ii. 302).

Immediately after Bertram's personality is revealed to the Court,
the exposure of Parolles begins. The superficial attraction of the
parasite is stripped away by the comically contemptuous attack of
Lafeu. In retrospect, both the structural pattern and the comedy
lighten the gravity of Bertram's defiance. The pattern is a common
device of Shakespeare to undercut the potential tragedy of a preceding or succeeding scene.[1] The confrontations of Bertram and the
King on the one hand and of Parolles and Lafeu on the other are
clearly parallel as indicated by the emphatic associations of Lafeu,
'Your lord and master did well to make his recantation' and 'Are
you companion to the Count Rossillion?' (II. iii. 186–95). Lafeu's
charge against Parolles reflects upon Bertram's offence, 'You are

1. See the discussion of the Clown and Falstaff above, p. 146.

more saucy with lords and honourable personages than the commission of your birth and virtue gives you heraldry' (II. iii. 256–8). The exit of Lafeu brings together on stage the two companions in folly. Despite the desperation of Bertram because of his marriage, the affected and ironically amusing greeting of Parolles maintains a comic tone, 'What's the matter, sweetheart?' (II. iii. 264). The childish conspiracy which grows out of their mutual frustration has not the cut of tragedy, nor of villainy. It is not viciousness but his immature concept of nobility that leads Bertram to exclaim:

> His present gift
> Shall furnish me to those Italian fields
> Where noble fellows strike. War is no strife
> To the dark house and the detested wife.
> (II. iii. 285–8)

The scene concludes with Parolles's humorous distortion of a proverb which replies to the Clown's 'no hurt done':

> A young man married is a man that's marr'd.
> (II. iii. 294)

The dismissal of Helena which ends the first part of *All's Well* is rich in echoes and foreshadowings. Helena, as the Countess had done, jests with the Clown, and the jests illustrate Shakespeare's continuing care in checking the dark potential of the plot. The entrance of Parolles recalls the Clown's warning about friends of the wife, for Helena says to Parolles, 'I hope, sir, that I have your good will to have mine own good fortune' (II. iv. 14–15). It is the friend of the husband in this instance who betrays the wife. The Clown, with more meaning than he intends, anticipates the drum scene, 'for many a man's tongue shakes out his master's undoing' (II. iv. 22–23) and defines its effect, 'and much fool may you find in you, even to the world's pleasure, and the increase of laughter' (II. iv. 33–35). In the presence of both the Clown and Parolles who earlier have commented upon the theme of woman's command and hurt, Helena asks, 'What more commands he?' (II. iv. 49). For the first time in the play, woman is at man's command and she will be hurt. Bertram's dismissal of Helena is handled with great dramatic skill. Shakespeare emphasizes Bertram's poor judgement before Helena enters. The hero defends Parolles against Lafeu's second attempt to expose the braggart.[1] As Bertram mistakes the folly of Parolles, so he mistakes the virtue of Helena. When Helena appears, Shakespeare preserves her from blame; she is entirely submissive to her husband's will.

---

1. Mr. Hunter objects to the Folio reading of II. v. 50 but Kittredge accepts the original line as indicating Bertram's indifference to Lafeu's reputation (ii. 52–53).

More surprising and yet quite natural, Bertram shows neither hostility nor contempt. How much more difficult would the reconciliation have been if Shakespeare had yielded to 'stagey excitement'. Instead, the warmly human and tenderly simple plea of Helena for a parting kiss excites Bertram to embarrassed irritation. The loving maiden and the abashed youth have led the audience far from fable. Psychological realism, ironic truth, and amusement are all served by Bertram's loud boast *after* Helena's exit:

> Go thou toward home, where I will never come
> Whilst I can shake my sword or hear the drum.
>   (II. v. 90–91)

In Act III, the revelation of the hero's intention produces the effects upon his mother and wife which we expect. The Countess is indignant and withdraws the title 'son' from him; Helena is despairing of her love. Shakespeare, however, cushions the condemnation of Bertram in several ways. Instead of a pathetic meeting between the two women, the playwright adds two French lords to the scene. Through them we hear that Bertram will receive great honours in war. With the support of their testimony, the Countess diverts her wrath upon Parolles and his evil influence. Furthermore, she entreats the lords to carry a message which serves as a clue to us, 'his sword can never win / The honour that he loses' (III. ii. 93–94). Finally, Shakespeare cuts short criticism of Bertram with Helena's third soliloquy in which we are made to see the hero through the loving eyes of the heroine. The speech is unique in this play in the extensive use of imagery. The reflective tone of the earlier soliloquies is swept aside by the vivid pictures of the terrified Helena. Images intensify the reality of Bertram's danger and Helena's fears; they heighten her selfless love and make creditable her self-exile. Where earlier she had feared the court as a learning place, she now chastises herself for driving Bertram from the 'sportive court, where thou / Wast shot at with fair eyes' (III. ii. 106–7). She imagines the harm which may befall him because he flees her 'command' and prefers her death to his harm in an image that recalls the mating of the hind with the lion:

> better 'twere
> I met the ravin lion when he roar'd
> With sharp constraint of hunger; better 'twere
> That all the miseries which nature owes
> Were mine at once.   (III. ii. 116–20)

If we are caught up in this soliloquy by the heightened emotion of a talented actress, we have looked upon Bertram with our own eyes for the last time.

Shakespeare makes several changes in his source which execute his intention in the characterizations of his hero and heroine. In Boccaccio, Giletta returns from court to Rousillon, puts the Count's estate into order with her usual efficiency, then writes to Beltramo to beg his return. He refuses and lists 'impossible' conditions for their marriage. Giletta, the clever wench, decides to fulfill those conditions and makes plans to visit Florence on the pretext of a pilgrimage. In *All's Well*, Helena responds to the flight of Bertram with fear for his safety. Imagining him in the midst of battle, she blames herself for his danger and resolves to flee Rousillon so that he may return to his home:

> Poor lord, is't I
> That chase thee from thy country, and expose
> Those tender limbs of thine to the event
> Of the none-sparing war? . . .
>   No; come thou home, Rossillion,
> Whence honour but of danger wins a scar,
> As oft it loses all; I will be gone;
> My being here it is that holds thee hence.
>
>   (III. ii. 102–5 and 120–3)

Helena's exile is prompted by unselfish love; she does not consider the fulfilment of the conditions. At the same time, the dramatist builds support for Bertram in a brief but important scene. In Boccaccio, Beltramo fled to Florence where he was 'made captaine of a certaine nomber of men' (p. 148). Shakespeare composes an impressive military ceremony in which Bertram is commissioned general of the troop. Not only does the scene mitigate the hero's offences, but it sharpens the dramatic contrast: when Helena's hope for her love sinks lowest, Bertram's fortunes rise highest. It sharpens as well the conflict between war and love and ironically foreshadows the resolution:

> Make me but like my thoughts and I shall prove
> A lover of thy drum, hater of love.
>
>   (III. iii. 10–11)

The letter in which Helena announces her self-exile to the Countess has occasioned much conflicting criticism. It begins:

> I am Saint Jaques' pilgrim, thither gone.
> Ambitious love hath so in me offended
> That barefoot plod I the cold ground upon,
> With sainted vow my faults to have amended.
>
>   (III. iv. 4–7)

Helena declares that she has undertaken a pilgrimage to make amends for the offences of her love. Some critics have pointed to these

lines as a confession of Helena's guilt, an admission of her un-
maidenly aggressiveness. Undoubtedly, from the heroine's point of
view, the lines are a confession. But is Shakespeare equating ambition
in Helena with the faults of Bertram? Are we to blame her for her
love? Critics who read the lines as Shakespeare's judgement upon
Helena make the common error of ascribing to the dramatist what
is the perfect psychological response of his character. That the letter
is not Shakespeare's judgement is demonstrable from the context. No
other character in the play blames Helena; throughout, she wins the
affection and admiration of all. The hint of the miraculous in the cure
of the King allies heaven with her. Both before and after the letter,
Shakespeare has guided our judgement. In the soliloquy just before
the delivery of the letter, we see Helena plan unselfishly for Bertram's
return; in the reaction of the Countess to the letter, we see not blame
but an affirmation of Helena's virtue and the purity of her love.
Helena's letter is simply a very natural and very human acceptance
of blame for the dangers faced by her beloved. We, however, know
that, even before the forced marriage, Bertram was eager for the
adventure and honour which he associates with war. Rather than
blaming Helena for 'ambition', we share the pity of the Countess
who is so moved by the confirmation of love. We share too the
realization of the Countess:

> He cannot thrive,
> Unless her prayers, whom heaven delights to hear
> And loves to grant, reprieve him from the wrath
> Of greatest justice.   (III. iv. 26–29)

The coupling of this realization with our pity for Helena brakes the
potential tragedy, and Shakespeare skilfully assures us that no harm
will be done. Despite this melodramatic moment, Helena is not a
pathetic victim, for Bertram can thrive only through her. The equation of the Countess which concludes the scene suggests a comedy in
which all will end well:

> Which of them both
> Is dearest to me I have no skill in sense
> To make distinction.   (III. iv. 38–40)

In the first scene at Florence, the several threads of the plot are
knotted. Helena had admitted in Act I that the court was a 'learning
place' and the young Count was receptive to such learning. As she
joins the group of Florentine women, she understands immediately
the mere hint passed by the Widow and asks:

> Maybe the amorous count solicits her
> In the unlawful purpose?
>   (III. v. 68–69)

The Widow's reply, couched in the language of war, confirms that Bertram, who has won honour in battle, now seeks a conquest in 'love'. Through the solicitation of Parolles, he would seduce a maiden whose name significantly is Diana. Helena now formulates a plan which weaves together much of the preceding action. She will fulfil the conditions of her husband's letter by substituting herself in the seduction. The sympathy expressed by the women for the Count's wife before Helena reveals her identity mollifies the boldness of the plan as does the Elizabethan awareness that Helena has the right to her husband. Shakespeare, however, does not leave the plan on a realistic level; he raises it through symbol. Helena, who has fled the service of the goddess Diana for Love's imperial throne, will now win that throne through the chaste Florentine maiden, Diana.

Shakespeare qualifies the dishonourable intention of Bertram by two tempering circumstances. The young Count makes his appearance in the scene at the head of an army as a hero who has 'taken their great'st commander, and . . . with his own hand . . . slew the duke's brother' (III. v. 5–7). The impression which he creates is described by Diana, who has reason to be indignant at his attack on her virtue. Instead, she cries excitedly:

> He—
> That with the plume; 'tis a most gallant fellow.
> I would he lov'd his wife; if he were honester
> He were much goodlier. Is't not a handsome gentleman?
>
> (III. v. 77–80)

This implies no coquetry in Diana as some critics have maintained; we cannot ignore her 'I would he lov'd his wife'. Diana simply expresses what should be brought out in any production: Bertram is very handsome; if he were more virtuous, he would be extremely attractive. The second circumstance is the recurring emphasis upon Parolles's influence. Even in Florence, the women have become aware that the faults of Bertram must be ascribed to Parolles. Diana exclaims:

> Yond's that same knave
> That leads him to these places. Were I his lady
> I would poison that vile rascal.   (III. v. 82–84)

The inference is clear: destroy the evil, and Bertram will thrive.

The two scenes which conclude Act III prepare for the expulsion of Parolles's influence and the cure of Bertram. The young lords persuade Bertram to test the braggart; Helena in the succeeding scene persuades the Widow to lure Bertram. The resultant exposure of Parolles is both a type and a cause of the exposure of Bertram. To emphasize the relationships, Shakespeare places arguments in the speeches of the lords which echo through the exposure of Bertram. In anticipating Parolles's betrayal of Bertram both in the drum scene and at Bertram's trial, the Second Lord warns, 'It were fit you knew him; lest, reposing too far in his virtue, which he hath not, he might at some great and trusty business in a main danger fail you' (III. vi. 13–15). The First Lord's prediction of Parolles's betrayal describes as well Bertram's desperation before the King:

if he do not for the promise of his life, and in the highest compulsion of base fear, offer to betray you and deliver all the intelligence in his power against you, and that with the divine forfeit of his soul upon oath, never trust my judgment in anything.   (III. vi. 26–31)

The Second Lord insists that Bertram's attitude will surely be changed when he sees 'to what metal this counterfeit lump of ore will be melted' (III. vi. 33–38). The dialogue after the entrance of Parolles equates the drum with the braggart's concept of honour and, by indirection, with Bertram's concept. Bertram unwittingly defines the significance of Parolles's failure to regain the drum, 'some dishonour we had in the loss of that drum, but it is not to be recovered' (III. vi. 52–54). Recovery of honour will come only with truth, the truth of self-knowledge which follows the wild lies at both trials. The Second Lord assures us of the inevitability of that knowledge, 'when you find him out you have him ever after' (III. vi. 89–90).

The identification of Parolles and Bertram is stressed in the fourth act. The exposure of the parasite occurs simultaneously with the supposed seduction of Diana. To emphasize this, Shakespeare informs the audience of the time of both actions. As he searches for the drum, Parolles muses, 'Ten a'clock. Within these three hours 'twill be time enough to go home' (IV. i. 24–25). As Bertram woos her, Diana agrees:

When midnight comes, knock at my chamber window.
                         (IV. ii. 54)

In delaying the trial of Parolles, the Second Lord explains that Bertram will not arrive 'till after midnight, for he is dieted to his hour' (IV. iii. 28–29). Parolles's search for the drum, of course, is not a success; he is seized by the disguised lords and led off to his trial. Neither is Bertram's intended seduction of Diana a success. He is captured by his disguised wife in a manner which leads to his trial. The exposure of the false soldier anticipates the exposure of the false lover. The structural irony which places the seizure of Parolles immediately before the wooing of Diana refutes those critics who defend Bertram's suit as sincere. Just as the soldiers use a mock language in binding the wordy Parolles, Diana mocks the artificial language of the false lover. Bertram argues against virginity in the affected speech of courtly love:

> Titled goddess;
> And worth it, with addition! But, fair soul,
> In your fine frame hath love no quality?
> If the quick fire of youth light not your mind
> You are no maiden but a monument.
> When you are dear you should be such a one
> As you are now; for you are cold and stern,
> And now you should be as your mother was
> When your sweet self was got.　　(IV. ii. 2–10)

Diana insists:

> 'Tis not the many oaths that makes the truth,
> But the plain single vow that is vow'd true.
> 　　　　　　　　　　　(IV. ii. 21–22)

Bertram's hypocrisy is evident in Diana's soliloquy:

> My mother told me just how he would woo
> As if she sat in's heart.　　(IV. ii. 69–70)

In his suit, the Count employs the same arguments against virginity which Parolles used with Helena.[1]

The relationship in the scene between Diana and Helena is not only established through the audience's foreknowledge of the bed-trick but through verbal association and symbol as well. Bertram's urging is phrased in terms which suggest the denouement:

> But give thyself unto my sick desires,
> Who then recovers.　　(IV. ii. 35–36)

Helena, not Diana, is the 'Doctor She' who will effect his recovery. The debate on honour recalls the earlier debate between the King and Bertram after Helena had chosen her husband. Now, however, the term 'honour' defines the conflict between Helena and Bertram. Setting aside his equation of honour with war, Bertram identifies his honour with his ancestral ring, the symbol of his noble birth, the symbol consequently of his objection to his low-born wife. On the other hand, Diana defines her honour as the jewel of chastity. The exchange of the symbol, the ring, for Diana's chastity is the surrender of Bertram's code to his 'sick desires'. But, the jewel which he receives is not Diana's chastity, not the fulfilment of his passion, but the love of his wife. Unwittingly, Bertram yields his hollow notion of nobility for love.

In order to make perfectly clear our comprehension of the night's

1. In Boccaccio, however, the Count is 'marvelouslye in love' with a Florentine maiden (p. 149). There are many meetings, 'the Count not thinkinge that he had lien with his wife, but with her whom he loved' (p. 151).

business, Shakespeare has added the commentary of the French lords. Critics who analyse the play as a struggle between youth and age ignore the judgement of Bertram's comrades.[1] We must not dismiss the attempted seduction as a harmless youthful escapade: 'He hath perverted a young gentlewoman here in Florence, of a most chaste renown, and this night he fleshes his will in the spoil of her honour; he hath given her his monumental ring, and thinks himself made in the unchaste composition' (IV. iii. 13–17). Because Bertram's peers disapprove, we cannot regard the affair as a light romantic episode which we might expect from soldiers in a foreign land. Yet, we are not to be outraged either. The lords agree that the Count has no self-knowledge, that he must learn from the exposure of Parolles: 'I would gladly have him see his company anatomiz'd, that he might take a measure of his own judgments wherein so curiously he had set this counterfeit' (IV. iii. 30–33). When Bertram realizes the folly of his model, he will begin to understand his own faults. To insure moderation in our judgement upon the hero, Shakespeare charges all of mankind with comparable flaws:

The web of our life is of a mingled yarn, good and ill together; our virtues would be proud if our faults whipp'd them not, and our crimes would despair if they were not cherish'd by our virtues.   (IV. iii. 68–71)

Our judgement is tempered also by the comic trial of Parolles which follows. The scene is comic. Critics who hold that Parolles is a Jonsonian character and the situation a harsh exposure of folly need only compare the tone to the caustic revelations of vice in *Volpone*. The mock language fashions a setting of unreality in which we cannot take seriously the cowardly replies of the braggart.[2] The exaggerations of Parolles heighten the unreality. When Volpone exposes Voltore, Corbaccio, and Corvino, we smile at the execution of justice. When Parolles absurdly calls Captain Dumaine 'a botcher's prentice in Paris', we laugh at the lie. Even his description of Bertram as a 'lascivious young boy' is an exaggeration which delights us. The discovery of a letter from Parolles to Diana in which he offers himself as her lover is pure farce. How realistic and satirical would have been a letter from Bertram in the hands of the pander, Parolles! Surely, there is an unquenchable spirit which charms the audience in Parolles's soliloquy after the exposure:

> Yet am I thankful [sic] If my heart were great
> 'Twould burst at this. Captain I'll be no more,

1. In addition, the Countess, the King, and Lafeu—all elders—favour the youthful Helena.

2. See the introduction to *All's Well* in the *Complete Works of Shakespeare*, edited by G. L. Kittredge, Boston, 1936.

> But I will eat and drink and sleep as soft
> As captain shall. Simply the thing I am
> Shall make me live. Who knows himself a braggart,
> Let him fear this; for it will come to pass
> That every braggart shall be found an ass.
> Rust, sword; cool, blushes; and Parolles live
> Safest in shame; being fool'd by fool'ry thrive.
> There's place and means for every man alive.
> I'll after them.   (IV. iii. 319–29)

From Act IV, scene iii, the trial of Parolles, until Act V, scene iii, the trial of Bertram, Shakespeare fixes our focus upon Bertram. He arrives for the trial of Parolles in a mood of youthful exhilaration:

> I have tonight dispatch'd sixteen businesses a month's length apiece. By an abstract of success: I have congied with the duke, done my adieu with his nearest, buried a wife, mourn'd for her, writ to my lady mother I am returning, entertain'd my convoy, and between these main parcels of dispatch effected many nicer needs; the last was the greatest, but that I have not ended yet.   (IV. iii. 82–89)

The summation of the night's business, however, resounds in the hollow style of Parolles who had boasted to the camp of his plans for the recovery of the drum:

> I'll about it this evening; and I will presently pen down my dilemmas, encourage myself in my certainty, put myself into my mortal preparation; and by midnight look to hear further from me.   (III. vi. 70–74)

Bertram's exhilaration passes quickly to harassment as Parolles spins out his lies, oaths, and betrayals. Against a farcical setting which conditions our later response, Bertram behaves precisely as he will at his own trial. The young Count must listen to his former idol describe him in terms which have been stressed throughout the play, 'a foolish idle boy'. But as Bertram begins his fall, Shakespeare already prepares for his redemption. Even Parolles, at this point of utter humiliation, is not rejected. The First Lord becomes amused at the wild extravagances of the cringing Parolles, 'I begin to love him for this' and shares Helena's judgement that the braggart is more attractive than the 'steely bones' of righteous virtue, 'He hath out-villain'd villainy so far that the rarity redeems him' (IV. iii. 253 and 264–5). The drum scene is followed by another interpretive scene of Helena. The entire night's activity simply confirms Bertram's self-deceit; like many men, he fails to recognize his own interests (IV. iv. 21–25). Recognition is the step to redemption.

Lafeu does much to sustain the comic mood of *All's Well* during the fall of Bertram. Through Lafeu, Shakespeare relieves Bertram of even the tragi-comic weight which Boccaccio had given to his hero. At Rousillon, Lafeu places the entire blame upon Parolles, whose comic chastisement the audience has just witnessed:

No, no, no, your son was misled with a snipp'd-taffeta fellow there, whose villainous saffron would have made all the unbak'd and doughy youth of a nation in his colour. Your daughter-in-law had been alive at this hour, and your son here at home, more advanc'd by the King than by that red-tail'd humble-bee I speak of.   (IV. v. 1–7)

Because the audience has seen the exposure of Parolles, because the audience knows that Helena is alive, the plot remains comic. Bertram's redemption is implied in the scene as well in Lafeu's acceptance of the Clown. Despite Lavache's faults which the Countess has just explained, Lafeu decides, 'I like him well; 'tis not amiss' (IV. v. 65). The comment helps to define Lavache's function in the play. Rather than an expression of Shakespeare's own cynical mood, Lavache is one of the three 'unsavoury' characters in the play who win acceptance despite their faults. The Countess has already accepted him out of love for her deceased husband just as Helena accepts Parolles out of love for Bertram. Lafeu, however, represents a more general, perhaps even a choral, approval. He likes Lavache; he takes Parolles into his household; he offers his daughter to Bertram as a token of general reconciliation. The fourth act ends with Lafeu eager to see the 'young noble soldier'.

The major problem in the denouement of *All's Well* is Bertram's reconciliation with Helena. Although the trial of Parolles prefigures the trial of Bertram, the braggart's exposure is merely a preparation for the solution of the problem, not a justification of it. Both men are crushed by plots, but the hero must rise to love. In Boccaccio's narrative, Giletta has many rendezvous with Beltramo in the guise of his Florentine love. When she is certain of her pregnancy, she hides herself from Beltramo and awaits the birth of her child in Florence. Beltramo, disappointed by the loss of his mistress, returns to his own home. Giletta delivers twins who strongly resemble the Count. After a while, she returns to France to confront the Count with the fulfilment of his conditions. On the Feast of All Saints, Beltramo entertains an assembly of knights and ladies. Giletta, in pilgrim's garb, rushes to the feet of her husband with the twins in her arms. Beltramo is astonished. Giletta's story wins the admiration of the Count and all the guests. Because of her wit and constancy, his delight over his sons, and the entreaties of the ladies Beltramo embraces Giletta and they live happily ever after. Boccaccio has solved the problem of the denouement through realistic plot details and literary legend.

Shakespeare solves the problem through realistic characterization.

Although the number of meetings in the *novella* increases the likeli-hood of pregnancy, although the proof which Giletta offers is a more obvious demonstration of the fulfilment, although her simple plea to the mature Count is a more plausible method of presenting her case, none of these details would induce the young Bertram to accept Helena in Shakespeare's version. Time and pressure are both vital to the dramatist's characterization.[1] Until Bertram matures, he cannot value his wife's virtues. His maturity must be forged under the successive strokes of adversity. To allow a number of years to pass, as in Boccaccio, destroys the entire effect of Parolles's exposure. In *All's Well,* before Helena can submit to Bertram, the young nobleman must submit to her. Only then can we believe in his love. Shakespeare has sacrificed realistic action for psychological motivation, but in the theatre the loss is inconsequential. The complications of the plot remain incredible even in Boccaccio; the many meetings between Giletta and Beltramo scarcely make the success of her disguise plausible.

The first step in the explanation of the psychology of Bertram is the reiteration of the strong influence which Parolles *formerly* held on him. Lafeu's insistence that, had it not been for Parolles, Bertram would have won advancement at Court by now makes evident the inherent capability and attractiveness of the young Count. The second step in the psychological justification for the denouement is the exhilaration of the hero as he comes before the King. His for-tunes have reached their apex. As I have noted, he has been received back into the household of his mother; he has been offered the daughter of a leading nobleman in marriage; he fears no conse-quences from his escapade in Florence; he has been assured of the King's pardon. His desertion of his wife, his disobedience to the King, his neglect of his mother's pleas, and his venture as a lover have had no consequences. Even the exposure of Parolles may bolster his ego; he has surpassed his former idol. For Bertram, his noble birth, his handsome appearance, his amiable personality, and his courage in war have overcome all obstacles. He has won 'honour' in the limited sense which the word has for him. Even the King acknow-ledges, 'I have letters sent me / That set him high in fame' (v. iii. 30–31). We can imagine Bertram's supreme confidence as he answers the King's question about Lafeu's daughter:

> Admiringly, my liege. At first
> I stuck my choice upon her, ere my heart
> Durst make too bold a herald of my tongue;

1. Dr. Johnson's note that Shakespeare is 'hastening to the end of the play', that he 'wanted to conclude his play', ignores the necessary pressure upon Bertram.

> Where, the impression of mine eye infixing,
> Contempt his scornful perspective did lend me,
> Which warp'd the line of every other favour,
> Scorn'd a fair colour or express'd it stol'n,
> Extended or contracted all proportions
> To a most hideous object. Thence it came
> That she whom all men prais'd, and whom myself
> Since I have lost, have lov'd, was in mine eye
> The dust that did offend it.   (v. iii. 44–55)

Bertram speaks of Lafeu's daughter in the same affected language with which he wooed Diana. He feels that he has mastered the courtly style. Psychologically as well as morally, Bertram is ripe for a fall. The series of events which follow in this last scene, so often condemned as contrived, are essential to the breakdown of Bertram's ego to the point where he has an awareness of self and an understanding of true nobility.

When Lafeu asks for a token of love for his daughter, Bertram hands to him a ring which he has received from Diana. Both Lafeu and the King identify it as Helena's. Bertram's first response is a matter-of-fact denial. But, as they press their questions, the youth passes to irritation and then anxiety that their 'mistake' may threaten his newly won prosperity. The significance which the King attaches to the ring puzzles both Bertram and the audience. The audience had not been informed of this second ring, and its place in Helena's plan creates suspense. Shakespeare deliberately compounds the action of this crowded scene in order to manage the total response of the audience.

Bertram's lies begin his exposure. Fearfully, he attempts to explain away the ring. The King, however, suspecting that Bertram has killed his wife, orders him to be seized and led into custody. (We are reminded of Parolles's seizure and exit under guard before his trial.) In a few minutes, Bertram has seen his fortune plunge and his very life endangered. While he is off-stage, the second blow strikes at his new fame. Diana accuses Bertram of seduction and dishonour; he is summoned before the King to answer this charge. In rapid sequence which recalls the wild lies of Parolles, he first denies intimacy with her, then brands her as a camp-follower, discredits any testimony of Parolles, and finally accuses Diana of seducing him. His desperation to salvage some remnant of 'honour' only reveals that same pride which initiated his predicament:

> She knew her distance and did angle for me,
> Madding my eagerness with her restraint,
> As all impediments in fancy's course

Are motives of more fancy; and in fine
Her inf'nite cunning with her modern grace
Subdu'd me to her rate.   (v. iii. 211–16)

The evidence, however, is overwhelming. With the entrance of Parolles, Bertram begins to crumble. He admits that he has lied, that the ring is Diana's. The entrance of the chastened Parolles at just this moment emphasizes the humiliation of the Count. But the play is not a tragedy, and Shakespeare moves swiftly for Bertram's redemption. The audience, because of its superior knowledge, has not taken seriously any of the charges and counter-charges. Even the mood, darkened by the grim desperation of Bertram, is now lightened. A rattled Parolles blurts out absurd replies to the questions of the King. Laughter at the scapegoat relieves the pressure upon the hero. In addition, the effect of Bertram's slanders is minimized by the new tone which Diana adopts. To the King's questions about the ring, Diana answers in exasperating riddles. Dr. Johnson concluded that there was no reason for puzzling the King, and, within the logical demands of the plot, he is correct. There is a most important reason, however, for the comic tone of the play. The banter of Diana dispels the potentially tragic atmosphere. The audience delights in the perplexity of the King, the bewilderment of Lafeu, and the amazement of Bertram.

Just as the King's anger mounts, Diana assures him that no harm has been done (v. iii. 293). The appearance of Helena solves the riddle and completes the transformation of Bertram. He who had lost all hope of favour, reputation, love, even of life, suddenly sees redemption. He does not understand the manner, but he knows that his wife lives and is somehow allied with Diana. In recognition of his own faults, he begs pardon of Helena. He realizes the virtue of his wife *before* he knows of its dedication to him. The explanation of the ring and the child increases his feeling; it does not cause it as in Boccaccio. All is well that ends well. Lafeu weeps for joy and turns to 'Good Tom Drum' for a handkerchief (how subtly does Shakespeare improve Parolles's fate!). Helena and the Countess embrace. And the King, in the spirit of romance which stresses the comic nature of the play, promises a husband now to Diana![1]

All's Well that Ends Well is a play which includes many elements, but they are not incongruous. To isolate a few examples, I point to the romance of the first act with its strong emotional sense of loss and frustrated love; consider the realistic characterization in the second

---

1. Critics who see this as sheer cynicism on Shakespeare's part disregard a similar ending in *The Comedy of Errors* where a new confusion between twin masters and twin servants comically concludes the play.

act as the characters respond to Bertram's rejection of Helena; consider the melodramatic moments of the third act, Helena's expression of selfless love, her exile, her discovery of her husband's passion in Florence; consider the fabulous elements of the fourth act with the fulfilment of tasks; consider the symbolism of the fifth act as it centres upon the ancestral ring and the jewel of chastity. These elements, however, cannot be isolated nor can any one be imposed upon the others as a unifying device without damage to Shakespeare's play. Shakespeare has given unity to *All's Well*. He has unified the play through its structure: the play is tightly knit through parallels, parodies, anticipations, and commentaries. He has unified the play through its theme: the word honour rings throughout the play and synonyms increase its force. As he does in other plays, Shakespeare weaves together character and incident with variations upon his theme in much the same manner as the composer of a symphony. Variations sound in Bertram, who misunderstands honour; in the King, who demands honour; in the Countess and Lafeu who have lived honour; in the Clown, who preaches honour; in the surprisingly serious young lords, who recognize the dilemmas of honour; and in Helena, whose virtue gains honour. The play is unified moreover by the development of its subject. *All's Well* is not the demonstration of an ideological struggle between male and female concepts of honour, as G. Wilson Knight suggests. More simply, Shakespeare tells the story of a foolish young man who is brought to a true understanding of honour through the love of a virtuous girl. She is aided by all the other characters of the play, *male and female, young and old*, with the exception of Parolles. The subject is unified by its tight progression from the Countess's opening comment to her son, 'Thy blood and virtue / Contend for empire in thee' (i. i. 58–59) to the final reconciliation of Helena and Bertram when nobility of birth shares the empire with nobility of virtue.

Perhaps the major factor in the failure of *All's Well* to rival *As You Like It, Twelfth Night*, or *The Tempest* is its mood. The great Shakespearian comedy is unified by a characteristic mood by which, in itself, we can identify the play. *All's Well* lacks that distinctive quality. But the imposition of a single mood from without, the adoption of a single approach to the play, may be more damaging than critical resignation to this lack. *All's Well* fares far better if each of its elements is exploited rather than ignored. I suggest that the director who draws out each character, each situation, each parallel, each seemingly diverse element, will solve many of the problems of past productions. I believe that the ideal production will trust to Shakespeare: the serious scenes will be played with respect for the gravity of the issues; the comic scenes will give full play to both wit and farce; the suspense of the plot will swing the audience along the road of high romance, untroubled by the fabulous complications; most important, the human qualities of all the characters will be affectingly unfolded. For *All's Well that Ends Well* is a very human play.

NOTES

CHAPTER 1

1. Among the most popular comedies of Beaumont and Fletcher during this period, four are realistic and only one romantic. *The Scornful Lady, Rule a Wife and Have a Wife, The Chances, Wit without Money*, and the romantic *Beggars' Bush* were played most frequently. See Arthur Colby Sprague, *Beaumont and Fletcher on the Restoration Stage*, Cambridge, Massachusetts, 1926, pp. 122–5.

2. *Shakespeare From Betterton to Irving*, i. 259–62. In his book, *Theatrical Criticism in London to 1795* (New York, 1931), Charles Gray notes that there are reviews in magazines of only two or three of the most important plays in the decade 1740–50. Newspapers carried only brief notices of performances among the other news items; often these notices were submitted by the theatres themselves (p. 98).

3. *Dramatic Miscellanies*, ii. 9. James Lynch, in *Box, Pit, and Gallery* (Berkeley, 1953, p. 99), accepts the Davies report that Mrs. Ridout and Mrs. Butler were taken ill during the production, but Genest (iii. 645–6) argues that their names continued in the playbills throughout this period. Neither Hogan (i. 88) nor Scouten (ii. 968–78) list substitutes for these actresses.

4. It appears that only Tate Wilkinson, who may be a prejudiced commentator on the acting of Woodward, disagreed with the general praise accorded to him. In his *Memoirs of His Own Life* (Dublin, 1791, iii. 247), Wilkinson recalls that Woodward was fond of acting Parolles, 'but I never remember any remarkable success or pleasure received from the representation of that play'.

5. See *Lloyd's Evening Post, & British Chronicle*, 3–5 Jan., 4–7 Feb., 4–7 March, 27–28 April, 5–7 Oct. 1763; 14–16 March, 16–18 May 1764. A few reviews give brief mention of other parts. The London *Chronicle*, 24–27 Jan. 1767, took notice of the 'judgment and propriety' with which Ross played Bertram and praised Shuter's acting 'the part of the witty Clown, with his usual, natural, and pleasing drollery'. For a performance of May 1772, which assembled a new cast for the minor roles, John Potter, in his *Theatrical Review* (London, 1772, ii. 184–5), found satisfaction only in the acting of Woodward and Miss Macklin.

CHAPTER 2

1. In the 1811 edition, Kemble eliminates references to the bed-trick and the conception of a child; he expurgates a larger number of lines than in the 1793 edition. In the 1811 edition, he shifts Bertram's introduction to the King from II. i to II. ii; II. i. becomes a brief scene in which Lafeu warns Bertram about Parolles (II. v. 1–13). He reinstated lines which had been dropped in 1793: Bertram's farewell before his departure for Court (I. i. 71–72); the Countess's highly effective interjection of her love into the speech of the Steward (I. iii. 97–101); Parolles's quibbles with the Clown (II. iv). In 1793, Mariana's lines had been given to the Widow; in 1811 Kemble restored her part. From the stage experience of his 1794 production, Kemble added an additional 'O Lord, Sir' as

an exit line for the Clown (II. ii). There are changes as well in stage directions and stage business.

In the Folger Shakespeare Library (catalogued as '866 Cage'), there is an interesting interleaved copy of the 1774 'Bell Acting Edition'. The Library has been unable to identify the copy except through a note inserted in the book and dated 1933, 'Mr. Paul [Henry Paul] says this is Kemble's "copy" from wh. "The first Kemble" 1793 was printed.' Certainly, the book was not used for the printing of the 1793 edition since lines are crossed out in the Bell copy which appear in the 1793 text; likewise original Shakespearian lines are written in on the leaves, yet do not appear in the 1793 text. Furthermore, the handwriting is not Kemble's nor is the method similar to other Kemble prompt-books. The copy appears to be a prompt-book, however, carefully worked out with elaborate stage machinery and detailed business. In general, it is an expansion of the Bell edition with only the Clown's role reduced. Surprisingly, it shows no concern for the increasingly rigid moral taste. I know of no performance which would suit this copy. See Charles Shattuck, 'Shakespeare Promptbook Collections', *Restoration and 18th Century Research*, Loyola University, Chicago, iii (May 1964), 10.

2. A. Aspinall (ed.), *Mrs. Jordan and her Family being the Unpublished Correspondence of Mrs. Jordan and the Duke of Clarence, later William IV*, London, 1951, p. 28. In surveying the correspondence, the editor concludes, 'Mrs. Jordan's frequent absences from the theatre were sometimes attributed by ill-natured journalists to caprice rather than their true cause, the calls of maternity.'

3. *The Dramatic Essays of Charles Lamb*, p. 70. As Lafeu, Munden may have felt a special sympathy for the hungry and tattered Parolles whom he welcomes into his household. While in similar straits as a young man, Munden had passed himself off as a soldier in order to obtain supper and bed from a military billet. He so delighted the militia with an evening of entertaining stories that he was hailed as 'king of his company' (Oxberry, ii. 75).

CHAPTER 3

1. 'All's Well that Ends Well, at the "Old Vic"', *The Spectator*, cxxvii (3 Dec. 1921), 744. The reviewer demonstrates none of the nineteenth-century resentment against Parolles, 'the Miles Gloriosus, the lovable Shakespearean rascal' who 'entirely compensates for the impossible part Helena has to play'. But Parolles is not entirely redeemed in the production, for Atkins retained the moral lesson of Phelps's interpretation, 'At the end of the scene, after his exposure as a cowardly braggart, this Parolles was as tragic a figure as Shylock outwitted by Portia.'

2. Alfred Harbage, *Theatre for Shakespeare*, Toronto, 1955, p. 85. In a conversation with Professor Harbage, Mr. Guthrie defended Mr. Benthall by maintaining that the interpretation has a basis in the diversity of Shakespearian criticism. *All's Well*, in particular, offers diversity in interpretation, but that diversity is still limited by the text and the guides which the text gives to the intention of the dramatist.

3. My interest in the unusual depiction of farce in this production has diverted me from Michael Hordern's Parolles. The interpretation has a place in the stage history of *All's Well* and is fortunately described for us by Mr. David (pp. 134–5):

> This Parolles was brimful of vitality, and a masterpiece of comic invention. As befits one who is to be found a sheep in wolf's clothing, he began by looking the opposite, his long hungry face in itself a contrast to the gay Florentine doublet with its huge hanging

sleeves. The wolf soon begins to look a good deal sillier, and Hordern was brilliant in inventing a series of mimes to express Parolles's attempts to maintain his dignity in face of Lord Lafeu's quizzing—hurt, and chilling at the first suspicion, a scraggy cockerel when trying to outface his tormentor, at last swallowing with anguish the sour plum of his inability to answer back without calling down retribution. His gait was as expressive as his face. His entry in procession with the victorious Florentine army, himself in dudgeon over the disgrace of the lost drum, brought down the house—a jobblin, unco-ordinated motion, head bobbing forward between limp shoulders from which the arms dangled, feet flapping carelessly down in the abandonment of utter disgust.

Despite the comic approach to the entire play, it is interesting to note that the exposure was not played entirely for laughs. The interrogation itself was marked by 'the anxious gabbling of the numbers as he tumbles over himself to betray the military strength of his own side, the confidential backing of his interrogator in order to impart one extra tidbit of lying scandal about his superior officers, the self-hugging satisfaction at getting through the interview, he thinks, so adroitly.' When he was exposed, however:

> Hordern managed an immediate and breath-taking transition from farce to deadly earnest. At the discovery he closed his eyes and fell straight backward into the arms of his attendants; then, as with taunts they prepare to leave him, he slithered to the ground, becoming vizened and sly on the instant, and with 'simply the thing I am shall make me live' revealed an essential meanness not only in Parolles but in human nature as a whole.

4. Ivor Brown (*Shakespeare Memorial Theatre: 1957–59*, London, 1959, pp. 15–6), for example, insisted that the play 'needs some added intervention to give pleasure now'. Eric Keown ('All's Well that Ends Well', *Punch*, ccxxxvi [29 April 1959], 593) agreed, 'Mr. Guthrie's interpretation of this difficult play is consistent, and it is great fun.' Keown had also approved Mr. Benthall's attempt to get 'as much fun as possible wherever it is to be discovered' (op. cit., n. 30).

CHAPTER 4

1. Advertisements were also carried in the *Massachusetts Mercury* on 5 and 8 March 1799; the 8 March notice expressed the hope that a 'genteel and numerous audience' would attend that evening's performance. The 1798–9 season is discussed by Ruth Michael in her unpublished dissertation, 'A History of the Professional Theatre in Boston from the Beginning to 1816,' Radcliffe College, 1941. The production's claim as the first American performance was disputed as late as 1933 by an editor of the St. Louis *Dispatch*; in answer to a correspondent's objection, he defended the Little Theatre of St. Louis's performance as the first since the 1799 production used Kemble's version. See the St. Louis *Dispatch*, 7 and 9 May 1933.

2. One scene is set in the King's Palace, another in the King's Gardens—'A Fountain over hung by a mass of foliage.' The Florentine scenes are to be staged impressively:

> A Public place in Florence, on the outskirts: A house on the R.—The Country at R & Beyond: Archway to the City and the City Walls at L. The City Within the Walls in distance. Balcony on the house R. The Gateway thronged with people (Trumpets & a march heard) Enter from house An old Widow & Diana: from the Gateway Marianna & Violenta.

3. The distinction between major and minor productions is undoubtedly arbitrary. In Great Britain, by necessity, I have limited my study generally to the London stage and Stratford on Avon. There were a number of productions in the nineteenth century in the provincial theatres, but the little evidence available suggests that they were based upon the Kemble text and present no innovations in the stage history. In America, I have investigated the professional companies travelling through the large cities of the country during the eighteenth and nineteenth centuries. In the twentieth century, I have been forced to consider only the two Stratfords and the Broadway theatre with its accompanying 'tryouts' and touring groups.

In the United States, there were early amateur productions of the play in St. Louis (1933) and Ann Arbor, Michigan (1933) directed by Thomas Stevens. B. Iden Payne did a production at the University of Iowa in the same year. An early professional performance was staged at the Pasadena Playhouse in 1937 under the direction of Mr. Maxwell Sholes. By the 1950s the number of such productions was considerable. Fortunately, many of the university, minor professional, and foreign performances are listed in the *SQ* and *SS*, often with interesting comments.

CHAPTER 5

1. John Munro (ed.), *The Shakspere Allusion-Book: A Collection of Allusions to Shakspere From 1591 to 1700*, i–ii, London, 1932. All the allusions are listed in the second volume of the collection; see pp. 49–52 for John Cotgrave's *The English Treasury of Wit and Language collected Out of the most, and best of our English Dramatick Poems*, 1655 and after; see p. 58 for the reference to T. Goff's catalogue of plays in his *Careless Shepherdess*, 1656; see p. 59 for Edward Archer's *An Exact and perfect Catalogue of all the Plaies that were ever printed . . .*, 1656; see p. 114 for Francis Kirkman's catalogue printed at the end of *Nicodeme A Tragi Comedy translated out of the French, of Monsieur Corneille by John Dancer*, 1670; see p. 360 for Gerard Langbaine's allusion in his *Account of the English Dramatic Poets*, 1691; see p. 418 for Charles Gildon's *The Lives and Characters of the English Dramatick Poets . . .*, 1698.

2. Mr. Hunter's excellent summary of the argument and his own conclusions are contained on pp. xviii–xxv of the 'New Arden Edition'. For my general history of the criticism of *All's Well*, it is sufficient to note that the first identification of the play with 'Love's Labour's Won' was probably made by Dr. Farmer upon a suggestion of Bishop Percy in 1767. The idea received wide-spread support until Malone withdrew his concurrence and concluded that *All's Well* was a late play (1606). Coleridge, however, had already proposed an alternative which would accomodate both views: *All's Well* was a later revision of 'Love's Labour's Won', which had been a sequel to *Love's Labour's Lost*. Since the date of the proposal, critics have applied internal and external criteria to demonstrate the theory, but Mr. Hunter's conclusion that the burden of proof is still upon those who argue a revision or a sequel seems justified. He himself assigns a tentative date 1603–4 to the play. Readers interested in the controversy may trace its major points in Verplanck, Charles Knight, Halliwell-Phillips, Gervinus, Kenny, Wendell, Brandes, Tolman, Masefield, Herford, Chambers, Lowe, Quiller-Couch, Elton, and Craig. Of particular interest is Robert Boyle's 'All's Well that Ends Well and Love's Labour's Won', *Englische Studien*, xiv (1890), 408–21.

CHAPTER 6

1. Frank Sharp, *Shakespeare's Portrayal of the Moral Life*, New York, 1902, pp. 145–7; Albert Tolman, 'Shakespeare's "Love's Labour's Won" ', *The Views About Hamlet and Other Essays*, Boston, 1906, p. 280; Walter Raleigh, *Shakespeare*, London, 1907, p. 175. In his work, Sharp argues that Shakespeare provides a solution to the plot difficulties which is 'simplicity itself. He merely makes us acquainted with the characters of Bertram's father and mother.' An emphasis upon heredity resolves any problem of reconciliation and reformation. Although Sharp oversimplifies, too few critics have failed to give due note to the stress which Shakespeare places upon Bertram's parentage.

2. 'Parolles', *Shakespearean Studies*, ed. Brander Matthews and Ashley Thorndike, New York, 1916, pp. 261–300. Krapp's view of Parolles as a serious character is typical of the criticism of this period. Ralegh (op. cit., n. 24) writes of the braggart's exposure 'Shakespeare dared to follow his characters into those dim recesses of personality where the hunted soul stands at bay, and proclaims itself, naked as it is, for a greater thing than law and opinion' (p. 147).

CHAPTER 7

1. *The Use of Rhyme in Shakespeare's Plays*, New Haven, Connecticut, 1941, pp. 28, 76, 77 n., 79, 84, 87, 88, 89, 103–4, and 142. In Appendix B, pp. 113–54, Mr. Ness lists the number of rhymed lines in the plays. Since many critics and editors have argued that *All's Well* is a revised play because the abundance of rhyme points to Shakespeare's early work, it is interesting to compare *All's Well* with several other plays. *Love's Labour's Lost* has 1,122 rhymed lines; *All's Well* has 267. *As You Like It* has 164; *Measure for Measure* only 82; but *Macbeth* and *Pericles*, both late plays, have 250 and 523 respectively. *Troilus and Cressida*, generally dated about the same period as *All's Well*, has 202 rhymed lines.

CHAPTER 8

1. The source of *All's Well* is the ninth novel of the third day of Boccaccio's *Decameron*; Shakespeare probably used the version, 'Giletta of Narbonna', the thirty-eighth novel in William Painter's *The Palace of Pleasure*, London, 1575. The characters of the Countess, Lafeu, Parolles, and Lavache are Shakespeare's creations. For discussions of the source and the playwright's modifications, see G. K. Hunter's 'New Arden Edition' of the play, London, 1959; Kenneth Muir's *Shakespeare's Sources*, London, 1957; and Geoffrey Bullough's *Narrative and Dramatic Sources of Shakespeare*, ii. London, 1958.

2. The apparently tragic atmosphere at the beginning of *All's Well* does not mark it as a 'dark play' or 'problem' comedy. Aegeon's sentence to death at the beginning of *The Comedy of Errors*, the banishment of Orlando in *As You Like It*, the decadent state of Vienna in *Measure for Measure*, the shipwreck in *The Tempest* demonstrate the tragic opening to be common to Shakespeare's comedies throughout his career.

3. The talk of a miracle is natural, however. The unexpected cure of a hopeless disease is popularly regarded as miraculous. Shakespeare carries the point no

further. Whether the cure is the result of divine intervention, a convention of fairy-tale, or the effect of natural causes may be decided individually by the audience. Regardless, the dominant impression is that Helena merits Bertram.

4. I am indebted to Professor Sprague for this observation. That Lafeu serves as a commentator is clear in that he reports to the audience the cure of the King, he describes the choice in this scene, he exposes Parolles immediately after this scene, and he announces to Parolles and the audience that Bertram and Helena are married. In all these cases, he reports accurately. Indeed, just before Helena's choice of Bertram, Lafeu correctly predicts Bertram's reaction (II. iii. 99–101).

5. The word 'honour' and its variant appear 51 times in the play and demonstrate the thematic stress. The heaviest concentration of usage occurs in this scene; the word occurs 10 times in 56 lines. The agreement of the King, the Countess, and Lafeu with Helena on the true meaning of honour disputes G. Wilson Knight's view that the play is a conflict between male and female concepts of honour.

BIBLIOGRAPHY

EDITIONS

1709   Nicholas Rowe (ed.), 'All's Well That Ends Well', *The Works of Shakespeere*, i, London.

1714   'All's Well that Ends Well', Bound in the *Williams Collection of Plays*, Folger Shakespeare Library, ii, London.

1734   'All's Well that Ends Well', *The Works of Shakespeare*. Printed for J. Tonson. ii, London.

1735   Alexander Pope (ed.), *Works*, ii, London.

1756   *All's Well, that Ends Well. A Comedy.* Printed for C. Hitch and L. Hawes, etc., London.

1765   Samuel Johnson (ed.), *The Plays of William Shakespeare, in eight volumes, with the Corrections and Illustrations of Various Commentators*, iii, London.

1767   Edward Capell (ed.), *Comedies, Histories & Tragedies*, iv, London.

1773   Lewis Theobald (ed.), *The Works of Shakespeare*. iii, London.

1774   *All's Well, that Ends Well, A Comedy, by* Shakespeare, *As Performed at the Theatre-Royal, Drury Lane*. Regulated from the Prompt-Book, With Permission of the Managers, By Mr. Hopkins, Promptor. Printed for John Bell, i, London.

1778   *All's Well, that Ends Well. A Comedy. As it is Acted at the Theatres Royal in Drury-Lane and Covent-Garden.* Printed for J. Harrison, ii, London.

1790   Edmund Malone (ed.). *The Plays and Poems of William Shakespeare*, iii, London.

1793   *Shakespeare's All's Well That Ends Well; With Alterations by J. P. Kemble. As it is performed by His Majesty's Servants, of the Theatre-Royal, Drury-Lane.* London. Bound in *Plays of the 18th Century*, xxv, Folger Shakespeare Library.

1793   J. P. Kemble (ed.). *Shakespeare's All's Well That Ends Well; With Alterations.* [MS. Notes by John Genest] London. This edition is in the Furness Library, University of Pennsylvania.

1795   'Shakespeare's All's Well That Ends Well: With Alterations by J. P. Kemble. As it is performed by His Majesty's Servants, at the Theatre Royal, Drury Lane', *A Collection of Much-Esteemed Dramatic Pieces*, i, London.

1811   *Shakespeare's All's Well that Ends Well, A Comedy; Adapted to the Stage by J. P. Kemble; And now first published as it is acted at the Theatre Royal in Covent Garden*, London.

1815   J. P. Kemble (ed.). *Shakespeare's All's Well that Ends Well*, London.

1821   Boswell-Malone Edition. *The Plays and Poems of William Shakespeare*, x, London.

1838   *All's Well That Ends Well: A Comedy, In Five Acts, By William Shakespeare. Printed from the acting copy, with Remarks, Biographical and Critical, by D.—G. . . . As performed at the Theatres Royal, London*, London.

1847   Gulian Verplanck (ed.), *The Illustrated Shakespeare*, ii, New York.

1850   J. Q. Halliwell-Phillips (ed.), *The Complete Works of Shakespeare*, i, London.

1853   Charles Knight (ed.), *The Comedies, Histories, Tragedies, and Poems of William Shakspere*, i, Boston.

1883(?)   'Augustin Daly production of AW with Notes by Winter'. 2 vols., Folger Shakespeare Library.

[n.d.]   'All's Well That Ends Well. Shakespeare's Comedy. Rearranged by Augustin Daly', Folger Shakespeare Library.

1904   W. Osborne Brigstocke (ed.), *All's Well That Ends Well*, The Arden Edition, London.

1905   William J. Rolfe (ed.), *Shakespeare's Comedy of All's Well That Ends Well*, New York.

1909   Helen A. Clarke and Charlotte Porter (eds.), *All's Well, That Ends Well*, New York.

1912   John L. Lowes (ed.), *All's Well That Ends Well*, The Tudor Shakespeare, New York.

1926   Arthur E. Case (ed.), *All's Well That Ends Well*, The Yale Shakespeare, New Haven.

1929   Sir Arthur Quiller-Couch and John Dover Wilson (eds.), *All's Well That Ends Well*. The New Cambridge Edition, Cambridge, England.

1936   George Lyman Kittredge (ed.), *The Complete Works of Shakespeare*, Boston.

1953   Charles J. Sisson (ed.), *The Complete Works of Shakespeare*, London.

1959   G. K. Hunter (ed.), *All's Well that Ends Well*. The New Arden Edition, London.

BOOKS

ADOLPHUS, JOHN, *Memoirs of John Bannister, Comedian*, 2 vols., London, 1839.

AGATE, JAMES, *Brief Chronicles; a Survey of the Plays of Shakespeare and the Elizabethans in Actual Performances*, London, 1943.

Airs, Duets, Choruses, &c. Introduced in Shakespeare's Revived Comedy of All's Well That Ends Well or Love's Labour Won! As Performed at the Theatre Royal, Covent-Garden, Friday, October 12, 1832. Music composed, selected, and arranged by Rophino Lacy, London, 1832.

APPLETON, WILLIAM W., *Charles Macklin: An Actor's Life*, Cambridge, Mass., 1960.

ARCHER, WILLIAM, *The Theatrical 'World' of 1895*, London, 1896.

ASPINALL, A. (ed.), *Mrs. Jordan and her Family being The Unpublished Correspondence of Mrs. Jordan and the Duke of Clarence, later William IV*, London, 1951.

BAILEY, JOHN CANN, *Shakespeare*, New York, 1929.

BAKER, HERSCHEL, *John Philip Kemble*, Cambridge, Mass., 1942.

DE BANKE, CECILE, *Shakespearean Stage Production: Then & Now*, New York, 1953.

BARTON, Sir DUNBAR PLUNKET, *Links between Ireland and Shakespeare*, London, 1919.

BELL, JOHN (ed.), *Annotations by Sam. Johnson & Geo. Steevens, and the Various Commentators, Upon All's Well That Ends Well*, London, 1787.

BENSON, Lady CONSTANCE, *Mainly Players*, London, 1926.

BENTLEY, GERALD EADES, *Shakespeare & Jonson: Their Reputations in the Seventeenth Century Compared*, 2 vols., Chicago, 1945.

BLACK, M. W., and SHAABER, M.A., *Shakespeare's Seventeenth Century Editors*, New York, 1937.

BOADEN, JAMES, *The Life of Mrs. Jordan*, 2 vols. London, 1831.

—— *Memoirs of the Life of John Philip Kemble, Esq.*, 2 vols., London, 1825.

BOAS, FREDERICK S., *Shakspere and his Predecessors*, New York, 1896.

BODENSTEDT, FRIEDRICH, *Shakespeare's Frauencharaktere*, Berlin, 1874.

BRADBROOK, M. C., *Shakespeare and Elizabethan Poetry*, London, 1951.

BRANDES, GEORGE, *William Shakespeare: A Critical Study*, 2 vols., New York, 1898.

BRIDGES-ADAMS, W., *The Irresistible Theatre*, i, London, 1957.

BROWN, IVOR, *Shakespeare Memorial Theatre: 1954–56*, London, 1956.

—— *Shakespeare Memorial Theatre: 1957–1959*, London, 1959.

BROWN, JOHN RUSSELL, *Shakespeare & His Comedies*, London, 1957.

BROWNSMITH, J., *The Dramatic Time-Piece*, London, 1767.

BULLOUGH, GEOFFREY, *Narrative and Dramatic Sources of Shakespeare*, ii, New York, 1958.

CHAMBERS, E. K., *William Shakespeare*, Oxford, 1930.

CHARLTON, H. B., *Shakespearian Comedy*, London, 1938.

CHILD, HAROLD, *The Shakespearian Productions of John Philip Kemble*, The Shakespeare Association, xix, London, 1935.

CLARKE, MARY, and WOOD, ROGER, *Shakespeare at the Old Vic*, London, 1954.

COGHILL, NEVILL, 'Wags, Clowns and Jesters', *More Talking of Shakespeare*, ed. by John Garrett, London, 1959.

COLE, JOHN WILLIAM, *The Life and Theatrical Times of Charles Kean, F.S.A.*, 2 vols., London, 1859.

COLLIER, J. PAYNE, *Notes and Emendations to the Text of Shakespeare's Plays from Early Manuscript Corrections in a Copy of the Folio, 1632*, New York, 1853.

COOK, DUTTON, *Hours With the Players*, 2 vols., London, 1881.

COOKE, WILLIAM, *Memoirs of Charles Macklin*, London, 1804.

CRAIG, HARDIN, *An Interpretation of Shakespeare*, New York, 1948.

CROSSE, GORDON, *Shakespearean Playgoing: 1890–1952*, London, 1953.

CURRY, JOHN V., *Deception in Elizabethan Comedy*, Chicago, 1955.

DALY, AUGUSTIN, *Woffington*, Troy, New York, 1890.

DAVIES, THOMAS, *Dramatic Micellanies*, ii, London, 1783.

DELIUS, NICOLAUS, 'Shakspere's All's Well That Ends Well', *Abhandlungen zu Shakspere*, Elberfeld, 1888, pp. 283–302.

DENT, ALAN, *Preludes & Studies*, London, 1942.

DOUNCE, FRANCIS, *Illustrations of Shakspeare*, London, 1839.

DOWDEN, EDWARD, *Shakspere: His Mind and Art*, New York, 1881.

DRAKE, NATHAN, *Shakspeare and His Times*, ii, London, 1817.

ECKHOFF, LORENTZ, *Shakespeare: Spokesman of the Third Estate*, Oslo, 1954.

EDWARDS, THOMAS, *A Supplement to Mr. Warburton's Edition of Shakespeare. Being the Canons of Criticism, and Glossary*, London, 1748.

ELLIS, RUTH, *The Shakespeare Memorial Theatre*, London, 1948.

ELLIS-FERMOR, UNA, *The Jacobean Drama*, London, 1936.

ELTON, OLIVER, *The English Muse*, London, 1933.

ELTON, OLIVER, 'Style in Shakespeare', *Essays and Addresses*, London, 1939, pp. 9–43.

EVANS, BERTRAND, *Shakespeare's Comedies*, Oxford, 1960.

FARJEON, HERBERT, *The Shakespearean Scene*, London, 1949.

FARMER, RICHARD, 'An Essay on the Learning of Shakespeare', *Eighteenth Century Essays on Shakespeare*, ed. D. Nichol Smith, Glasgow, 1903, pp. 162–215.

FELDHEIM, MARVIN, *The Theater of Augustin Daly*, Cambridge, Mass., 1956.

GALE, CEDRIC, *Shakespeare on the American Stage in the Eighteenth Century*. Unpublished Dissertation, New York University, 1945.

GAYLEY, CHARLES MILLS, *Shakespeare and the Founders of Liberty in America*, New York, 1917.

GENEST, JOHN, *Some Account of the English Stage from the Restoration in 1660 to 1830*, 10 vols., London, 1832.

GERVINUS, G. G., *Shakespeare Commentaries*, trans. F. E. Bunnett, London, 1883.

GILDON, CHARLES, *The Life of Betterton*, London, 1710.

GLOVER, ARNOLD, and WALLER, A. R., (eds.), 'Dramatic Essays from The London Magazine', *The Collected Works of William Hazlitt*, viii, London, 1903, 383–484.

GODDARD, HAROLD C., *The Meaning of Shakespeare*, Chicago, 1951.

GOLDSMITH, ROBERT HILLIS, *Wise Fools in Shakespeare*, East Lansing, Michigan, 1955.

GORDON, GEORGE, *Shakespearian Comedy and Other Studies*, Oxford, 1944.

GRAHAM, WALTER, *English Literary Periodicals*, New York, 1930.

GRAY, CHARLES HAROLD, *Theatrical Criticism in London to 1795*, New York, 1931.

GRIFFITH, Mrs. ELIZABETH, *The Morality of Shakespeare's Drama Illustrated*, London, 1775.

GUTHRIE, TYRONE, *A Life in the Theatre*, New York, 1959.

—— ET AL., *Renown at Stratford: A Record of the Shakespeare Festival in Canada, 1953*, Toronto, 1953.

HAIG, ROBERT L., *The Gazetteer: 1735–1797: A Study in the Eighteenth-Century English Newspaper*, Carbondale, Illinois, 1960.

HALLIWELL-PHILLIPS, J. Q., *Memoranda on All's Well That Ends Well*, etc., Brighton, 1879.

HANEY, JOHN LOUIS, 'Shakespeare and Philadelphia', *An Address Delivered before the City Historic Society of Philadelphia, Nov. 28, 1934*, Philadelphia, 1936.

HARBAGE, ALFRED, *As They Liked It*, New York, 1947.

—— *Theatre for Shakespeare*, Toronto, 1955.

HARRIS, FRANK, *The Women of Shakespeare*, New York, 1912.

HAZLITT, WILLIAM, *Characters of Shakespeare's Plays & Lectures on English Poets*, Macmillan Library of English Classics, London, 1920.

HERFORD, C. H., *Shakespeare's Treatment of Love & Marriage and Other Essays*, London, 1921.

HITCHCOCK, ROBERT, *An Historical View of the Irish Stage*, 2 vols., Dublin, 1788.

HOGAN, CHARLES B., *Shakespeare in the Theatre: 1701–1800*, 2 vols. Oxford, 1952–7.

HOOKER, EDWARD NILES (ed.), *The Critical Works of John Dennis*, 2 vols., Baltimore, 1939.

HORNE, HERMAN H., *Shakespeare's Philosophy of Love*, Raleigh, North Carolina, 1945.

HOUTCHENS, LAWRENCE H., and HOUTCHENS, CAROLYN W. (eds.), *Leigh Hunt's Dramatic Criticism. 1801–1831*, New York, 1949.

HUDSON, H. N., *Lectures on Shakspeare*, i, New York, 1948.

HURSTFIELD, JOEL, *The Queen's Wards: Wardship and Marriage Under Elizabeth I*, London, 1958.

JAGGARD, WILLIAM, *Shakespeare Memorial; Stratford-on-Avon*, Stratford on Avon [1925?].

JAMESON, ANNA BROWNELL, *Characteristics of Women, Moral, Poetical, and Historical*, New York [18–?].

JERROLD, CLAIRE, *The Story of Dorothy Jordan*, London, 1914.

KEMP, T. C., and TREWIN, J. C., *The Stratford Festival*, Birmingham, 1953.

KENNY, THOMAS, *The Life and Genius of Shakespeare*, London, 1864.

KENRICK, W., *A Review of Doctor Johnson's New Edition of Shakespeare: In Which the Ignorance, Or Inattention, of That Editor Is Exposed, and the Poet Defended from the Persecution of His Commentators*, London, 1765.

KILBOURNE, FREDERICK W., *Alterations and Adaptations of Shakespeare*, Boston, 1910.

KITTREDGE, G. L., 'Unpublished Lecture Notes on *All's Well that Ends Well*', prepared by Arthur Colby Sprague, 1921; 1925.

KNIGHT, CHARLES, *Studies of Shakspere*, London, 1849.

KNIGHT, G. WILSON, 'The Third Eye', *The Sovereign Flower*, New York, 1958, pp. 93–160.

KNIGHT, JOSEPH, *Theatrical Notes*, London, 1893.

KRAPP, GEORGE PHILIP, 'Parolles', *Shakespearean Studies*, ed. Brander Matthews and Ashley Thorndike, New York, 1916, pp. 291–300.

LAMB, CHARLES, *Specimens of English Dramatic Poets*, Bohn's Standard Library, London, 1901.

LAWRENCE, W. J., *Old Theatre Days And Ways*, London, 1935.

—— *Speeding Up Shakespeare*, London, 1937.

LAWRENCE, WILLIAM W., *Shakespeare's Problem Comedies*, New York, 1931.

LENNOX, CHARLOTTE, *Shakespear Illustrated: or the Novels and Histories, On which the Plays of Shakespear Are Founded*, i, London, 1753.

LOUNSBURY, THOMAS R., *Shakespeare as a Dramatic Artist*, New York, 1901.

LOVETT, DAVID, *Shakespeare's Characters in Eighteenth Century Criticism*. Unpublished Dissertation, Johns Hopkins University, 1935.

Lowe, Robert W., *Bibliographical Account of English Theatrical Literature*, London, 1888.

Lynch, James J., *Box, Pit, and Gallery*, Berkeley, Calif., 1953.

MacMillan, Dougald, *Drury Lane Calendar, 1747–1776*, Oxford, 1938.

Marston, Westland, *Our Recent Actors*, 2 vols., London, 1888.

Masefield, John, *William Shakespeare*, New York, 1911.

Mason, John Monck, *Comments on the Last Edition of Shakespeare's Plays* [Johnson & Steevens, 1778], London, 1785.

Matthews, Brander (ed.), *The Dramatic Essays of Charles Lamb*, New York, 1891.

—— *Shakspere as a Playwright*, New York, 1913.

Matthews, John F. (ed.), *Shaw's Dramatic Criticism (1895–98)*, New York, 1959.

Michael, Ruth, *A History of the Professional Theatre in Boston from the Beginning to 1816*. Unpublished Dissertation, Radcliffe College, 1941.

Morgann, Maurice, 'An Essay on the Dramatic Character of Sir John Falstaff', *Eighteenth Century Essays on Shakespeare*, ed. D. Nichol Smith, Glasgow, 1903, pp. 216–303.

Morris, Corbyn, *An Essay Towards Fixing the True Standards of Wit, Humour, Raillery, Satire, and Ridicule*, London, 1744.

Muir, Kenneth, *Shakespeare's Sources*, London, 1957.

Munden, Thomas Shepherd, *Memoirs of Joseph Shepherd Munden*, London, 1844.

Munro, John (ed.), *The Shakspere Allusion-Book: A Collection of Allusions to Shakspere from 1591 to 1700*, 2 vols., London, 1932.

Murry, John Middleton, *Shakespeare*, New York, 1936.

—— 'Shakespeare and Love', *Countries of the Mind*, London, 1922, pp. 9–28.

Ness, Frederic W., *The Use of Rhyme in Shakespeare's Plays*, New Haven, Connecticut, 1941.

Nicoll, Allardyce, *A History of Restoration Drama: 1660–1700*, Cambridge, England, 1923.

—— *A History of Early Eighteenth Century Drama: 1700–1750*, Cambridge, England, 1925.

—— *A History of Late Eighteenth Century Drama: 1750–1800*, Cambridge, England, 1927.

Odell, George C. D., *Shakespeare from Betterton to Irving*, 2 vols., New York, 1920.

Ogburn, Dorothy and Charlton, *This Star of England*, New York, 1952.

Oulton, Walley C., *The History of the Theatres of London . . . From the Year 1771 to 1795*, 2 vols., London, 1796.

—— *A History of the Theatres of London . . . From the Year 1795 to 1817 Inclusive*, 3 vols., London, 1818.

Oxberry's Dramatic Biography, 5 vols., New Series, i, London, 1825–27.

Parrott, Thomas Marc, *Shakespearean Comedy*, New York, 1949.

Pascoe, Charles Eyre, *The Dramatic List*, Boston, 1879.

Pedicord, Harry William, *The Theatrical Public in the Time of Garrick*, New York, 1954.

PHELPS, W. MAY, and FORBES-ROBERTSON, JOHN, *The Life and Life-Work of Samuel Phelps*, London, 1886.

PHELPS, SAMUEL, *The Samuel Phelps Collection of Shakespearean Prompt Books* [n.d.].

POTTER, JOHN, *Theatrical Review; or, New Companion to the Play-House*, 2 vols., London, 1772.

POTTS, ABBIE FINDLAY, *Shakespeare and the Faerie Queene*, Ithaca, New York, 1958.

RALEIGH, WALTER, *Shakespeare*, London, 1907.

RAYSOR, THOMAS MIDDLETON (ed.), *Coleridge's Shakespearean Criticism*, 2 vols., London, 1930.

RHODES, R. CROMTPON, *Shakespeare's First Folio*, Oxford, 1923.

RIDLEY, M. R., *Shakespeare's Plays*, London, 1957.

ROACH, JOHN, *Authentic Memoirs of the Green Room*, London, 1796.

ROSENFELD, SYBIL, *Strolling Players & Drama in the Provinces. 1660–1765*, Cambridge, England, 1939.

ROWE, NICHOLAS, *Some Account of the Life of Mr. William Shakespear (1709)*, The Augustan Reprint Society, Extra Series, no. 1, #17, 1948.

SCHLEGEL, AUGUST WILHEIM, *Lectures on Dramatic Art and Literature*, trans. John Black, London, 1883.

SCHÜCKING, LEVIN L., *Character Problems in Shakespeare's Plays*, New York, 1922.

SCOTT, CLEMENT, and HOWARD, CECIL, *The Life and Reminiscences of E. L. Blanchard*, 2 vols., London, 1891.

Scrapbook for Drury Lane and Covent Garden, ii (1763–4). Uncatalogued at the Folger Shakespeare Library.

Scrapbook of Sir William Augustus Fraser. #1327 in the Folger Shakespeare Library Catalogue of Scrapbooks.

SEILHAMER, GEORGE O., *History of the American Theatre During the Revolution and After*, 3 vols., Philadelphia, 1889.

SEN GUPTA, SUBODH CHANDRA, *Shakespearian Comedy*, Oxford, 1950.

SHARP, FRANK CHAPMAN, *Shakespeare's Portrayal of the Moral Life*, New York, 1902.

SHAW, BERNARD, *Our Theatres in the Nineties*, 3 vols., London, 1932.

SITWELL, EDITH, *A Poet's Notebook*, Boston, 1950.

SMITH, LOGAN PEARSALL, *On Reading Shakespeare*, London, 1933.

SPEAIGHT, ROBERT, *William Poel and the Elizabethan Revival*, London, 1954.

SPENCER, HAZELTON, *The Art and Life of William Shakespeare*, New York, 1940.

—— *Shakespeare Improved*, Cambridge, Mass., 1927.

SPRAGUE, ARTHUR COLBY, *Beaumont and Fletcher on the Restoration Stage*, Cambridge, Mass., 1926.

—— *Shakespearian Players and Performances*, Cambridge, Mass., 1953.

SPURGEON, CAROLINE F. E., *Shakespeare's Imagery And What It Tells Us*, New York, 1935.

STAUFFER, DONALD A., *Shakespeare's World of Images*, New York, 1949.

STEVENS, THOMAS WOOD, *Shakespeare's All's Well That Ends Well As Produced in Brief at the Globe Theatre, Century of Progress, Chicago*, New York, 1934.

STOCKWELL, LA TOURETTE, *Dublin Theatres and Theatre Customs (1637–1820)*, Kingsport, Tennessee, 1938.

STOLL, ELMER EDGAR, *From Shakespeare to Joyce*, New York, 1944.

—— *Shakespeare Studies*, New York, 1927.

—— *Shakespeare's Young Lovers*, Toronto, 1937.

STONE, GEORGE WINCHESTER, *Garrick's Handling of Shakespeare's Plays and His Influence Upon the Changed Attitude of Shakespearian Criticism During the Eighteenth Century*. Unpublished Dissertation, Harvard University, 1938.

TERRY, Dame ELLEN, *Four Lectures on Shakespeare*, ed. Christopher St. John, London, 1932.

THALER, ALWIN, *Shakspere's Silences*, Cambridge, Mass., 1929.

THISELTON, ALFRED EDWARD, *Some Textual Notes on All's Well, That Ends Well*, London, 1900.

TILLYARD, E. M. W., *Shakespeare's Problem Plays*, London, 1950.

TOLMAN, ALBERT H., ' Shakespeare's "Love's Labour's Won" ', *The Views About Hamlet and Other Essays*, Boston, 1906.

TREWIN, J. C., *The Birmingham Repertory Theatre: 1913–63*, London, 1963.

VAN DOREN, MARK, *Shakespeare*, New York, 1939.

VICTOR, BENJAMIN, *The History of the Theatres of London and Dublin, From the Year 1730 to the present Time*, 2 vols., London, 1761.

WALDER, ERNEST, *Shakespearian Criticism: Textual and Literary: From Dryden to the End of the Eighteenth Century*, London, 1895.

Was Shakespeare a Lawyer? London, 1871.

WATKINS, RONALD, *On Producing Shakespeare*, London, 1950.

WATSON, CURTIS BROWN, *Shakespeare and the Renaissance Concept of Honor*, Princeton, 1960.

WEISS, JOHN, *Wit, Humour, and Shakspeare*, Boston, 1876.

WENDELL, BARRETT, *William Shakspere*, New York, 1895.

WEST, E. J. (ed.), 'How to Lecture on Ibsen', *Shaw on Theatre*, New York, 1958, pp. 53–58.

WESTFALL, ALFRED VAN RENSSELAER, *American Shakespearean Criticism. 1607–1865*, New York, 1939.

WILKINSON, TATE, *Memoirs of His Own Life*, 3 vols., Dublin, 1791.

WILLIAMS, E. HARCOURT, *Four Years at the Old Vic*, London, 1935.

WILLIAMS, J. M. (ed.), *The Dramatic Censor: or, Criticial and Biographical Illustration of the British Stage. For the Year 1811*, London, 1812.

WILLIAMSON, AUDREY, *Old Vic Drama*, London, 1948.

—— *Old Vic Drama 2*, London, 1957.

WINTER, WILLIAM, *Shakespeare on the Stage*, New York, 1911.

WRIGHT, HERBERT, *Boccaccio in English*, London, 1957.

YELLOWLEES, HENRY, 'Medicine and Surgery in the 1955 Season's Plays', *More Talking of Shakespeare*, ed. by John Garrett, London, 1959.

PERIODICALS

ADAMS, JOHN F., 'All's Well That Ends Well: The Paradox of Creation', *Shakespeare Quarterly*, xii (Summer 1961), 261–70.

ALVEREZ, A., 'My Fair Helena', *New Statesman*, lvii, n.s., no. 1467 (25 April 1959), 573–4.

ARTHOS, JOHN, 'The Comedy of Generation', *Essays in Criticism*, v (April 1955), 97–117.

Athenaeum: 4 Sept. 1852; 4 June 1920.

BABCOCK, WESTON, 'Fools, Fowls, and Perttaunt-Like in *Love's Labour's Lost*', *SQ*, ii (July 1951), 211–19.

Bell's Weekly Messenger: 7 July 1811; 4 Sept. 1852.

BLISTEIN, E. M., 'The Object of Scorn: An Aspect of the Comic Antagonist', *Western Humanities Review*, xiv (Spring 1960), 209–22.

BOYLE, ROBERT, 'All's Well That Ends Well and Love's Labour's Won', *Englische Studien*, xiv (1890), 408–21.

BRADBROOK, MURIEL C., 'Virtue Is the True Nobility', *Review of English Studies*, i, n.s., no. 4 (Oct. 1950), 289–301.

BRIEN, ALAN, 'All's Well That Ends Well', *The Spectator*, ccii, no. 6826 (24 April 1959), 578–9.

BROWN, IVOR, 'All's Well That Ends Well', *Punch*, cxcix, no. 5195 (16 Oct. 1940), 388.

BROWNE, RAY B., 'Shakespeare in American Vaudeville and Negro Minstrelsy', *American Quarterly*, xii (Fall 1960), 374–91.

BYRNE, MURIEL ST. CLARE, 'The Shakespeare Season at The Old Vic, 1958–9 and Stratford-upon-Avon, 1959', *SQ*, x (Autumn 1959), 545–67.

CARTER, ALBERT HOWARD, 'In Defense of Bertram', *SQ*, vii (Winter 1956), 21–31.

CASE, ARTHUR E., 'Some Stage-Directions in *All's Well That Ends Well*', *Modern Language Notes*, xlii, no. 2 (Feb. 1927), 79–83.

The Court Journal: 13 Oct. 1832; 20 Oct. 1832; 4 Sept. 1852.

CRAIG, HARDIN, 'Shakespeare's Bad Poetry', *Shakespeare Survey*, i (1948), 51–56.

The Critic: 15 Sept. 1852.

Daily Advertiser: 28 July 1785.

DAVID, RICHARD, 'Plays Pleasant and Plays Unpleasant', *SS*, viii (1955), 132–8.

DOWNER, ALAN S., 'A Comparison of Two Stagings: Stratford-upon-Avon and London', *SQ*, vi (Autumn 1955), 429–33.

EDINBOROUGH, ARNOLD, 'A New Stratford Festival', *SQ*, v (Jan. 1954), 47–50.

EHRL, L., and STROEDEL, W., 'International Notes—Germany', *SS*, vii (1954), 111–12.

ELLIS-FERMOR, UNA, 'Some Functions of Verbal Music in Drama', *Shakespeare Jahrbuch*, xc (1954), 37–48.

European Magazine and London Review: Aug. 1785; Jan. 1795; June 1811.

The Examiner: 28 July 1811; 4 Sept. 1852.

FLEMING, PETER, 'All's Well That Ends Well', *The Spectator*, cxciv, no. 6619 (6 May 1955), 586.

The Gazetteer and New Daily Advertiser: 26 July 1785; 27 July 1785; 28 July 1785.

GUTHRIE, TYRONE, 'Shakespeare at Stratford, Ontario', *SS*, viii (1955), 127–31.

HALIO, JAY L., 'All's Well That Ends Well', *SQ*, xv (Winter 1964), 33–43.

HEWES, HENRY [All's Well at Stratford, Conn.], *Saturday Review*, xlii (22 Aug. 1959), 23.

Illustrated London News: 4 Sept. 1852.

J. Russell's Gazette (Boston): 7 March 1799.

JACKSON, Sir BARRY, 'Producing the Comedies', *SS*, viii (1955), 74–80.

JEROME, JUDSON. 'Shakespeare at Antioch', *SQ*, vii (Autumn 1956), 411–14.

John Bull: 4 Sept. 1852.

KEOWN, ERIC, 'All's Well That Ends Well', *Punch*, ccxxv, no. 5896 (30 Sept. 1953), 416.

—— 'All's Well That Ends Well', *Punch*, ccxxxvi, no. 6194 (29 April 1959), 592–3.

LANG, ANDREW, 'All's Well That Ends Well', *Harper's Magazine*, lxxxv (July 1892), 213–27.

LAWRENCE, WILLIAM WITHERLE, 'The Meaning of "All's Well That Ends Well" ', *Publications of the Modern Language Association*, xxxvii (Sept. 1922), 418–69.

LEECH, CLIFFORD, 'The "Capability" of Shakespeare', *SQ*, xi (Spring 1960), 123–36.

—— 'The "Meaning" of *Measure For Measure*', *SS*, iii (1950), 66–73.

—— 'The Theme of Ambition in "All's Well That Ends Well" ', *English Literary History*, xxi (March 1954), 17–29.

LERICHE, KATHLEEN, 'Shakespeare in Essex', *Essex Review*, lxi (Oct. 1952), 187–91.

Lloyd's Evening Post, & British Chronicle: 1763–4.

London Chronicle: 1 Dec. 1757; 24–27 Jan. 1767.

London Daily Telegraph: 22 April 1959.

London Evening Post: 13–15 March 1764.

London Star: 13 Dec. 1794.

London Times: 11 Oct. 1832; 13 Oct. 1832; 16 Oct. 1832; 1 Sept. 1852; 2 Sept 1852; 3–4 Sept. 1852; 8–9 Sept. 1852; 22–23 Sept. 1852; 22 Jan. 1895; 27 Sept. 1924; 11 May 1955; 22 April 1959; 26 April 1959.

McGLINCHEE, CLAIRE, 'Stratford, Connecticut, Shakespeare Festival, 1959', *SQ*, x (Autumn 1959), 573–6.

MONSEY, DEREK, 'All's Well That Ends Well', *The Spectator*, cxci, no. 6535 (25 Sept. 1953), 322.

NEWMANN, JOSHUA H., 'Shakespearean Criticism in the *Tatler and the Spectator*', *PMLA*, xxxix (Sept. 1924), 612–19.

The New Age: 15 Dec. 1921.

New York Herald-Tribune: 19 July 1953.

New York Times: 22 April 1959.

PRAZ, MARIO, 'Shakespeare's Italy', *SS*, vii (1954), 95–106.

RAYSOR, THOMAS M., 'The Study of Shakespeare's Characters in the Eighteenth Century', *MLN*, xlii (Dec.1927), 495–500.

SCHOFF, FRANCIS G., 'Claudio, Bertram, and a Note on Interpretation', *SQ*, x (Winter 1959), 11–23.

SCOUTEN, ARTHUR H., 'The Increase in Popularity of Shakespeare's Plays in the Eighteenth Century', *SQ*, vii (Spring 1956), 189–202.

SISSON, CHARLES J., 'Shakespeare's Helena and Dr. William Harvey: With a case-history from Harvey's practice', *Essays and Studies*, xiii (1960), 1–20.

SMITH, ROBERT M., 'Interpretations of Measure for Measure', *SQ*, i (Oct. 1950), 208–18.

The Stage: 10 Aug. 1949; 28 April 1955.

The Stage and Television Today: 23 April 1959.

The Sun: 13 Dec. 1794.

TARN, 'All's Well that Ends Well, at the "Old Vic" ', *The Spectator*, cxxvii, no. 4875 (3 Dec. 1921), 744.

'The Theatres', *The Spectator*, xxv (4 Sept. 1852), 845–6.

The Theatrical Observer; and Daily Bills of the Play: 11–13 Oct. 1832; 17 Oct. 1832.

Times Literary Supplement: 24 Oct. 1929.

Town & Country, Sept. 1774, p. 497.

TURNER, ROBERT Y., 'Dramatic Convention in All's Well that Ends Well', *PMLA*, lxxv (Dec. 1960), 497–502.

TYNAN, KENNETH, 'Stratford-upon-Avon', *New Yorker*, xxxv (26 Sept. 1959), 119–21.

Universal Magazine of Knowledge & Pleasure, lv (1774), 153.

Westminster Magazine: or, Pantheon of Taste, ii (1774), 488–9.

WHEATLEY, HENRY B., 'Post-Restoration Quartos of Shakespeare's Plays', *The Library*, Third Series, iv (July 1913), 237–69.

WILSON, HAROLD S., 'Dramatic Emphasis in *All's Well That Ends Well*', *Huntington Library Quarterly*, xiii (May 1950), 217–40.

WORSLEY, T. C., 'The Dark Not Dark Enough', *The New Statesman and Nation*, xlix, N.S., no. 1260 (30 April 1955), 611–12.

—— 'The Old Vic', *The New Statesman and Nation*, xlvi, N.S., no. 1177 (26 Sept. 1953), 344–5.

WRIGHT, HERBERT G., 'How Did Shakespeare Come to Know the "Decameron"?' *Modern Language Review*, l (Jan. 1955), 45–48.

INDEX